THE UNIONS

THE UNIONS

by

Guy Arnold

HAMISH HAMILTON LONDON

First published in Great Britain 1981
by Hamish Hamilton Ltd
Garden House 57–59 Long Acre London WC2E 9JZ

Copyright © 1981 by Guy Arnold

British Library Cataloguing in Publication Data

Arnold, Guy
  The unions.
  1. Trade unions—Great Britain
  2. Power (Social sciences)
  I. Title
  331.88′0941   HD6664

  ISBN 0–241–10107–7

Printed in Great Britain by
Willmer Brothers Limited Rock Ferry Merseyside

Contents

Acknowledgements

I wish to record my thanks to the many people who generously gave their time and knowledge to help me in writing this book. In particular I want to thank those who allowed me to record and quote their views:

John Biffen MP; Albert Booth MP; David Buckle; Ray Buckton; Lord Carr of Hadley; Kenneth Castle; Geoffrey Chandler; William Daniel; Moss Evans; John Garnett; John Gorst MP; Eric Heffer MP; Bob Hughes MP; Jim Hendry; Tom Jackson; Sir Alex Jarrett; Tom Jenkins; Leo Kramer; Sir Hector Laing; Alan Leather; Pat Lowry; Iain Macdonald; Jim McConochie; Willie McFall; Roy Moore; Jim Mortimer; Lionel Murray; Sir Richard O'Brien; Sir Peter Parker; L. H. Peach; Sir Raymond Pennock; Ian Pirie; James Prior MP; Bob Ramsey; Reg Race MP; Ruskin College; Nicholas Scott MP; Michael Shanks; Lord Sieff of Brimpton; William Speirs; John Stokes MP; L. J. Tolley; Professor (Lord) Wedderburn; Sidney Weighell; Keith Wickenden MP; Jack Wotherspoon; Kenneth Young.

Preface

The unions constantly make the news; the popular perception of them is of great power which is often misused. They do have great power which is sometimes used disruptively or defensively rather than constructively. The media are uninterested when the unions are constructive. There are many misconceptions about the unions and their place in British Society. Since there are twelve million trade unionists, half the adult workforce, this is hardly surprising.

This book is an attempt to find a consensus of views on what the role of the unions in Britain is, and what it ought to be; how their power is used in fact, and how it ought to be used.

It is not possible to discuss the unions in isolation: they must be considered in two broad contexts. The first, of course, is their industrial setting which is their *raison d'être*. The second, equally important, and possibly more important in some people's estimation, is their political context.

I have talked with a wide range of trade unionists, industrialists and politicians across the broad spectrum of views from left to right in an attempt to achieve a balance of ideas and judgements and in order to dispel some of the misconceptions.

I should like to make two points. The first, that it would have been quite impossible to interview all the people I should have liked to include in this exercise—the book would never have been completed. There are, therefore, inevitable gaps and critics will no doubt be quick to point these out. I had to be selective; I hope the selectivity has been sufficiently widely based to ensure that the resulting picture, despite its particular biasses, is nonetheless a fair one.

The second point which I believe goes to the heart of many of the problems discussed in this book, is the discovery which I personally made in the course of my research: the extent to which British public life is dominated by partisanship. Again and again people assumed I had to be writing from a particular standpoint:

for the union case or for the management case; for the Labour Party or for the Tory Party. If I insisted, as I sometimes did, that this was not so I then met either disbelief or incomprehension.

Guy Arnold
London, March 1981

The Union Image

It was appropriate that the 1980 Granada Guildhall lectures had as their theme 'The Role of the Trade Unions', for in Britain over recent years few subjects have caused so much interest or concern as union power and the position the unions hold in our society. Three distinguished speakers delivered these lectures: James Prior, Tony Benn and Lionel Murray, and each man in his own way epitomised a particular viewpoint.

It was also symptomatic of the British democratic disease that Mr Prior's lecture was chaired by Lord Scanlon, Mr Benn's by Sir Monty Finniston and Mr Murray's by Sir John Greenborough. The British love to show how democratic they are; equally they can be amongst the most partisan people in the world. Few subjects are cause for greater partisanship, frustration, anger, arrogance, blindness, conservatism and plain misconception than are the trade unions. The misuse of trade union power, the readiness of workers to strike first and bargain afterwards, the arrogance of trade union leaders—these are some of the accusations thrown at the movement from its enemies to be found more or less on the political right. The guardians of working conditions, the only check to unbridled capitalism, the democratic safeguard for the working man, are the counter-claims for the unions.

As in any major debate there is a great deal to be said for both sides of the argument: of course unions sometimes misuse their power; of course they need to reform themselves—or be reformed; of course they employ restrictive practices. Too often, however, those who criticise take such ills to be the sum total of union behaviour and so go on to argue that we should be better off without unions at all—or at least with unions whose powers have been so emasculated as to make them unrecognisable.

Those who defend unions can be equally extreme, reacting to criticisms as though they are still fighting industrial battles of the nineteenth century or at the very latest of the depression years of the 1930s. Some 450 trade unions representing more than twelve million workers are affiliated to the TUC: that is almost half the total workforce of the country and roughly equivalent in numbers to the voting membership of either of the two main political parties. It is not, therefore, surprising that, no matter what the realities, the public perception is one of great if amorphous union power so that when there is an irruption of strikes and confrontations of the kind which occurred in the so-called 'winter of discontent', people see their prejudices or fears confirmed. That particular winter did the union movement little good and contributed substantially to the Tory election victory of the following May.

In the opening part of his lecture Mr Prior enumerated four areas where change was needed if British industrial performance is to improve: the second of these areas where he thought change to be essential was 'in the basic attitudes deeply ingrained in our industrial relations. We must move away from the "trench warfare" which has all too often characterised them.' Here, indeed, he touched upon the nub of the problem: the ingrained British habit of treating industry as a battleground in which rival ideologies are in a state of perpetual confrontation. The question, of course, is how confrontation may be turned to industrial co-operation.

Mr Prior suggested that a primary task for the unions in the 1980s should be to 'face squarely what is sometimes done in the name of union loyalty and brotherhood'. He suggested five tasks for the unions: that they should put their own house in order; that they should reconsider the rules governing industrial action; that they should improve their own organisations; that union leaders should lead; and finally, that unions should reappraise their political role.

On the other side of industry, James Prior suggested that management must now be prepared to disclose information and take employees into its confidence in order to secure active and wholehearted co-operation.

These are not unreasonable demands coming from a 'consensus' Tory more interested in the middle ground of British politics than any of its extremes. Finally, on the subject of productivity, James Prior pointed out that, while in the mid-1950s British productivity was 15 per cent higher than that of France or West Germany, by the mid-1970s theirs was 30 per cent higher than Britain's. What, then, has happened to put Britain near the bottom of the productivity league among the top industrial nations?

The arguments presented by Tony Benn in his Granada lecture are logical and go far closer to the roots of political and ideological divisions in Britain than do most others on this theme. He said, in effect: that the consensus politics which achieved their high water mark under Harold Macmillan have not worked, although they did wean the Labour Party away from its commitment to a programme of Socialist transformation; that a declining capitalism can no longer afford to maintain either full employment or the welfare state; that incomes policies (in their various forms) were all designed to contain the bargaining power of the unions; and that, increasingly, more and more of the country's industrial and productive problems came to be blamed by 'industrialists, the City, the Civil Service and the Establishment' upon the trade unions, while the media hammered home this message on every possible occasion.

After the analysis, Tony Benn enumerated the increased powers and rights he believes should be accorded to the unions. These include: the extension of collective bargaining to cover the whole range of company decisions; joint control of pension funds (which are deferred wages); joint union-management planning of company policies including research, development, marketing, investment, mergers, manpower planning and the distribution of profits. Broadly, Tony Benn argues that, contrary to popular belief, the unions have too little power and most of that is of a negative, reactive nature; he wants them to have a great deal more power over a wide range of issues which at present they are hardly able to affect at all.

Lionel Murray, the General Secretary of the TUC, gave the third of the Granada lectures; he presented a remarkably balanced view of trade union power and responsibilities and made the point that 'Britain's poor economic record since the war is due much more to the ineffective use of our resources than to excessive wage settlements.' He said: 'Workers will accept changes in manning and working practices only if they are convinced of the need for the benefits of change, and if they are protected against its adversities. They ask—fairly enough in my book—why they should accept the adverse consequences of decisions made by faceless boards of directors, or by managements, or indeed by governments for their own purposes.'

The views of these three men are instructive of the problems that Britain faces in relation to its unions and the political passions which they arouse. James Prior is cautious, perhaps acutely aware

13

that the forms of restraint upon union power which many members of his own party as well as management would like to see imposed, are in fact politically impractical. Tony Benn, whose socialist and egalitarian politics have been erected into a major bogey by the political right—and not least the right of his own party, would like to see changes that give the unions a far greater absolute say in both the control and direction of industry and within the policy making of the Labour Party itself.

Lionel Murray, who sits in the hot seat of TUC General Secretary, is only too well aware of the limitations of union power, the difficulty of the TUC actually being able to provide the leadership which it is often exhorted to provide, and perhaps more than Mr Benn he is aware of the inherent conservatism of the working man whom the union movement represents.

The 1979 Conservative Manifesto devoted considerable attention to the trade union movement. 'In bringing about economic recovery,' the manifesto argued, 'we should all be on the same side. . . . Yet at the moment we have the reverse—an economy in which the Government has to hold wages down to try to make us competitive with other countries where higher real wages are paid for by higher output.' The manifesto went on to consider intended reforms covering picketing, the closed shop and the subject of wider participation or the use of the secret ballot. The manifesto said: 'Labour claim that industrial relations in Britain cannot be improved by changing the law. We disagree. If the law can be used to confer privileges, it can and should also be used to establish obligations.'

The thrust of the Tory argument was for a 'return to responsibility', a loaded enough political phrase but understandable in a party manifesto. How this was to be achieved was by people retaining more of what they earned; effort and skill receiving larger rewards; and the state leaving more resources to industry.

Although the Conservative Party and many individual Tories argue that 'we should all be on the same side', the theory does not match the practice. So ingrained has the two-party approach become in this country, and so much has that approach accepted the thesis that the broad mass of the working population—despite the much-vaunted Tory claim that there are four million and more trade unionists who vote for the party—is committed to one side of the political divide, that Tories who argue to the contrary hardly appear to believe themselves.

Conversely, capital and management are committed to the Tory

14

Party in this political divide, despite occasional if not very convincing arguments to the contrary advanced half-heartedly from time to time in order to persuade a doubting public of managerial impartiality. The public perception in Britain is that capital and management are firmly in support of the Tory Party and the broad 'free enterprise' policies associated with it. This divide is central to an understanding of the constant confrontations that take place on the British industrial front.

When the new director general of the CBI, Sir Terence Beckett, spoke harshly of the monetarist policies of the Thatcher government at the November 1980 CBI conference and said industry would have to fight 'with the gloves off', he was quickly taken to task by other 'loyal' industrialists, aghast that so influential a person should be seen publicly to attack the Tory Party. Sir Terence climbed down but, having recovered his breath, he returned to the attack a few weeks later when he spoke of large numbers of the nation's industrial companies 'disappearing down the plughole faster than we can stop them'.

The most interesting aspect of these CBI attitudes towards the Tory Government lies in the fact that, while both Tory politicians and businessmen constantly deplore the close political tie-up between organised labour and the Labour Party, at the same time they try to give the impression that there is not an equally close tie between the Tory Party and the other side of industry—ownership and management. This is an exceptionally difficult fiction to maintain.

The fact of these two close liaisons—the labour movement with the Labour Party, and capital and management with the Tory Party—lies at the heart of a great deal that bedevils the smooth and productive operation of British industry.

The de-industrialisation of Britain is a phrase which came into the popular currency during the 1970s. The figures which led Sir Terence Beckett to make his second attack upon the Government at the beginning of December 1980, were certainly frightening: 921 company liquidations occurred in October 1980, while unemployment was rising at the rate of 3000 jobs a day. Sir Terence compared redundancies in manufacturing and in local government: for every 100 in the former only 5 occurred in the latter; and while British manufacturers were expected to cut investment in 1981 by 10 per cent, Japanese investment was expected to go up by 28 per cent.

15

The *Employment Gazette* of September 1980* carried a special feature on apprenticeship and training in the manufacturing industries. The figures it provided again bore out the theme of the de-industrialisation of Britain. The manufacturing sector employed 8·3 million people in 1964; this figure had dropped to 6·7 million in 1980. Numbers undergoing formal training in all manufacturing industries increased from 390,000 in May 1964 to 450,000 in May 1968, but by 1980 had fallen to 240,000. Such figures needed to be carefully analysed: methods of training change, the duration of apprenticeships has been shortened and so on, yet the overall picture that emerges is discouraging: de-industrialisation—and if that is the case trade union defensiveness in response to the fear of redundancy becomes a major, if not the major motivation for union behaviour.

The Labour Party obtains about 85 per cent of its funds from the trade unions. This close political dependence is a source of strength and weakness both ways: for the Party it means financial stability and organisational help at the grass roots level, especially during elections. It also means the unions—as paymasters—can and do exercise restraints upon party policy, which politicians sometimes find irksome if not intolerable.

For the unions, the relationship means that they have at Westminster a party which is always likely to press their case when it is in opposition, and will sometimes both legislate and otherwise devise policies broadly to the benefit of the organised labour movement when it is in power. The relationship is an uneasy one, and its complications can be gauged according to how Labour leaders behave towards the unions. If they fall out, as did Wilson and Barbara Castle over the 'In Place of Strife' legislation at the end of the 1960s, then the Party is in trouble. But conversely, so also are the unions. They were happy enough to see Wilson return to power in 1974, and this time round the Labour Party went for the 'social contract' approach rather than the introduction of more curbs. Callaghan's miscalculation over the general election timing in 1978 and his insistence upon a five per cent norm between them not only made the 'winter of discontent' a certainty, but also ensured that it contributed to Labour's electoral defeat in 1979. In 1980 the unions were paying the price of Labour's defeat as they faced an unsympathetic Tory government. One result of the manifest failure of the social contract

* *Employment Gazette* (September 1980, Volume 88, No. 9), Department of Employment.

politics of the period 1975–9 was the growing disarray within the Labour movement, that came to a head in 1980 as the Party examined new ways to elect the leader and control its parliamentary members. As long as this argument continues, it will be important for both the Party and the unions to recall Eric Heffer's dictum of 1973: 'Labour is nothing without the trade unions but the trade unions can survive without the Labour Party.'

Attempts to weaken, strengthen, come to terms with or persuade the unions to alter their practices were a major feature of British politics for the fifteen years from 1965 to 1980. These years witnessed the Donovan Report, which argued that the main problem of industrial relations concerned the growth of shop-floor power. Donovan rejected the idea of legal sanctions, yet first Labour and then the Tories opted for such sanctions. Barbara Castle's 'In Place of Strife' was withdrawn under TUC pressure, and the Heath government's 1971 Industrial Relations Act was repealed when Labour came back to power in 1974. Thereafter, the Labour Goverment passed the 1975 Employment Protection Act, and then first Wilson and later Callaghan embarked upon the road of the Social Contract.

The Social Contract worked quite well for two years but broke down in the third. Basically this approach can only work in the conditions of an expanding economy and when there is a real *quid pro quo*; the trouble with all attempts at incomes policies has been that, whatever the theory, in practice they have come to be seen as no more than a means to restrain wages while prices and other economic factors have escaped from similar control. Once that becomes apparent the contract—or the wages policy bargain—is, and is bound to be, dead.

Views upon the place of the unions in British society are many and varied but, whatever people may think, the unions are here to stay, though their structure may change and their nature alter under the economic pressures and storms which are likely to come during the 1980s. But the union problem—if it is a problem—is only part of a much wider question: Britain's industrial and commercial life, her performance and productivity. In this, of course, the unions play a vital and sometimes a preponderant part—but always *only* a part. The trade union movement is inextricably intertwined with the fortunes of one political party, yet, more important, the unions are also one part of the industrial structure of the country of which management and capital (including the public sector) make up the other, so that any search

17

for a solution to the 'right' place the unions should have in our society must also ask comparable questions about management. As Lionel Murray says of the unions: 'We are handy, we hang about in huge lumps, we are very conspicuous and therefore we are natural targets.'

Many people argue that union weaknesses and faults which are not denied, play an important and sometimes overwhelmingly important part in Britain's industrial and other failures, yet the unions are only one element to be considered alongside management, government, education and cultural attitudes. The *them* and *us* approach to industrial (and other) problems is all too apparent in British life. Some people blame the unions for this and say, quite rightly in many cases, that they are fighting past battles and sticking obstinately to a 'labour' role that modern developments have bypassed. Yet it takes two to make a confrontation, and if there is a *them* and *us* mentality in Britain and the unions are the *them*, who, one must ask, constitutes the *us*?

The factors controlling British industrial life are immensely complex. One of those factors, amorphous, irritating, old-fashioned and reactionary, is the trade union movement: it has immense if often unharnessed power at its disposal—the capacities of twelve million of Britain's adult working population. It can stop things—or its members can—and often does. But it consists of people: the people who vote both Labour and Tory; the people who make British industry work. Moreover, increasingly, they are to be found in all walks of life—unions today include members up to managerial level and those with incomes well into five figures. Trade unionists are also consumers, the 'average' men and women in the street, and the practice of regarding the trade union movement as though, somehow, it stands on the outside of British society and poses a threat to it, is exceptionally dangerous.

The trade union movement and individual trade unions are a part of the entire body politic and economic of Britain. How they are regarded; how they behave; how they should be reformed and who will do it; and above all, how they interact with management are at the centre of the most compelling political question for the 1980s. Strong, effective trade unions working with strong, effective managements could transform the British economic scene during the course of the 1980s. Whether anything of the sort is practicable and, even if practicable, remotely likely is perhaps the most significant question facing British politicians and British industry at the present time.

18

2

Carr and Prior

Lord Carr of Hadley, formerly Robert Carr MP, was a leading member of the Heath Administration of 1970–4, starting in June 1970 as Secretary of State for Employment, becoming Leader of the House in 1972 and then Home Secretary. He was created a Life Peer in December 1975. He was responsible for the 1971 Industrial Relations Act and is one of a relatively small number of Tories who become MPs from an industrial background. In 1980 he became chairman of The Prudential Assurance Company.

Speaking in the House of Lords in January 1979, Lord Carr said: 'Finally, we must look at the problem of union power firmly, but also calmly. We must keep it in perspective. Do not let us forget that we need strong unions. We do not want weak ones. The real problem in Britain is not so much the actual strength of union power, but the way in which it is used. There is also a great problem in Britain in the balance of power within the unions. The constitutional power of our British unions tends to be too weak, and the unofficial power within them too strong. Unions in other countries also have great power, but in other countries the power of the unions is made much more accountable both to the community as a whole and to the unions' own members. This surely is what all of us ought to want to achieve in Britain as well.'

Lord Carr does not share the view of those Tories who would like to see union power weakened and unions excluded from an active part in the political affairs of the country. Rather, he is of the Macmillan school of Tory, those who were deeply affected by the sufferings they witnessed as a result of the recession of the 1930s and would like to see a reasonable consensus in industrial affairs. Lord Carr comments wryly that he is regarded as a 'wet'.

In a wide-ranging appraisal* of union-government relations

* In a discussion with the author, perhaps ironically on the Day of Action, 14 May 1980.

during the Heath Administration as well as later, Lord Carr starts by looking at unions in politics: 'I do not think you should try to exclude trade unions from an active part in the political affairs of the country, lobbying to further their interests. How they do it is another matter; their right to do it is a soundly based one since all sections in a free society can participate. The trade unions are a special case because of their industrial power.

'When I first got involved in politics the trade unions had considerable political power because of their industrial strength and because of their organic link with the Labour Party. But then they always reserved industrial action for industrial purposes; and that is where the trade unions have gone wrong in recent years: they now tend to use their industrial power for political purposes, which is both wrong and dangerous. It is wholly objectionable for the trade unions—or any other interest groups—to blackmail a democratically elected government and say: we will not recognise the actions of such a government, approved by Parliament, unless it does certain things. On the other hand it is not improper for the trade unions to enter into discussion and consultation with the government and press their point of view. It is a matter of degree.'

Lord Carr is concerned, as are many other Tories, with the predominantly political, as opposed to industrial, role that he believes unions have taken on in recent years. As he says: 'Previously trade union leaders had strong political convictions, but when it came to using industrial action they were trade unionists first and politicians second. They had a strong traditional belief that you did not use industrial action to further political objectives. Now we have some trade unionists who are politicians first and trade unionists second, and this is a very important reversal of roles. It is when there is the element of blackmail backed by the threat of industrial action that trade union power becomes dangerous.

'It is not that the power of trade unions is too great; rather, it is how they use that power. In other countries unions also have great power but use it with much greater discretion. They resort to strike action with much greater reluctance as a last resort. Quite large sections of the British trade union movement use the strike or the threat of a strike as the weapon of first resort. What we want to look at, therefore, is the way trade unions use their power rather than the extent of that power. In every other country except Britain trade union power is used within a framework

20

of rules, accepted on the whole by the unions themselves, by the employers, the government, the community: these rules have been defined in law. In this country we have tended to withdraw the operation of the law in relation to the trade unions, which is an unfortunate historical accident. Increasingly, however, as the 1950s and then the 1960s passed it became clear to many people in this country (by no means only Conservatives), including many people in the Labour Party and the trade union movement themselves, that the old voluntary concordat was breaking down. More and more of us began to feel there was a need for a legal framework within which trade union power would not be diminished but controlled and channelled. This is what the struggles of the last fifteen years have been all about.

'It should not be forgotten that it was Mr Wilson's Labour Government which, contrary to all their normal instincts decided in 1968 to have a comprehensive framework of legislation: hence 'In Place of Strife' and hence also the Conservative Government's commitment in 1970 to introduce the Industrial Relations Act, for which I was responsible. I believe that some such framework is necessary.'

Thus Lord Carr, clearly, does not believe that the problems of labour relations can be solved by emasculating trade union power. Laws should only be used to control and channel that power, not to break it. He believes that in some respects the unions are too weak rather than too strong. Thus in the Tory Party conference prior to the 1970 election, Mr Heath said: 'The trouble in Britain today is not that the trade unions are too strong but that they are too weak in this important sense: that compared with other countries it is getting more and more difficult for employers to make firm agreements with trade unions which they will keep, because well over 90 per cent of all the strikes that take place in Britain start as unofficial strikes and then subsequently are blessed by the unions.'

Lord Carr would like to see a return to the old situation, as he puts it, that when a trade union leader signed on behalf of his members then that was an agreement which had the full backing of the union, which would subsequently do its best to see that its members kept to it. This, he believes, is an essential ingredient of more stable and peaceful industrial relations.

There is another, closely related trade union weakness: that while trade unions never seem to be reluctant to use their rule books against members who refuse to follow a direction to strike,

21

they are extremely reluctant to do so in the case of members who strike contrary to union instructions. The failure to exert their authority to discipline members in the latter case is, Lord Carr argues, a clear example of union weakness rather than strength and one he would like to see rectified.

Government-union relations during the Heath Administration of 1970–4 came close to catastrophe: they included the 1971 Industrial Relations Act, the pay policy ending in the three-day week and the final confrontation with the coal miners. Lord Carr, who had the major responsibility for government-trade union relationships during the first part of that administration, speaks of the paradox of extremely good and extremely bad relations at the same time.

'In a very paradoxical way relations between the unions and the Heath Government were both better than they had ever been with any government before, and worse. The confrontations which occurred were not, as popularly supposed, over the Industrial Relations Act but over pay policy. There was a great deal of hassle over the Industrial Relations Act, and our problem there had been greatly increased by the fact that our immediate predecessors had first of all said that such legislation was absolutely essential in the national interest, and then had caved in and not enacted it, so that when we came to power in 1970 the trade unions undoubtedly thought: we have knocked a Labour Government off its perch and we are all the more determined to knock a Tory one off theirs too. It would have been healthy for the country if the Labour Government had got its act through. Their failure made our position very much more difficult: as a result we started those negotiations (about the 1971 Act) in a more head-on situation than otherwise might have been the case because of what had gone on in the preceding year. And that of course led to demonstrations, one-day strikes and a great deal of public hassle. Beneath the surface, however, very constructive and close consultations were going on between the government and the trade unions. Before the government, unfortunately, felt compelled to introduce a statutory incomes policy in the autumn of 1972, more detailed and fundamental discussions were held between the Heath Government and the trade unions than had ever been held before between any government and trade unions, in a desperate attempt to get some broad consensus—not a bargain —between government and unions.'

Lord Carr maintains that whatever went wrong between the

Heath Government and the trade union movement, that Government had made a greater effort to bring the unions into the picture on national affairs than any of its predecessors. In support of this contention he describes how, at a major American trade union convention of 1973 at which many British trade unionists were guests, a number of them told both their hosts and members of the British press who were covering the convention that 'no British Prime Minister of either party had ever treated them on such equal terms as had Mr Heath or been so prepared to consult with them and take their views into account over all the major issues.' This union attitude to Heath was also brought out at a public meeting in Kent, when Vic Feather was asked who, in his opinion, had been the best Prime Minister for the trade unions to deal with in the sense of really being prepared to understand, discuss things that really mattered and take their views seriously. To this Feather replied: 'That is the easiest question I've had—without doubt, Mr Heath.'

If this was the case, one is bound to ask what went wrong, for when Heath went to the country in 1974 the election was substantially fought in terms of 'Who runs Britain?'—the unions or the government, and in the event that particular government was thrown out. The fact that the election could be presented in such terms, and still more that the Tory Government should then go down to defeat, has clearly imprinted itself deeply upon the political consciousness of many Tories and undoubtedly had much to do with the very different attitudes to unions which emerged among ministers and the rank and file of the party when the Tories returned to power in 1979 under a new leader, Mrs Thatcher.

The close political relationship of the trade union movement with the Labour Party is one of the key factors in British public life. Lord Carr believes it to be a tragedy that the trade union movement felt compelled to form an organic link with, and indeed almost to found, the Labour Party. As he says: 'Historically the two old traditional parties—the Liberals and Tories—must take a great deal of blame for allowing this to happen, because had they been more responsive to organised labour in the conditions of the nineteenth century—the weakness of employees as individuals in those days and their consequent need for collective action—; had one or both those parties in the early days of this century been more sympathetic to the plight of employees in the industrial situation so that the trade unions had felt that people in those parties would at least listen to their case, then I believe

23

that the Trade Union–Labour Party tie-up would not have taken place.'

In today's mixed and still predominantly private enterprise economy, most unions go for the biggest slice of the economic cake they are able to obtain for their members and in effect argue that as long as it is a capitalist economy, they will act accordingly whatever their commitment to eventual socialism may be. Against this background, the Tory Party seems to have missed many opportunities over the years of coming to work more closely with the trade union movement rather than having confrontation with it.

Lord Carr in part accepts such an analysis yet also argues: 'In the 1930s the Tory Party, on the surface, appeared to be indifferent to the real aspirations—not simply unemployment—and collectivist feelings of people in industry, although there were many men in the party such as Macmillan, Butler, Eden and Baldwin himself, and of the later generation McLeod and Maudling, who did understand this very deep social feel of the community. After the war we had the Industrial Charter which Butler had played a major part in preparing; then in 1951 when Churchill won the election, he made Walter Monckton Minister of Labour and he built up a great rapprochement with the trade union movement. By the end of the 1950s the Tory Party had got its relationship with the trade unions right.'

As a major Tory figure in the Lords not offered any office in the Thatcher Government, Lord Carr is understandably cautious about what he says in terms of that Government's policies. He emphasises that he supports the overwhelming majority of its policies. At the same time, he makes no bones about his disquiet at what he describes as the government's manner of talking in a separatist way about trade union problems. This, he says, is dangerous. Dialogue between government and unions appears to have come to a standstill. Thus he says: 'It is an art of government to act strongly, sometimes even harshly, but always to be prepared to talk. The present government seems—no doubt in part spurred on by natural exasperation with the trade union movement (and here it reflects the general feeling in the country) —unwilling to talk enough. It is,' he continues, 'the easiest thing in the world today to say that the trade unions are too powerful and ought to have their power reduced; or that we (the public) are fed up with them. The trade unions should take very serious note of their unpopularity, which spreads to millions of their own members. But having said this, there should be more dialogue.

'It is not good to hear what was said this morning [14 May 1980, "The Day of Action"],' Lord Carr said, quoting Len Murray, ' "that we have got to go on the streets because we cannot talk to this government". There is an atmosphere (even though such a statement is not true) which has been created that makes people feel such a remark is credible. Now the more strongly a government or a minister feels he needs to resist what the trade unions are demanding, the more he ought to go out of his way to find time to talk with them.'

It is a paradox of British political life that the Tory Party, which is generally assumed to represent the interests especially of employers and industrialists, has so few members of parliament with real industrial experience. Lord Carr, who does have such a background, says: 'One of the troubles is that there are so few people in the Tory Party, at least in Parliament, who have had genuine experience in industry, particularly of manufacturing. This is a very great lack. It is not only the trade unions that feel this lack. Management is always grumbling that politicians including the Tories know nothing about industry, and that the responsible ministers are also ignorant about industry. It is vital,' he thinks, 'that employers and managers do something about this lack and, for example, encourage people on their staff who are inclined to go into politics to do so, because Parliament needs more people with direct industrial experience.'

Lord Carr says it is easy enough to make the trade unions scapegoats. 'There are too many people who try to put all the blame for things that go wrong in industry upon the trade unions, and not enough upon management. Some people, of course, would put it all the other way round.' Examining the question of overmanning which is often cited in relation to the unions—making some international comparisons then of course it is true—Lord Carr says, 'that we have got overmanning at the shop-floor level. But one of the interesting things is that we have also got overmanning at managerial level, at the secretarial level and so on, although far too many people appear to think that all overmanning is on the shop-floor.'

A disastrous example of bad management occurred when Lord Carr had his first ministerial job as Parliamentary Secretary to the Ministry of Labour (1955–8), when the Austin Motor Company, as it then still was, had its first major post-war redundancy.

25

It was the first set-back in demand for motor cars after the war and the Austin Motor Company declared a very big redundancy 'just like that'. 'There was,' Lord Carr says, 'no effective consultation and some of the people made redundant were old service employees. At that time the company had not even got a member of its Board with special responsibility for personnel relations.'

Many of the problems of British industry and the clashes between unions and employers or unions and government, come down to a question of attitudes. In the eyes of many people on the shop-floor, for example, managers and directors are equated with the Tory Party. Lord Carr certainly insists that management must take much of the blame for what is happening in British industry.

The question of productivity recurs throughout this book. Many reasons for Britain's poor performance when compared with her principal trading rivals are advanced. Poor management, restrictive union practices, inadequate investment, too much government interference are all blamed with different degrees of emphasis, depending upon the viewpoint of the speaker. Lord Carr sees a wide range of reasons for this poor performance.

'Possibly the basic fault lies with our culture: look at our schools. How many people are encouraged to go into industry? Industry is not held in sufficient esteem. Then there is the question of government responsibility, because since the war we have suffered from lack of stability in government policies: it is not possible to plan modern industry on the basis of having a policy for five years after which it is likely to be reversed. For example, look at the number of tax changes for industry in this country compared with West Germany: for every one change they have, we have between ten and twenty. Governments have served industry very badly.

'Then examine regional policies in this country: there are tax incentives, grants, tax subsidies, yet the base for these is constantly changed and areas qualifying for support and the type of support available constantly change, so that before it is possible to build a new factory in a development area there have probably been two or three changes in the conditions governing the venture. Thus governments are a lot to blame, and all this is apart from interventionist policies.

'The whole question of nationalisation is another matter. Of course we have got a poor steel industry when it has been under the threat of nationalisation or denationalisation or renationalisa-

26

tion: How can anyone run an industry under such conditions? Government as an institution—not any particular one—has a great deal to answer for in these respects.'

Finally, on the performance of management itself, Lord Carr says he is an uncompromising believer in the Napoleonic saying that there are no bad soldiers but only bad generals; following from that, directors and senior managers must accept first responsibility for what happens. 'Having said that, there are great difficulties: outdated trade union attitudes, having to deal with a dozen trade unions in a factory where Britain's counterpart in West Germany would deal with one union, so that the trade unions too must shoulder a lot of the blame. But in the end it comes back to company management: some companies overcome these attitudes and are among the best in the world; there is no real reason why others should not do as well.

'Another major criticism I would make of British employers, is that they have been very bad—(the Austin example quoted above) —in not really telling their employees what they are doing and why—explaining profits and the need for profits. From 1947 onwards, for example, I worked in a relatively small company with about 4000 employees in five factories, and from that year onwards one of the Board always went round to hold a meeting in each of the factories as soon as possible after the annual general meeting to explain results, profits, how they were used, what the plans were for the future. Had every company in Britain done that sort of thing over the last thirty years, we would face a very different situation today. Now more companies are doing it, yet so far too few companies have seen the importance of explaining the business to their workforces. You cannot have universal education for a few decades and not end up with different attitudes to management; people no longer do things simply on someone else's "say so"; they require an adequate explanation.'

James Prior, Secretary of State for Employment in Mrs Thatcher's Government, was one of the contenders for the leadership of the party at the time when the Tories chose Mrs Thatcher in place of Edward Heath. He is a moderate, middle-of-the-road Tory who has been dubbed 'chief wet' in the curiously expressive slang of the hard right of his own party. Should the monetarist policies of Mrs Thatcher, Sir Geoffrey Howe and Sir Keith Joseph collapse, then Mr Prior would be a leading contender for the leadership of a revamped Tory Party. It is an interesting political sidelight upon Mrs Thatcher that the job of employment was

27

given to Prior at all, especially as he had been and remained a close associate of Mr Heath and had views upon the unions at marked variance with the hard anti-union attitudes that seemed to dominate the Tory Party in 1979. One result was that during 1979 and 1980, when Prior was piloting his legislation through the House of Commons, he found some of the toughest criticisms coming from his own right wing on the grounds that he was not going far enough to restrict union power.

Looking first at the political power of the unions, James Prior argues that since they have a great deal in Britain—and more than in many other countries—there has to be a fairly close relationship between government and unions. This, he believes, should be based mainly upon discussion of industrial matters. The great problem in Britain, however, is that the unions were the founders of the Labour Party; as a result they have become deeply involved in party politics. It is, therefore, never easy for a Conservative government to have the sort of relationship with the unions that, for example, a Republican President or a Republican administration in the USA might have; or even a Christian Democratic government in West Germany.

It is not particularly easy for a Labour government to deal with the unions for if it determines upon action the unions might resent, it is aware of the fact that they are its paymaster. Looking back over the fifty years following the General Strike, Mr Prior believes there was a fairly good understanding between unions and the government of the day, which was chiefly Conservative. Then in the 1950s, when Walter Monckton was responsible for employment and labour relations, there existed a reasonable basis for discussion between unions and a Conservative government. Searching for the ideal government-union relationship at the present time, Mr Prior says: 'A situation in which there is discussion between the government of the day and the unions on all matters involving industrial and employment policy is what you want, with as little reference to the doctrinal aspects of policy as is humanly possible.'

On the subject of union structure, James Prior sees the growth of the power of the shop steward in recent years as one of the more startling and in many respects, he thinks, more damaging aspects of British trade unionism. As he says: 'We need strong trade union leadership which is able to control the rank and file. At present we have far too many unions: what is needed is much more development of the industrial union; although there will be no quick change for the present union pattern is embedded in the prejudices and emotions of the past, and it may be a long time before necessary changes can be effected.'

The trade union movement which will not allow a Labour government to reform it is certainly not going to allow the Tories to do so. Nor, it seems, are they about to do so themselves. Commenting on such attitudes, Mr Prior says they put government in great difficulty with the result that great patience as well as firmness is required from the government.

On the question of legislation to effect changes in trade union behaviour, Mr Prior is fundamentally cautious, although accepting that there is a powerful case for some kind of pressure upon the unions to make them change. But one attempt was made by the Tory Party in 1971 and that followed what Barbara Castle's 'In Place of Strife' had sought to achieve in 1969. Mr Prior's Bill in 1979, therefore, represents the third such attempt in ten years. Of his own approach to the unions, Mr Prior says: 'It has to be a combination of approaches so as gradually to change the whole attitude and the way unions organise themselves without mounting a frontal assault, for frontal assaults are pretty fruitless exercises.'

Although the operation of the American and German trade union systems is often held up as a possible example for Britain to emulate, Mr Prior is doubtful that Britiain should go for either. In his view, the American system is not especially satisfactory although, he says: 'The only thing that is more satisfactory in America is the attitude of the American people towards work, money and enterprise. In Germany, on the other hand, there is a much more disciplined society which makes the operation of trade unionism much easier.'

On the subject of the legislation for which he is responsible, Mr Prior says: 'The Government's legislation is an attempt, for the first time for many years, to prove that it is possible to pass legislation on industrial matters through the House of Commons which can be regarded as doing something to restore the balance of bargaining power. They must, therefore, be acceptable measures which will stick. The measures,' he says, 'are designed to help restore the balance of bargaining power; the present imbalance has not done the unions any good. It could be argued, for example, that if the excessive extent of their bargaining power had been good from a union point of view then the workers they represent would be much better off than they are; however, they are in fact worse off than in almost any other of the major western industrialized nations. The Government, therefore, is seeking to achieve a number of specific measures: making secondary picketing unlawful; easing some of the worst excesses of the closed shop; making it more difficult for new closed shops to be set up; gently bringing in secret balloting and postal balloting; and taking other action on such forms of secondary union action as blacking and secondary striking.'

Part of Mr Prior's caution about passing legislation stems from the experience of the Heath Administration. 'It is no good passing laws,' he says, 'unless employers are going to use them. One of the great mistakes about the 1971 Industrial Relations Act was that it brought in laws, for example, covering the closed shop, more or less making that illegal yet no employers except for a few mavericks did anything about it.

'This time,' Mr Prior argues, 'we have approached the subject in a quieter and more practical way: the Act will confer certain rights on individuals so that at least they may obtain damages for unfair dismissal. However, there appears to be a more robust attitude developing among employers even with regard to the closed shop, and though a lot of employers of the big companies will continue to have a closed shop they will now also have to recognise that we are conferring certain rights on individuals within closed shops.'

On the question of whether or not the unions may be seen as some sort of estate of the realm, Mr Prior gives an unequivocal 'No'. He does not believe that any grouping outside Parliament should have special status. Enlarging upon that theme, he says: 'One of the great problems about modern Britain—and it has happened a few times before in our history—occurs when it is seen that a group of people outside Parliament are able to exercise more power than Parliament itself. Many people feel this about the trade unions today in the same way they felt it about the industrial barons of the nineteenth century or the landed barons of the seventeenth and eighteenth centuries. The unions should not be seen as constituting an estate of the realm; yet obviously because of their powerful position, they exercise, and have a right to exercise pressures upon Parliament and government. They should not, however, try to usurp the position of those elected to run the country.'

On the subject of current Tory attitudes towards the trade unions, Mr Prior does not pull any punches. He argues con-

30

vincingly: 'A major problem at the moment is the existence of a good deal of Tory hostility to the unions, and in recent years Tories appear to have lost sight of an earlier tradition of regarding the working man as a natural ally. In the last twenty years in particular we have lost touch very badly with the working class Tory. I have spent a good deal of time in the last five years trying to do something about this, which is part of the reason why, in certain sections of the Conservative Party, I am so unpopular.

'As a result, I think we have lost the vision which Disraeli had of the working man being a Tory as also of the whole 'one nation' concept. The attitude of the Tory Party through most of the years I have been in Parliament towards the trade unions, has been an entirely negative one. Instead of trying to embrace the trade unionist and change the trade union movement into something helpful to us because we were a part of it and seen to be a part of it, we have done nothing but attack the movement the whole time. I do not believe that this is the way you ever get the best out of the British because once any organisation, and particularly a conservative organisation, feels it is under attack it digs in its heels and changes even less.'

Mr Prior believes that the fact that he has been able to withstand some of the more extreme pressures that have been put upon him from within the party, is because support for his line towards the unions is growing within the Parliamentary Party and, to a much lesser extent, in the constituency parties.

For those who are very much laissez-faire in their views, the unions are regarded as obstacles, since they wield monopoly power. The growth of nationalisation, moreover, has encouraged the growth of monopoly trade unions as well. Such an inbuilt monopoly position in society does not allow market forces to operate in the way they used to do, so that it is less a question, for example, of trade unions bargaining in a market society for their share of the 'cake' and getting what they can out of the economy as a result of their own endeavours, than of coming into their position by sheer monopoly power or brute strength. The biggest and strongest unions can well argue, 'Fine, leave the market forces at work, we are part of the market and we shall therefore use our strength to get the biggest share we are able of what is going.'

Such an approach would not be the Disraelian answer to what Toryism is about, Mr Prior argues, because such an attitude would really divide the nation. 'Should this happen, then the political,

31

economic and social pressures to bring about a fairer society will certainly bring about changes in the policy. You cannot forever have the miners getting 20 per cent and some people nothing. The result of that sort of thing must be that if miners get 20 per cent then civil servants have to get 15 per cent, and so on. The Wages Council structure which goes back to the early 1900s, was designed to ensure that workers without bargaining strength are not exploited.'

On the subject of productivity Mr Prior sees the great worry as the fact that for every one hundred pounds of new investment, Britain gets less out of it as a nation than do all our principal trading rivals. It is not simply that British productivity growth is low: in fact productivity measured over the whole economy has increased rather more than, for example, that of the USA over the last fifteen to twenty years. But Britain starts from a much lower base level. In terms of responsibility for low productivity, Mr Prior says: 'The failure to achieve greater productivity is more than half the fault of management and rather less than half the faults of governments and unions. Obviously unions have a very great responsibility, though. What has done an enormous amount of damage to productivity in Britain is the constant incomes policies which have always had a loophole for spurious productivity.'

Expatiating upon the subject of incomes policies, James Prior thinks: 'There may be much to be said in favour of incomes policies just as long as they are not statutory and as long as they are not so close to statutory that they are virtually an imposed policy, since then they can be very damaging. On the other hand, to get the maximum degree of voluntary acceptance of what the country can afford, perhaps some form of concerted action for accord type policies might help, because you can then develop some concept of fairness in society, although not an absolute concept of it.'

Mr Prior is a great believer in talking with people so as to develop a spirit of working together; he would like to see a round table or forum approach to industrial problems and thinks there is much to be said for an annual debate on the state of the economy. He also thinks it might prove valuable for trade union leaders, bankers and industrialists to have to come before parliamentary select committees so as to justify their actions. Possibly such an annual debate should start with the National Economic Development Council (NEDC) and a select committee discussing

32

with each other the problems the country faces. Such an initial discussion could then be followed by a more inquisitorial affair with trade union leaders and others taking part.

In some of his answers Mr Prior may sound 'un-Tory-like', at least to his own right wing. Yet he does not pull any punches with the unions and, for example, in answer to the question of whether—as unions often argue—they are made scapegoats, he says tartly: 'They have brought a lot of it upon themselves. Many people feel they have become arrogant, unsympathetic, bullying and thoroughly badly organised and oriented in recent years. They are inefficient beyond measure and the quality of the provincial or regional structure is not good. They have become deeply unpopular with wide sections of the community.'

On the other hand he is equally ready to dissect faults of management. 'It is far too easy,' Mr Prior says, 'for everyone to parcel their frustrations and ineptitudes together and simply say it is union structure. I am a believer in the saying that there are no bad men, only bad officers, and I think it is really British management that has allowed us to get into this mess. Further, the political business of throwing together disparate groups in nationalised industries (I do not think the British operate very well in enormous groups) has led to the growth of union power; it has led to bad management structure; poor management and lack of communication by management. One result is that today too many managements simply rely upon the trade unions to communicate their message to the shop-floor.

'Results condemn management. It is not individuals, because they are snapped up all over the world and do extraordinarily well. Quite often, moreover, British management of multinationals based in Britain also does well and sometimes achieves productivity higher than in sister companies in other countries. But the tragedy about British management is its general level and the ingrained, thoroughly bad practices which have almost worked their way through to the top of it.'

At the Tory Party Conference of October 1980 there were demands for further government action to restrict trade union activities. Mr Prior resisted these pressures and made plain he would not be pushed into any precipitate actions. The mood of a good deal of the party was clearly against him, yet he argued that reviving Britain was 'not just a matter of economic management but the re-establishment of the harmony of wills which can only come through reasoned political discussion.' On union

33

'abuses', he said: 'We mean to deal with abuses as we identify them and as we think the time is right. But our main objective must be to go at a pace acceptable to public opinion, to carry with us the support of the shop-floor for what we are doing, and in that way to make our changes in the law stick.' And finally he said: 'Because we are a truly national party we cannot be against or hostile to the idea of trade unions.'

Lord Carr and James Prior each at ministerial level represent the broad middle approach to trade union and labour questions of the Tory Party.

3

Some Tory Opinions

Five Tory MPs provide an interesting spectrum of the views to be found within the party. The first, Nicholas Scott (member for Chelsea) has been cast in the role of chief 'wet' by hard liners of the Thatcher Government. Throughout his period in the House, Scott has been associated with the backbench committee on employment; he was, briefly, Under-Secretary of State in the Department of Employment, having been appointed in the middle of the coalminers' strike of January 1974. He has also worked in the print industry, which sees some of the more extreme union attitudes and exercises of power.

A second Tory, Keith Wickenden (member for Dorking) might be described as a middle-of-the-road businessman backbencher. He is executive chairman of European Ferries, which owns Townsend Thoresen Car Ferries and harbours, including Felixstowe harbour, and in his business capacity has had dealings with the National Union of Seamen, the Merchant Navy and Airline Officers' Association and, to a limited extent, ASTMS, Apex and the TGWU.

A third Tory, John Stokes (member for Halesowen and Stourbridge) has had industrial experience in ICI, British Celanese and Courtaulds although only dealing with staff. He now runs his own personnel selection business. Mr Stokes has distinctive views upon the relations of management and employees and in a *Guardian* leader of mid-1980, for example, entitled 'The Adorable Mr Stokes', he was savaged—in kindly fashion—for his apparently extreme right wing views. Among them is his contention that the House of Lords is beloved not least by British working men.

John Gorst (member for Hendon North), another Tory backbencher, first became involved with union affairs in the House of Commons when he took up the rights of George Ward, the employer in the notorious Grunwick dispute. As a public relations consultant he had also advised BALPA, the airline pilots' union, both when they were on strike and working to rule, so he claims a certain knowledge, if untypical, about the workings of unions.

Finally John Biffen, Principal Secretary to the Treasury* in Mrs Thatcher's Government, who is generally regarded, and regards himself, as a high Tory. Intellectually he is one of the most stimulating and challenging men in the House of Commons.

Their views, broadly, may be seen to represent a spectrum from left to right across the Parliamentary Tory Party.

The central concern of many Tories in terms of industrial affairs is with union power; a majority of Tories consider the unions to be too powerful, although there are many variations on this theme. Nicholas Scott, for example, argues that trade unions and trade unionists have great power to inflict damage on others and on society as a whole; yet in other ways he says they are not powerful enough, that is, in relation to their own members, since something like 90 per cent of the stoppages that occur in Britain are unofficial, taking place without union authority. Subsequently the appropriate unions do nothing to stop these strikes. Members of unions who strike unofficially do not use the procedures the unions have negotiated on their behalf; a habit has grown up of simply stopping work and ignoring procedures. On the other hand, Scott sees the unions as having too little power: for example, although they sit as equal partners with government and industry on the NEDC he would prefer to see all unions and employee organisations—not just those affiliated to the TUC—develop a way of electing representatives to sit on some form of economic and social committee or council of the kind that exists in almost every other EEC country. This, moreover, was something the Conservative Party talked of before the 1979 election.

Keith Wickenden's concern with union power is somewhat different: he would like to see the legal immunities of unions restricted. There is no reason, he says, why one corporate entity or group of corporate entities should enjoy immunities that are not available to everybody else. He is opposed to the right to engage in secondary and tertiary picketing and blacking. The strongest power the unions possess is the strike weapon: he stresses that it is the threat of the strike rather than the strike itself which constitutes this power, since once a union actually strikes he believes that it has (usually) lost; the threat, however, particularly if the timing is right, can be very effective. The strike, indeed, is a two-edged weapon: once a union strikes, its members cannot win because, whatever happens, they lose income which they will

* He became Secretary of State for Trade in Mrs Thatcher's 1981 cabinet reshuffle.

take a great deal of time to make up—if they ever do. So it is the strike threat the employer fears.

The media generally have a great deal to say about union power. Like many Tories and businessmen Wickenden sees two sides to the power question: on the one hand, he thinks the trade unions as such do not have too much power; on the other hand, he believes that shop stewards do have too much power and that it is too easy for the politically motivated, or simply the bad shop stewards, to persuade their men to walk out with appeals to union solidarity. This may be on an unofficial basis; subsequently the national union leaders find they cannot persuade the men to go back.

John Stokes is unequivocal in his belief that unions are too powerful. He thinks most of their immunities should be reduced or got rid of but that, owing to Home Office weakness, even existing laws are not adequately enforced. He thinks no picket should be more than three or four strong and that they ought not to have the right to stop lorries, for example, although these may choose to stop. Picketing, he says, has turned into blockading of ports and factories and is accompanied by far too much violence. He also believes that all secondary picketing and the picketing of customers should be made illegal.

Stokes is also scathing about the general level of union leadership and believes it is generally of a very poor calibre compared with union leaders in many other countries, and does not act in the best interests of either its members or of the country. He thinks one reason for this is that union leaders are badly paid; at the same time he feels that union leaders have not thought deeply enough about the problems which are facing British industry: they take the short term view of trying to safeguard jobs instead of, as for instance in the USA, trying to act as a stimulus to management to make it more efficient so that in the end there will be more jobs and pay for everybody. In a somewhat contradictory vein, he says that union leaders are unpopular but nonetheless their members go along with them because in the end, so far, these leaders have got them the money.

John Gorst maintains there is an imbalance between the power of organised labour and the power of the people they negotiate with: it is an imbalance he wants to see redressed. He argues the unions have too much power, especially as many of them hold to the concept that the interests of the unions are paramount when weighed in the balance against the interests of the nation—

'My members right or wrong'—without respect to the effect this attitude has on the national interest or on the interests of people outside the union. He goes on to argue that industrial disputes and their consequences should be confined to the primary participants. Consequently he is opposed to all secondary action: if a dispute begins to affect people other than the primary participants, then the wider interests of the nation should be seen as paramount rather than the narrow interests of the disputants. Like many Tories, Gorst thinks that union leadership has considerable difficulty managing its lower echelons.

The unions are too strong again according to John Biffen, because the authority they wield cannot effectively be cast within a legal framework as long as there is no corresponding sense of moral responsibility which attaches to them, as has been the case in the past in relation to other large corporate entities within the state. Biffen thinks that many people in the Labour Party sympathised with the initiative taken by Barbara Castle with her 'In Place of Strife'. However, those who are hard-headed, he argues, know that the cause of union reform is, broadly speaking, electorally popular while the fate of being identified as the political spokesman for the union movement is, if anything, unpopular.

While no one argues against the right to strike there are wide variations of view as to when the strike weapon should be used, and, still more, how it should be used. Strikes are the union activity which most often make the headlines; when coupled with periods such as the 'winter of discontent', they easily evoke the anger of those affected by them.

Nicholas Scott claims that the unofficial strike is more than anything else the British 'disease' and says: 'If you look at our record of strike days lost we are only about half way in the league table. But I think the difference here is that it has widespread effects in industry in inhibiting the attitudes of the first line of management who are always playing safe, never going for the bold move, because they are frightened the men will just down tools and walk out.'

The reasons for this British readiness to strike unofficially are not easy to pinpoint. Scott believes they are the result of a mixture of causes: 'Cumbersome procedures which union members do not have enough faith in, a legacy of bad management as well as a legacy of union leadership being out of touch with its members. Furthermore, at the present time a sizeable part of all union leadership is on the left of the political spectrum and unrepresentative.

38

On the other hand, the seeds of this may well have been sown in the post-war period when union leadership was very authoritarian and right wing, as was the leadership of the Labour Party, so that (both) were out of touch with the grass roots membership.'

Keith Wickenden believes that a strike is justified when a majority of the workforce feel they have a real grievance. But he does not think a national strike is ever justified on the 'say-so' of national officers or even local officers; they should, in his view, always test their workforce and the only way to get its real views is by using the secret ballot. More generally, however, he believes that if a majority of the workforce really feels strongly about a matter then a strike is justified almost whatever the consequence: in such circumstances strikes would be shorter. The only exception to this rule would be a strike that renders the country defenceless: only the police, nurses, doctors or people connected with defence work should have removed from them the right to strike.

Similarly, John Stokes thinks that striking is to be justified under many headings: bad conditions, bad treatment, unfairness, other reasons—and for money.

The Labour Government attempted to curb union power by law in 1969 with Barbara Castle's 'In Place of Strife': it failed and the attempt was undoubtedly a contributory cause of Labour's election defeat in 1970. The Heath Government introduced the Industrial Relations Act of 1971 and then became bogged down in a bitter conflict that ended with the miners' strike, the three-day week and electoral defeat for Heath in 1974. Back in power Labour then tried the different road of the Social Contract, which undoubtedly achieved considerable impact. Yet Callaghan's inept timing over the election of 1979 contributed to the 'winter of discontent', while public reaction to what was generally presented in the media as gross misuse of union power again contributed to the electoral defeat of the Labour Party in May 1979. By December 1979, the House of Commons was debating the Thatcher Government's Employment Bill. James Prior, the Secretary of State for Employment, was the architect of the Bill and despite some powerful pressures and lobbying from more right wing elements in his own party, insists upon going gently over union affairs. He has withstood very tough criticisms from his own side in his determination to avoid a confrontation with the unions if this is at all possible.

Hardliners on union matters inside and outside politics would like to see far more stringent laws governing union behaviour and there is resentment that unions should enjoy exemptions denied to other groups or individuals. Many people, however, of both right and left are dubious of the extent to which the law can achieve more than providing at most a certain framework within which it may be possible to modify the behaviour of unions. It is unrealistic to suppose that simply by passing laws a radical transformation will be achieved in the way British unions operate and behave.

Scott claimed that the 1971 Industrial Relations Act which made closed shops illegal, had little or no impact. And he says: 'I worked in the printing industry and it made not the slightest difference to the operation of the closed shop in the printing industry or anywhere else; it simply went on being operated. You cannot, simply by passing a law, change that sort of thing.' On the other hand, he suggests that by giving greater protection to individuals in a closed shop the Prior Bill will make it much more difficult to come to arrangements for a new closed shop—and that is the kind of way in which to use the law—gently so as to alter a situation. Scott does not think it possible in our society fundamentally to change the position of the trade unions by passing a law.

Keith Wickenden says: 'I am always loathe to involve the law more than one has to. I think that laws—before they could have any hope of working—would require a much more responsible attitude in this country than we have at the present time. If we had a disciplined society as in West Germany and to a slightly lesser extent the USA, I think such laws would work very well; but of course you do not need them once you have got a society as disciplined as that.' Wickenden sees as undisciplined those elements which consider that the contract between an employer and the unions on behalf of the workforce can be broken with impunity by the employee side, although it must always be adhered to by the employer side.

Wickenden does not believe that union reform can be achieved easily by law though he would like to see secondary picketing controlled by law and the requirement for secret ballots introduced. More important, perhaps, he says: 'If we can make the union leadership more reflective of the views of their members, then I think most of the other things would flow from that.'

John Stokes is stronger on legislation. He thinks there must be laws covering union behaviour because 'there has been so much legislation already giving them the absurdly protected position they enjoy in British public life which no other body has and which we know the public and most trade unionists themselves dislike and deplore.' Although doubtful as to how effective legislation may be, Stokes says: 'I fully realise the difficulties and pitfalls; nevertheless an attempt must be made to cut union power down to size.'

John Gorst would like to see much tougher legislation than that encompassed in the Prior Bill. He wants to see some of the immunities which unions enjoy removed: the abolition of the closed shop (though he is not opposed to 100 per cent union membership); he is less certain of the efficacy of enforced ballots; most of all he would like to see a reduction of picketing. While accepting that a man has a right to withdraw his labour and a further right to induce others to join him and therefore the right to picket, Gorst insists that the process of picketing must be one of peaceful persuasion. Consequently he argues that anyone subjected to picketing should not also be subjected to the intimidation of numbers in the background. In the debate of December 1979, Gorst moved an amendment (which was not accepted), the effects of which would have been to 'anaesthetise the area of the industrial dispute in the same way that a polling station is anaesthetised at election time: nothing should be done in sight or sound of the industrial dispute.'

In the years since the Second World War organised labour has become in people's minds something of an 'estate of the realm', a phrase which was applied to unions by Robert Taylor in his book on Britain's unions in the seventies which he called *The Fifth Estate*. Calling unions an estate of the realm highlights attitudes to their power: are they that powerful, do they merit such a description and should they be treated as special within our society—that is, as a corporate group that carries and ought to carry more weight than other corporate groups? These are questions that disturb many Tories—though not all.

Nicholas Scott, for example, is not worried at the idea and in answer to whether he thinks the unions should be regarded as an estate of the realm says: 'I do. This worries some people who think it smacks of a drift towards corporatism, but I think that if the trade unions were able to put their house in order, to see they were really representative of their members and to ensure that it was not simply those unions who chose to affiliate to the TUC who are counted in this context but those outside as well, including staff bodies and others, then I believe they ought to be treated,

41

if not quite as an estate of the realm, certainly as having a constructive part to play in decisions of an economic and social nature.' He sees no objection to what he calls a civilised corporate state in which the real powers and interests in the land have representation in bodies that influence and make social and economic decisions. In any case Britain is governed to a considerable extent by pressure groups.

Such views may appear heretical to some of Mr Scott's colleagues. The relationship between unions and government is seen in a totally different light by Tories and members of the Labour Party, many Tories disliking any political role for unions and wanting them instead to confine themselves solely to industrial matters—wages and conditions. That at least is the logic of the monetarist approach of the Thatcher Government. Such a view towards the unions is not held by Scott. On the free market, for example, he argues that 'where you have union monopoly bargaining power then in many areas the free market does not actually work. You can have a free market, but if in one part of it you have monopoly power that distorts the whole thing.'

Unlike many of his Tory colleagues, Scott believes in the concept of an incomes policy. He says: 'I do not see any chance at all that you can run an economy such as ours over a sustained period without an incomes policy of some sort. Indeed, the present Conservative Government [1980] could be said to be operating an incomes policy by cash limits, but they are leaving it for people to learn the lesson: that increased income will raise unemployment.' Scott also favours some form of annual debate on the state of the economy. He would particularly like to see the annual round of wage settlements concertinaed into as short a period as possible so as to minimise the leap-frogging that goes on when settlements are reached, with one union trying to get a one per cent higher settlement than the previous union to demonstrate that it is doing that much better by its members.

Keith Wickenden opposes the idea of an incomes policy, although conceding that the economic situation might at times be sufficiently bad to warrant one as a temporary expedient: he would, however, regard that as an emergency situation. Like Scott, he favours some form of annual debate on the state of the economy to involve all interested parties before the annual wage settlements take place.

John Stokes says: 'I am not particularly keen upon government having a special relationship with anybody—whether CBI, unions, churches or any corporate body. I believe government has to govern in the interests of all the people and these special pressure groups should be kept at a distance; the same applies to the CBI.' He is unequivocally opposed to an incomes policy which he says is: 'Absolutely futile and dangerous. What we are trying to do now [1980] is get the nation's economy right for the first time since 1945, and that is going to be a very difficult job. Realism is starting to break in,' Stokes says, 'and it is breaking in much more on the shop-floor than it is among intellectuals, among *Guardian* readers and among weak managers in the City. My father and grandfather were in the City so I am not anti-City, but the City is often very silly; so also are some managers who say: "give them the money". Those days are over for ever.' Stokes is opposed to an annual debate on the state of the economy, believing that wages and salaries should be fixed by the market—by supply and demand, which is the only efficient and fair method.

On what constitutes an ideal union-government relationship, John Gorst says: 'It would be one in which trade unions confined themselves to negotiations about the terms and conditions of employment of their members and did not involve themselves in matters which are more properly left to the elected representatives—in other words, political issues.' Amplifying this view, he says: 'I have in mind the social contract in which the unions made demands for cuts in defence expenditure, nationalisation of certain undertakings and so on; these were very remotely connected with terms and conditions of employment. I have in mind the Post Office workers' strike, or threatened strike, to prevent the mail going through to South Africa: that was totally political in its intentions. These are the sort of things I do not believe the trade unions should be involved in: apart from anything else there are substantial sections of the trade union movement which do not necessarily vote for these political ideals, and I think it is divisive within the trade union movement itself.'

Gorst, too, is opposed to an incomes policy: 'It may have attractions as a temporary expedient, but it is the floodgates that get opened after you release them that seem to argue against such a policy.' He divides the market in terms of the private and public sectors: with regard to the former he says the criterion should be the ability to pay. 'But where you have non-productive activities going on where you cannot apply the creation of new wealth and resources as a criterion, then I think you have got to have some form of cash limits arranged in which you either have

43

a lowish paid workforce which enables you to provide a large amount of service, or you have a highly paid workforce but are limited in what you can supply.' Returning to the unions, he says: 'I would like to have a trade union movement which was sophisticated and educated about the realities of what the "goose" can pay.'

John Biffen wants to see a diminution of union membership as a starting point—'If by virtue of large sections of the population choosing not to be unionised, then in character union behaviour might become more analogous to what happens in France or the USA rather than what happens in Britain. In other words, I should like to see us starting from a position where the membership of the unions has diminished and where as a consequence the unions play a much more passive role in formal relations with government and do not have the same almost preponderant voice in pay determination with employers.' Biffen feels that a social contract is broadly undesirable, although he concedes that it is short-sighted to assume there will not be formal relations between governments and outside corporate interests.

British productivity is among the lowest overall of the major industrial powers; repeated analyses demonstrate this to be so though debate as to the causes is wide ranging and inconclusive. Union practices, bad management, lack of investment, outdated machinery, outmoded attitudes of both management and unions and lack of competitive spirit are some of the main reasons advanced. There are others. In 1979 the Dresdner Bank, for example, produced a productivity comparison in which if West Germany were 100 then the USA was 128, France 78 and Britain 52.

Nicholas Scott lays a fair proportion of the blame for this upon the unions: partly because of restrictive practices but more because, since 1965, unemployment has been steadily growing in Britain and the climate for productivity has been commensurately declining. 'No one,' he says, 'is going to bargain for increased productivity which means less jobs when there are few new jobs being created so that unemployment seems inexorably to rise.' On union practices, he argues that the tendency in Britain not to go through the normal procedures to resolve a dispute but instead to stop work first and argue afterwards, has meant, for example, that both lower and middle management tend to play safe, avoiding decisions that would lead to increased productivity for fear that the production line could come to a halt and they would then find themselves in trouble with senior management.

Keith Wickenden has some scathing comments to make about management. 'It is very easy to blame the unions for everything; we have got some rotten management in this country as well, which is one of the other factors to examine. In particular, we have had a very complacent management for a very long time. I sometimes think with horror that it is perhaps only fifteen years ago that I was personally rather amused at the thought that the Japanese could produce cars. It was a very superior attitude and eventually I thought—"Well, I am sure they will be able to copy ours but the cars will be tinny and not very good." Now we accept that the Japanese make magnificent products of all sorts.'

Perhaps most surprising, coming from a Tory, are his reflections upon the Empire. Speaking of its effects upon British business, Wickenden says: 'We had our own captive market for too long. I think the Empire has a tremendous lot to answer for. Quite apart from the fact that it gave us all the wrong attitudes, it also gave us protected markets and drained us of some of our best talent, particularly between the wars when we had lost a million young men anyway and we had to keep sending people abroad to administer it.'

John Stokes also thinks management is primarily responsible for poor productivity. He says: 'It has been bad management and bad leadership. In this country a job in a merchant bank commands twice the salary of a factory manager. There is the depression and low esteem of engineers. The nineteenth-century idea that you went into a factory and made your way is gone, and now the careers master will tell a young man to go into the City, the professions, the public service, or anything but industry. Manufacturing industry is not getting a fair share of people of ability in this country.'

John Gorst says that while poor productivity is considerably affected by union activity, 'I would not on all occasions say it was unjustified from a psychological point of view, because I think it is based on fear. We suffer from obsolete plant in industry and the fear of innovation and consequent loss of jobs is a real one. We did not have the "advantage" of defeat at the end of World War Two that our competitors did, who were thus enabled to start afresh.' He concedes that bad management plays a part.

Looking at a particular union-company situation, Gorst makes the further point: 'If, for example, you take BL where any further inroads will lead to the collapse of the undertaking, they have

45

reached the end of the road; the unions know there are no more demands they can make without doing themselves out of a job. And one of the sad things about our present industrial relations scene is that management can only now manage if they are on the knife-edge of viability.' This situation, he argues, has been brought about where unions are very strong and in an overwhelming bargaining position where it is possible to maintain overmanning and other indefensible activities.

John Biffen is more cautious about the reasons for low productivity and believes it necessary to have an analysis almost industry by industry to find the causes. However, he does say: 'Where you are dealing with the older industries, I think there you find the most intractable problems; and there you do happen to find a tradition of strong union representation. It could well be that the intractable problems derive from the age of the industry every bit as much as from unionisation. It could well be, too, that in quite a lot of modern industries—petrochemicals especially, for example—it is possible to have quite a substantial degree of unionisation and also a high degree of innovation, so I do not want to be too dogmatic about this. On the whole, I think that the low productivity which is alleged to be a characteristic of the British, does in part derive from the substantial trade union influence across most of the areas of manufacturing industry. If you look at the financial services or agriculture where, broadly speaking, we have got a good record relative to other countries, there you will find a very low level of unionisation.'

Many observers of the union scene—and certainly not just from the ranks of the Tory Party—would like to see industrial unions: one union to an industry. But almost everybody concedes that the chances of this are minimal at the present time: the way the unions have grown up, their large numbers and the multiplicity that are to be found operating in a single industry and often in a single factory, simply make it unrealistic as a short-term or even medium-term aim.

The question of industrial democracy was given a major setback by the Bullock proposals, which the Tories and management generally regarded as being so politically one-sided that they rejected them out of hand. Nonetheless, the concept of industrial democracy in other forms is certainly welcomed by Keith Wickenden. 'I think it is desirable. I think that larger businesses such as my own have a great deal to learn from smaller businesses in a sense of consultation, even though the owners of the business

46

may not realise they are doing it. In fact, in the small concern there is a great deal of consultation on every aspect of the business between the manager, who is usually the owner in such circumstances, and his workforce. In larger businesses we tend to pay lip-service to the concept rather than practise it. The form industrial democracy should take is very debatable. I dislike the Bullock proposals intensely: largely because it was not a plan for employee participation; it was a plan for union participation. The effect would be greatly to increase the power in the hands of a few trade union leaders without necessarily supplying the employee participation that I think most businesses require.' In an industry which is only part unionised, Wickenden argues that employees should be balloted for their representatives across the board—both union and non-union members of the workforce.

John Stokes, on the other hand, is completely opposed to industrial democracy; he is not even certain he believes in democracy anyway. He says: 'You must have checks and balances. That is why I am a close supporter of the House of Lords. I think the best democracy was de Gaulle's where you had a "oui" or "non" vote every five years and then for the next five years he just got on with it. I am in favour of putting people in the picture much more fully than is done by management now. I am also in favour of consulting: for instance, if you are putting in new machine tools you must ask the skilled workmen what they think about it. But that does not mean Bullock and that does not mean having all these chaps in the boardroom.' Stokes does not favour worker representatives in the boardroom either from the unions or from the workers as a whole, and he doubts that they in fact want it themselves.

Though sceptical of the concept of worker representatives in the boardroom, John Gorst is in favour, although he adds the rider: 'I do not think that those who have a very narrow view of the enterprise are qualified to make global decisions about it. On the other hand there may be one or two people who, though carrying out a minute aspect of the total enterprise, can yet see the wider issues and so contribute to them.'

The subject of shop-floor power—shop stewards—as opposed to the national union leadership, is one that exercises the minds of many Tories and businessmen. Keith Wickenden has a good deal to say on this subject and feels there is perhaps more of a divide between members and their shop stewards than members and their national leadership. He considers that, in some cases,

47

the local union leadership has been systematically infiltrated by the far left and feels there are far too many communists and worse at that level. Of the approximately 300,000 shop stewards in the country he reckons that between 30,000 and 50,000 are doing the job for what he calls 'political ends', while the remainder do it because they believe in it. The trouble, he says, is that the 30–50,000 are more militant, more articulate and therefore get their way more often than the moderate shop-floor stewards. He believes that being a shop-floor steward is a very quick and easy way to obtain power at the local level—and sometimes quite a strong local level if he can bring a factory to a halt: at such a point a shop steward has a lot of power—both political power and power to disrupt. The economic weapon, he says, is one of the main weapons of the far left.

John Stokes has a similar fear of left wing shop-floor activities: 'The left wing get on and up at shop-floor level by holding meetings on Sunday afternoons, by reading the rules, by attending constantly when most other chaps are going fishing or watching football and so a tiny minority, quite unrepresentative of the mass of the trade unionists, get the power.'

The press especially but the media more generally are consistently singled out by trade unionists as being unfair to their case. Keith Wickenden, however, attacks the press from a somewhat different angle. Talking of the difficulties in getting issues across to the average person, including the average trade unionist, he says one reason is that 'our press is almost indescribably trivial compared with the American press, which tends to be rather serious and sombre on the whole.' Although in Britain we have a national rather than a local press, 'The Chancellor of the Exchequer will have to produce something very startling to get on the front page of the *Daily Mirror*.' The trouble with such an attitude on the part of the press is simply that, since, the average person does not read serious documents, the extent to which they become informed about issues too often depends upon press or television coverage.

Disraeli told Lady Chesterfield (quoted in Robert Blake, *Disraeli*) that the legislation (the Employers and Workmen Bill which made breaches of contract normally no longer liable to criminal prosecution, and the Conspiracy and Protection of Property Bill that changed the law of conspiracy in favour of the trade unions and legalised peaceful picketing, both introduced by Cross in 1875), 'will gain and retain for the Conservatives the

48

lasting affection of the working classes'. Much of Disraeli's reputation and a great deal of subsequent Tory myth-making have been
based upon his concern for the working classes and the picture
he painted in *Sybil* of their miseries under the effects of capitalism.
What is of greatest interest today is that his 'one nation' concept
appears to have been lost by the present leaders of the Tory Party.

The unions, despite endless political rhetoric about socialism,
are in many respects quite profoundly conservative. They are
prepared to work the capitalist system; they believe in and
encourage the principle of differentials which is a fundamental ingredient of capitalism; they seek—quite properly in terms of their
mandates—the largest slice going of the economic cake that they
can obtain on behalf of their members. In all these respects they
are acting—though they may well deny it—in a manner which
ought to make them the natural allies of both business and the
Tory Party rather than its opponents. And yet this apparent
affinity between the interests of trade unionists and the Tory Party
causes acute unease among many Tories.

Reflecting upon this question, Nicholas Scott argues that the
Tory Party-trade union relationship was better in the post-war
era at the time when Churchill appointed Monckton to deal with
labour. During that period, there was a very healthy relationship
between the Tory Government and the trade union movement.
Partly, that resulted from the more conservative nature of trade
union leadership at that time while the Tory Party then went
out of its way to get on good terms with the unions. 'Then during
the late 1950s and 1960s,' Scott says, 'the worry began to emerge
about the overmighty subject: the unions did have powers to
inflict damage on other people and were not really accountable
in any sort of way. Even the Labour Government was forced to
bring forward proposals under Wilson to reform the trade unions,
but was bullied out of it by the trade union leadership of the day.
It ought to have been possible for a Labour Government to enact
sensible reforms of the trade union movement, and it was the
abandonment of that by Wilson that made the present [1980]
situation very much worse.'

Though defending the attitudes towards the trade unions of
Robert Carr and Maurice Macmillan in the Heath Government
of 1970–4 and of James Prior in that of Mrs Thatcher, Scott also
admits: 'Perhaps it is true that in recent years we have lost sight
of that rather philosophical notion of one nation and we have
gone rather too much for the idea of every man for himself. What

49

I mean by the concept of one nation is that we are all part of it and therefore have got to make concessions to the other person's point of view. We have got to give up something that we might be able to win for ourselves in the market place just because we care about keeping a cohesive society. Now that isn't what free market economics are about. Of course, if you look at what most trade unionists want then Conservative governments since the war have delivered the goods a deal better than have Labour governments. I would like to see a much more independent trade union movement that would be perfectly free to deal with and that would seek to influence governments of either side.'

On the question of monetarism as a policy, Scott believes it acts as an invitation to the unions to go for a free for all. 'I think a hands off, totally free market economy is an invitation to the unions to go for everything, and of course if you really go into the arguments of Hayek and Friedman, ultimately they depend on breaking union monopoly bargaining power and, if not abolishing the trade unions, certainly radically diminishing the power they have. I do not think that is possible and therefore you have to find countervailing forces and ways of channelling that power.'

Keith Wickenden says that, while the average working man is a most conservative person and ought to have a natural identity of interest with the Tory Party, it will take a long time to reverse present attitudes. He puts forward the almost revolutionary notion that he would like to see trade union sponsored Tory MPs, and suggests it would also make sense if business were to sponsor union members for parliament.

John Stokes believes that much of the apparent antagonism between the Tory Party and unions is based upon historical folklore, arguing that up to 1900 the Tories were supported by the working classes while the Liberal Party was the party of the upper and middle classes. In terms of the modern Tory Party, he distinguishes what he calls the blue book chaps and the technocrats who tend to be antagonistic to unions and working people and those members in industrial seats (like his own), although he admits there are not very many industrial seats that are Tory.

John Gorst, however, is unequivocal in his admission that there is antagonism in the Tory Party to the unions. The reasons, he believes, are ideological: 'Basically the ethos of the Labour Party is collectivism and what the crowd does or what large masses of people do takes precedence: the psychology is one of solidarity. In the Tory Party, with considerable variations, we believe the individual is more important than the group.' He concedes that James Prior's approach to the unions is designed to win over those within the trade union movement who are the natural allies of the Tory Party. Admitting that there has been a measure of Tory failure in capturing union support, Gorst returns to his individualist thesis: 'If you are outer directed you will be trade union minded, you will be group minded; if you are inner directed, which is the alternative that Tories tend to be, then you will be an individualist.' This conflict in part explains Tory antagonism to the trade union movement.

John Biffen also accepts that, in theory, trade unionists and Tories have much in common. But, looking at union support for a continuing policy of nationalisation, he says: 'I think the unions have seen state control and state ownership as being one of the mechanisms whereby they are able to bargain for real wages to the detriment of the other components such as investment, and they do so more effectively where the state is owner than where the state is not. As a consequence, if you want to see how industry has become organised increasingly for the benefit of trade union members rather than for the public which they might be presumed to serve, then you have to look at the operation of the Post Office or the National Coal Board. Of course, you cannot forever hold out the prospect of repelling realities if you are in an internationally traded commodity like steel or shipbuilding. Sooner or later you have to adjust to the external competitive forces. But in substantial areas it does seem, where you have got industries which are heavily unionised and are state owned, that the privileges which then attach to the workers in such industries are disproportionate relative to all the other factors that might be expected to come into the equation. That situation helps explain why, to me at any rate, the trade union movement has committed itself fairly unequivocally to the promotion of public ownership of industry.'

The arguments are valid yet it is possible to detect a sense, if not quite of bewilderment certainly of puzzlement among Tories that, despite the affinities—real and potential—between the Party and organised labour, they so clearly have such little rapport with it.

Much of the discussion about the unions in the end comes down to questions of attitude: to work, to the profit motive, to competitiveness—and here there would appear to be a growing unanimity in a number of circles that, consciously or not, the

British people may have made some form of choice to opt for an easier lifestyle than that perhaps pursued by the people in countries which today are Britain's principal trading rivals. This is a notoriously difficult area to pin down.

Nicholas Scott says: 'There is also in this country an attitude which puritans would find intolerable, but I am not sure that I do entirely: that people do opt for more leisure and less work— and they do—whether that is going for longer holidays, or closing the country down for a fortnight at Christmas, or going off to the golf course on Friday afternoons. We are not here to flog ourselves to death for forty-eight years of our lives for forty-eight weeks of the year forty-eight hours in the week. I think a more relaxed attitude has merits as long as we keep a decent civilised society and we create enough wealth to keep our people having a rising standard of living for themselves.'

John Stokes says the unions do not really understand capitalism and are not really behind it, while the unions do understand capitalism in France, West Germany and the USA. He thinks it much pleasanter living in Britain than, for example, in the USA.

On the other side of the Tory Party from Nicholas Scott, John Biffen nevertheless says much the same thing about motivation: 'I hesitate to deprecate a level of low motivation if in fact it derives from those who say consciously: "I would sooner have a lifestyle that did not push the last five per cent because I think that there is something frenetic about Britain today or indeed the western world today." You may (by being frenetic) gain something in the actual quantity of goods and services, but you miss somewhere in the quality of life. There is a balance between these two things which is very much a matter of personal judgement.

'What I deprecate,' Biffen continues, 'is low motivation nonetheless demanding the full rewards that might come from high motivation, and that is quite different. Perhaps, therefore, in a very opaque way the British are saying: we are not Japanese, we are not German and we are not Americans, but we are British and that means that probably we will be less materially motivated in many instances. I am not sure that this is true, but I can perfectly understand if it is, and then my anxiety would be that such an attitude becomes confused with inconsistent demands so that, instead of arguing as part of the whole balance of quality versus quantity that motivation need not be so high, people will rather demand that "they"—which usually means the politicians—hand out the goods and services consistent with high motivation while the performance of the country is at a lower level.'

There are many stereotypes of what different groups of people are supposed to think of the unions. This, too often, is the contribution of the media which slots people into neat packages—right wing or left wing and so on. A Tory-union confrontation would seem to be an inevitable part of politics in the 1980s, and yet the range of views about unions in the Tory Party is infinitely wider than the popular image would suggest.

John Biffen, who is on the right of the Tory Party, holds far from orthodox views about the unions. He says: 'I think intellectually I am against them and in a funny way emotionally I am for them, in that I think the unions have been corporate entities which have been profoundly conservative in their social and industrial outlook, although obviously not in their political outlook. And that is something which has appealed to the high Tory in me. But intellectually I think that they have been a perverse influence in industrial life and so I would start off with a hope that we could have a society in which there would be a great deal less unionisation.'

Expanding on the idea of their perverse influence, he says: 'I think two things: first of all, I believe that they have been to some extent Luddite in their resistance to industrial change, though I do not want to overstress that, and I certainly would not want to try to draw a balance or make a judgement between where the faults lie for our poor level of commercial and industrial performance as between management and labour. But, secondly, I think, because of the very substantial corporate privileges that they possess and which I do not think evoke a sense of moral responsibility, they have been able to be rapacious in the conduct of collective bargaining. Part of the explanation of the low levels of profitability and the low levels of investment in Britain lies in the extent to which the demands of labour have had to be satisfied as a prerequisite for the continued existence of industry and commerce.'

Perhaps of greatest interest in political terms is Biffen's attitude towards the results of the two-party system upon industry. 'I think,' he says, 'that what a lot of businessmen regret is the lack of a broader consensus in Britain between the competing political parties about the direction in which economic management should proceed. There is no doubt that is so when you compare what is happening in other countries with Britain: either there is greater agreement between those who are contesting for power, or else there are long periods of unchallengeable authority by one dominant party, as we are seeing in France. In Britain we have not had this experience. Perhaps the most obvious problems have been tax changes in this country that have been essayed and then, if not rescinded at least substantially altered; patterns of public ownership which have been disputed and then eventually grudgingly accepted, and so forth. I think these matters create an anxiety within the business community which is extremely well founded: the lack of underlying continuity in basic attitudes towards industry.

'I myself very much hope that we might come to a settled acceptance of a social market economy: I would concede a very substantial role for government in that; not merely in terms of social services but to some extent in terms of economic management. In return, my opponents would have to accept broadly the case for private ownership so that the political control did not come by the root of actual equity ownership, but much more in the relationship between government and those who managed industries.'

Here Biffen has touched upon one of the most crucial aspects of the entire industrial scene and indeed of British political life. The chances of such a political consensus during the 1980s hardly appear encouraging.

4

Some Labour Views

The range of attitudes towards the unions within the ranks of the Labour Party is perhaps not as wide as in the Tory Party: at least all members of the Parliamentary party accept as a starting point the close union-party tie-up which is an aspect of Labour history. Thereafter, their attitudes will vary, depending upon whether they view trade union involvement as a necessary backdrop to Party power to be accepted as such, or whether they see the Labour Party today as the political spearhead of the demands of organised labour as represented by the trade unions.

Four Labour MPs whose interests spread fairly widely across the spectrum of the Party, here discuss union power, the role of the movement and its links with Labour. The members are Albert Booth, Bob Hughes, Reg Race and Eric Heffer.

Albert Booth (member for Barrow-in-Furness) was Secretary of State for Employment from 1976 to 1979. A lifelong trade unionist himself, he joined the AEU as an apprentice fitter and turner, aged seventeen, and is a sponsored MP.

Bob Hughes (member for Aberdeen North) may be described as on the middle left of the Party; he also became a union member as an apprentice in the engineering section of the AUEW. He, too, is a sponsored MP.

Reg Race (member for Harringey—Wood Green) started working for NUPE at head office in 1972 as a research assistant and later as senior research officer responsible for servicing the union's executive council. He also acted as secretary of the National Steering Committee Against Cuts during the period prior to the 1979 election. Since entering Parliament he has been sponsored by NUPE.

Finally, Eric Heffer (member for Liverpool, Walton) is one of the more influential members on the left of the Party and a powerful voice on the side of change in the constitution and selection of party leader.

The interrelationship of the Labour Party and the trade union movement is a factor of immense importance in British political life: many people both inside and outside the Party object to this close association for a wide range of reasons, yet there is absolutely no prospect in the foreseeable future, even despite current turmoil within the Labour Party, of the relationship changing. Attitudes to the trade union movement, therefore, in large measure are often also attitudes towards the Labour Party. There are great strains between the two groups and, for example, Eric Heffer is on record as saying that the Labour Party is nothing without the unions. At the present time, approximately 200 Labour MPs are sponsored by unions: this and the fact that the Party's funds are overwhelmingly derived from union fees are the two most concrete links between the trade union movement and the Party. The third is the presence of the unions at the Labour Party Conference, where they wield their bloc votes.

Members did not see sponsorship inhibiting their freedom as MPs. Albert Booth felt that sponsorship makes a member conscious that he has resources to contact, and gives him some sense of obligation to find out how his union will be affected by proposals in the House. Otherwise, members make their own judgements. Bob Hughes was surprised after reaching Westminster, he says, at the relative lack of liaison between the executive council of his union and the sponsored MPs. On the other hand, such pressures as exist vary from union to union and depend upon what policy the government, certainly if it is a Labour one, is pursuing. Reg Race thinks some sponsored MPs take very little account of their sponsoring organisation; on the other hand he does not believe unions tell their sponsored members how they should vote. The relationship in fact seems a very loose one.

Union-Labour relations can be stormy: to most Labour MPs the relationship is an inescapable one, an accepted part of the political set-up in this country. Of this relationship, for example, Albert Booth says: 'There is a tremendous overlap of the industrial and political aims and interests of the unions and the Labour Party; it is inconceivable that any major British union would hold an annual conference at which it would only talk about wages and the conditions of its membership. It is inevitable that people organised in a body which is big enough to cover any industry or craft, will use that organisation to express something of their social concerns as well. Such a body needs a strong link in political representation that only the Labour Party can provide.

Whether this is done by a bloc voting system or something else, in practice, once people are involved in that sort of partnership, they in fact have the power to determine to a very considerable extent the policy of the Party.'

Bob Hughes regards the union link as essential. When the Labour Party was founded, it was called the Labour Representation Committee. This was an early recognition by the trade unions that, however powerful or weak they might be in terms of wage bargaining, they needed a wider perspective: that required parliamentary action to improve the lives of working people. 'To that extent the Labour Party certainly is the creature of the trade union movement. The Labour Party needs the strong base the unions provide; at the same time the unions are coming to realise that they cannot operate without the Labour Party.'

Hughes, however, would like to see some examination of the power trade unions wield in the Labour Party conference. There, he says: 'Trade unions are represented on a membership which is almost as fictitious as constituency parties in terms of Labour Party members, because automatically, if you join an affiliated trade union you become a member of the Labour Party by virtue of paying the political levy, and you can only contract out of that. This means that the number of people in the trade union movement who are actually committed to the Labour Party is much smaller than the affiliation. Three unions (the TGWU, the AUEW and the GWMU) provide something in the order of 60 per cent of votes cast at the Labour Party conference and, in consequence, have too big a say in Labour Party policy.'

On the crucial relationship of unions and Party as the present decade opens, Hughes sees considerable difficulties ahead for both sides. 'I think,' he says, 'one of the saddest things about Labour Party-trade union relationships (as well as between rank and file of the Party and the parliamentary party) is a hostility which is obviously apparent between the Parliamentary Labour Party and the trade unions. The Party has always been a very critical one which never hides its differences, but at the present time there is a hostility as well.'

This hostility, Hughes thinks, relates to the performance of Labour Governments in 1964–70 and 1974–9; he suggests these governments did not play fair with their supporters. 'After all, we came into office in 1974 on the basis that there would be no incomes policy, and it was not long before we had one. We came in on the basis of high public expenditure; it was not long before that was cut back. There were clarion calls about what the Party would do in foreign policy, that it did not in fact live up to. Thus there is the feeling that the Party takes up positions without due regard for what its supporters think.'

It is a matter of keeping the commitment of Labour Party voters after they have voted the Party into power. As Bob Hughes says: 'People's expectations these days are very high, and they remain high. There are a number of people in my constituency who say, almost with admiration—a sneaking admiration—that there is one thing about the Tories: they look after their friends and they do it quickly. It is much easier to have tax cuts, to cut public expenditure in order to change the thrust of government policy that way, than to do things in a reverse direction. It is easy to follow a non-interventionist policy, and that I think is one of the things that the trade unions have to understand, that Party members have to understand. It is not going to be an easy process.'

Commenting on Eric Heffer's remark that the Labour Party was nothing without the unions, Reg Race says: 'I agree with that. The Labour Party is structured on the basis of constituency party organisation and the trade unions; if the trade union involvement was taken away, the Party would be a far less credible force in society than it is now. It is not simply the financial support the unions provide the Party—that is easy enough to ascertain—but the qualitative relations which exist both at national and local levels. The Party is much better as a result of trade union involvement: there are more real discussions about real problems because that relationship exists.'

Elaborating upon his own remark, Eric Heffer said: 'I meant that the Labour Party is distinct and quite unique and very different from the social democratic parties of Europe, in the sense that the trade unions actually formed the Labour Party so that the Party is based upon them and always has been. As a consequence, the Party cannot get on without the unions since they are an integral, essential part of it. They are the basis of the Labour Party. Individual membership and constituency organisations actually came later.

'I do not think it is a question of whether the relationship is good or bad: its exists, and in a sense I think it is a very good relationship since it provides the party with a very broad base that relies upon ordinary working people. Thus the Party reflects the strengths and weaknesses of the trade unions, and the unions tend to keep it on a broad socialist base although they tend to be a rather conservative force in the Party. Of course, the Party could exist, and perhaps go even further to the left without the trade unions than is the case at present, yet that way it might end up having no electoral consequence. We must, therefore, live with the reality that we are a broad based party which is essentially dependent upon the trade unions.'

The sheer numbers represented by the trade union movement—more than twelve million members—lead people to assume there is great union power; such assumptions are always enhanced when particular unions use their power in ways that antagonise the general public. A consensus of Labour opinion, however, demonstrates the belief that the unions have too little rather than too much power.

Albert Booth thinks this. Recalling how Frank Cousins once said he would give his right arm to be able to guarantee that every one of his members had a wage above £15 a week, but that he had not got the power to deliver, he says: 'In some ways, unions in other countries have much more power than they do in Britain. In West Germany, for example, unions occupy 90 per cent of the working places on the boards which determine the corporate strategy of the companies in which the members work; that is a kind of power outside the experience of most British unions, with only one or two rare exceptions. In this country, unions have not even begun to argue for any degree of economic power in terms of the ownership of industry which you find in other countries: in Israel, the Histradut owns about 40 per cent of the country's industry. There has been no demand in Britain for economic democracy comparable to those that have been advanced in Denmark: there they are saying that in return for a deal with government over wages policy, what they call the "forfeit in wages" should be made available to them in terms of the right to buy a place in the industry. This has not yet been conceded, but it is a practical policy which unions in other countries are prepared to advance. In Britain, the power of unions depends very much upon their relationship to government: that is, the ability to influence policy. Whether or not that is power is another question.'

Bob Hughes thinks the unions are surprisingly weak. He would like to see them more powerful in two ways: first at the level of decision making. As he recalls: 'My industrial experience is in a fairly small engineering company which employs about 300 men and in which the managing director was on the shop-floor as much as he was in the office. Nevertheless, there was really no contact, and decisions affecting the company's future, affecting the lifestyle and work of the people within the factory were made exclusively in the boardroom with no discussion or consultation with the workforce.'

Reg Race says: 'I do not believe the trade unions have more substantial power now than they did thirty years ago. If you ask whether a shop steward or convenor can sack a managing director, the answer is clearly no: I have yet to discover any case of that happening. If it were the case, it could be argued the trade unions now possessed powers they did not have thirty years ago. Take another measure of their importance in the economy: the distribution of national income. The distribution has not changed very much for the last fifty or sixty years, so that in a very real sense the impact of trade union collective bargaining has been neutral over that period of time as far as the distribution of national income is concerned. All that the trade unions are doing, is reacting in a defensive way to the problems of the economy: that is why collective bargaining is of course important to the trade unions. But, because of the crisis of capitalism we are in, trade unions cannot simply restrict their activities to collective bargaining, because they have to take account of everything the government does.'

Returning to the question of the share of national income, Race says: 'The wages share of the national income has not changed more than about 0·1 per cent since the early 1900s, so that in an objective sense the role of unions in collective bargaining has been to defend wages against the increasing desire of employers to obtain higher profits, and in that defensive sense I think they have been successful. But this defensive operation is completely misunderstood by many conservatives because they see it as an aggressive form of bargaining, designed to undermine industry.'

Race wants to see the unions more powerful and, for example, regarded the need for a 'Day of Action' as a sign of weakness. He believes the only way to change society is by a combination of political and industrial action. 'What I would like to see,' he says, 'is the trade union movement acting on behalf of working people and doing so in democratic fashion: having a major say in a planned economy and, in particular firms, over questions such as the setting of price levels, over the setting of employment levels, over the setting of import penetration ceilings and questions about investment, and so on. At present, none of these questions are discussed in an effective way by the trade union movement at all.'

Finally, Eric Heffer thinks a great deal of nonsense is talked in Britain about union power. 'For example,' he says, 'we used to hear a great deal about too much power on the shop-floor, that there were too many unofficial strikes and that trade unionists did not take any notice of their leaders and that those leaders ought to be more powerful. Now we hear that the leaders are far too powerful and that they are irresponsible. I think this is propaganda put out—and possibly genuinely believed—by those who do fear the trade unions. I think the trade union movement is a very responsible one; I do not think it has too much power. Probably the power is about right. The movement could do with a little more power in certain respects.'

The possession or lack of power by unions leads on to the question of participation and the extent to which the union movement at local (industry) and national level should be involved in decision making processes. Albert Booth says: 'Of course they should be drawn in: I think the present Tory position is an absolute nonsense and totally impracticable. They say the job of the unions is to look after their membership: in British terms, this means dealing with sectional interests and it is precisely on that narrow basis that the unions frustrate many of the things the Tory Government wants to do. If you are fighting for the position of one group of workers in relation to others it is not only the workers who get hurt: the industries in which they work get hurt as well, and it is a never ending process.

'As Secretary of State for Employment I tried to build up the agency function of the Department and get unions and employers actually involved in shaping employment policies, training policies and so on through ACAS and the Manpower Services Commission. If you get the two sides working in a tripartite relationship with government then they are more likely to make policies work which they helped frame, and what they establish in such circumstances cannot be shrugged off when they come to talk about terms and conditions.' After that sort of relationship has been established, Booth thinks moves should be made towards industrial democracy.

Bob Hughes believes industrial democracy to be vital for the whole of industry: 'Although I said unions were weak I do not necessarily say they never abuse their power or go on strike for silly reasons; it would be futile to say that. But, by and large, I believe that if there were a much better consultation process things would work better. I have a great deal of contact with a shipyard in my constituency where there has been a transformation in the past twenty years. Twenty years ago there was hardly a week when they were not on strike; now this seldom happens for both work-force and management have agreed that for the industry to survive there has to be co-operation.'

The form such co-operation takes is the subject of much debate: few people, Labour, Tory or management, for example, have much faith in the efficacy of so-called worker directors on the board though some concede that may be a first step.

Bob Hughes believes it is a proper role for unions to be involved in political agitation for change. As he says: 'Quite apart from the direct connection between wage levels and conditions in factories, there is obviously a political role for unions. We are moving more and more towards a social wage where unions have an interest in how the health service is run, what the levels of unemployment pay or social security benefits should be and indeed the general thrust and strategy of the economy. My own union membership card, for example, makes plain that the union exists for two purposes: first, to protect members' living standards at the workplace; and second, to change society from a capitalist one into one where (they do not actually call it a socialist society) poverty and inequality will be eradicated.'

Such statements are included in the rules of almost all unions which have been political since their inception. Hughes adds a rider that, while he believes unions should be politically involved, they ought not to be captive of governments or vice versa. The unions should retain their political independence while taking a political stance.

Dealing with the line, popular with the political right, that unions should confine their activities to matters relating to conditions and wages of members, Reg Race says: 'I understand the line: it is purely a position of self-interest. The only thing that stands in the path of the Tory Government, preventing it changing the mixed economy to a predominantly market economy, is the power of the trade unions and so they have to break that power in many ways: that is why we have got the employment bill, restrictions on the right of picketing, the abolition of schedule eleven of the Employment Protection Act—in order to break the power of trade unions over collective bargaining. Naturally the Tories want to see the trade unions play a lesser role in the political affairs of the country, because they know the unions are a major force in society and probably one of the few forces that can bring about a change of direction as far as they (the Tory Party) are concerned.'

Race then poses a crucial question, when he asks: 'Who sets the parameters of discussion? The parameters of discussion about politics and the role of trade unions in politics? Those parameters are set by governments, by newspapers and television, and most trade unionists in the absence of that information—like anybody else in society—tend to accept the parameters which they are given. I think, therefore, that it is quite legitimate for trade union organisations and trade union activists to seek to undermine those parameters and say to their members: these are not in your interest, there are other parameters to which you ought to pay attention.'

Race believes that the trade unions should automatically be a part of the pressure group establishment of the country. On the 'Day of Action', for example, he says that while other groups can do things without asking permission of government, the unions were obliged to take a 'Day of Action' in order to make their voice heard. He refers to the example of the City refusing to finance the Labour Government's public sector borrowing requirement in 1976 before the IMF visit. That, he says, 'was a classic case of a relatively small group of people deciding they were not going to buy government gilt-edged stock until either the price was increased (with a rise in the interest rates) or until massive public expenditure cuts were initiated. This was a case of a tiny group of people acting on behalf of another small group and in fact dictating to government what it should do: I think far more naked political power is exercised in this country by such groups than by the trade unions in years.'

Eric Heffer points out that most trade unions have clear rules which state they are in favour of building a socialist society, while some go further to say they are in favour of workers' control. These union rules were drawn up, in the main, prior to the First World War. The TUC, moreover, used to have a rule to the effect that in the event of war a special congress should be called to determine the attitude of the TUC. Thus the unions have always been involved in politics: everybody has a political voice.

The question of what constitutes an ideal relationship between the union movement and governments, is one that must exercise the minds of many politicians at the present time. Albert Booth clearly favours tripartism: 'I think the employers have to be in on it. Given private ownership of a large part of the economy (and even without it), there is a specified management role that needs to be defined. I should say, therefore, that the ideal relationship would be one in which the trade union movement says: we are prepared, through an industrial democracy approach, to pursue a series of agreed objectives as to industrial growth and investment, realising the implications of these objectives for the wages and claims of our membership. Where the two sides conflict we come to you, government, to see how things may be sorted out. Thus, if an industry is embarked upon massive capital investment this should not mean no increase in wages takes place: rather, in such circumstances, there should be an approach to government for additional investment. That is the sort of dialogue we are looking for.

'Second, there should also be some dialogue to indicate the proper relationship between the public and private sectors and particularly the civil service, the health service and those kind of organisations, because we have to earn the means to finance services which do not finance themselves.'

Bob Hughes makes a very different point in this respect, arguing for the removal of the mystique that surrounds the budget. 'Instead of finding that for months preceding the budget further dialogue about economic decisions is precluded on the grounds that it is a budget question, rather the government or the Treasury should advance a series of options: that one kind of policy must have the following results, a different policy another set of results, and so on. Should such options be advanced six months before the budget (assuming an annual budget is a necessity anyway), they could be properly debated and lead to far more open government and greater public discussion. Thus an ideal government-trade union relationship would result if government made known its intentions well in advance and the TUC and individual unions (and of course other bodies) had the opportunity to discuss them and make their own constructive suggestions.'

Eric Heffer argues that, increasingly since World War Two, the trade unions have been consulted by both Labour and Conservative governments, at least until the Thatcher Government. The unions have expected to be called to No. 10 on a regular basis to discuss matters, and a sort of democratic corporate state concept has developed: that the government has its role, the trade unions have their role, the CBI has its role, the press has its role and so on. They should, therefore, all meet and try to reach agreements as far as possible.

'I do not think we can stop trade unions wanting that kind of consultation,' Heffer continues, 'and in general terms it is right. But we have to be careful they do not lose their independence. Even if we had a full-blooded socialist society in this country, I think it would be terrible if the unions, as they are in the Soviet Union and other Communist countries, were to become integrated in the state apparatus as a sort of transmission belt for government policy. That is not the role for the unions: they must be independent all the time so that they can act as one of the checks or balances in our society. They must remain totally free so they can oppose government policy; and, even if we achieve worker control of industry or democratic management, they should still be able to oppose their own democratically elected management as they do from time to time in Yugoslavia. The ideal union position, therefore, is one in which they remain totally independent.'

Britain's low productivity compared with that of her chief industrial rivals is cause for endless debate: no single reason for it is advanced. Albert Booth doubts that it is as bad as it is often made out to be. 'Very few other countries export as many manufactured products in relation to their size, their GNP and population as does Britain. One reason for the false comparisons is very often that like is not compared with like. Sometimes a British factory provides a range of services while similar factories abroad "buy in", so there are differences that way. Where there are unfavourable comparisons—and I do not deny their existence—it is often due to lack of industrial democracy, and that in turn relates back to lack of investment in times of high profitability.

'In the 1950s, British shipyards were producing half the world's shipping, which hardly betokened low productivity; but through the 1950s and 1960s Japanese and other yards made superb strides and took over our role. They were prepared to plough enormous investment into their yards. Had there been that kind of investment in British yards, proposed on the basis of industrial democracy with each side standing to gain from the investment and working out together ways of increasing output, then there would have been a different response.'

'The failures of different sectors of British industry to maintain their lead—car or motor-cycle manufacturers—were due in large measure to the absence of industrial democracy. Short-sighted or bad management would not have been able to ignore the evidence of change, for example, in Japan, if reports had been presented to boards of fifty-fifty composition so that workers' representatives had been able to argue that if we do not invest now we will be without jobs in a few years' time.'

Lack of investment and fear of unemployment are the two principal causes of low productivity according to Bob Hughes: 'Primarily it is a matter of investment; and second it arises from a very deep-rooted fear of unemployment which is growing now. To a large extent we have lost the battle on the argument about productivity because of this fear. You can only achieve proper productivity if people feel part of their organisation. And incidentally, if the best mathematicians in the world are on the shop-floor amongst the people who have to operate on bonus schemes—they can calculate their bonus to the last moment—they make sure they do not produce too much so the ratings get changed.'

To criticisms from the management side that union practices nullify the value of investments, Hughes says the basic union reply would be that too often investment has been automatically followed by redundancies: the fear of unemployment again, so that there is no welcome as there should be from the shop-floor for new investment.

Reg Race sees a multiplicity of causes for low British productivity: one has been the way successive British governments have exercised deflationary pressures upon the economy, so that capitalists have not been certain of selling their goods in the fairly restricted British market from the early 1960s onwards and therefore have invested less. Then there has been the tendency for British capital to seek investment outlets other than in manufacturing—in the early seventies in fringe banking and property—and the readiness to export capital. At the present time (1980), the combination of a policy of deflation and the abolition of exchange control will together mean even less home investment. Some unions have been particularly effective in resisting the implementation of technical changes, another factor, but always in declining industries.

Finally, on productivity, Eric Heffer says: 'We have to recognise that both unions and employers in this country are being somewhat old-fashioned. We were the first industrialised country in the world, we were the workshop of the world, we have always done things that way and so why on earth change them. Such an attitude has meant a reluctance on the part of employers actually to introduce new machines to increase productivity. There are some marvellous pace-setting groups, but if we look at our old industries we are really only now getting down to proper modernisation—the steel industry, the ship-building industry—yet so late that we have almost been competed out of world markets. That is the fault of management. But equally, because of fears of what happened in the 1930s, trade unions have been reluctant to accept change, which is why governments should have done more to intervene: not as between employers and trade unions but by making certain that, if there were to be wholesale redundancies because of modernisation, alternative employment would be created. Although there were some minor efforts along such lines, they were not enough, which I believe is the real key to what has happened.'

Tripartism and greater co-operation between management and unions, rather than the mistrust and confrontation that too often appear to dominate the British industrial scene, lead to a consideration of some form of social contract. A social contract of a kind was tried during the Wilson-Callaghan period of 1974-9: in the end it broke down. That is not to say it could not be tried again and be managed in a different fashion.

Bob Hughes favours such an approach, but he thinks that the social contract broke down (and voluntary incomes policies always break down) because of the lack of an incomes policy, in the sense, he says, that it was first agreed in the Labour Party conference of the early sixties. An incomes policy ought to be part of a planned growth approach; in fact there have been attempts to hold down wages. 'And the more rapid the rate of inflation then the more difficult it is for that to be a tenable proposition. What you must have is an open dialogue with the unions on the levels of income to be sustained, and how in fact industry is to be directed.'

Speaking of the period of the social contract, Reg Race says: 'When the Labour Government was in power, my union (NUPE) in common with every other union had to take account of the Labour Government's wages policy; take account of the £7000m cuts in public expenditure and the wider aspects of its economic and social policies. The government wanted the social contract to be a trade-off: wage restraint in return for certain political actions or direction. Now, during that period, some trade unions like mine did not believe that the Labour Government was implementing sufficiently strongly many parts of the social contract—if at all. And certainly the coming to power of the Tory Government has made the importance of politics to the trade union movement far clearer: only through political action, it would appear, can trade unions possibly protect their members against many of the policies being introduced by this Tory Government or, indeed, by the last [1974–9] Labour Government.'

Eric Heffer thinks the social contract was killed because there was too much emphasis upon a wages policy rather than on other aspects of the contract: 'In the end the social contract was interpreted, certainly by government, simply as a way to control wages, even if not by legislation. I think the Government went a fair way to meet the demands of the trade unions, but it certainly did not go the whole way and in the end the trade unions were trying to extricate themselves from a voluntary incomes policy. At that stage the whole contract collapsed because the Government insisted upon continuing with norms, rigid norms, and these simply did not work. There has to be agreement between Labour governments and trade unions in particular or we are never going to make any real progress.

'We must be very careful about this: some people seem to believe that inflation is caused solely by high wages. A number of economists take a very different view and believe that there are other ways in which inflation can be controlled.'

Considering the great attention as well as hostility that the trade unions attract, it is interesting how often both defenders and critics point to weaknesses rather than strengths in the movement. For example, to the question: What do you see as the movement's greatest weakness? Albert Booth replies, perhaps surprisingly, for many: 'In the political arena. I think the unions in this country probably devote 99 per cent of their efforts to industrial issues and one per cent to political issues. This is not a proper balance in terms of the needs of their membership. Unions ought to be organised in such a way that they give far more time to considering those political decisions that have a direct effect upon their membership. One often sees it in the House of Commons: an issue arises, perhaps a bill, say a transport bill, that will have a major effect upon transport workers and very few unions have the resources immediately to step in and work out the options, discuss how they should tackle the question or learn political lessons from it so that they can shape better policies for the future.'

In part this weakness is a question of education; but it also involves money and research facilities. It requires a better liaison and a better machinery for talks between trade unions and parliamentarians. While there is liaison at top levels between Labour members and union officials, lower down at the sub-committee level trade unionists are not always available even when it is a matter of discussing issues that could lead to major changes affecting the unions.

From a different standpoint, Reg Race is far more scathing of trade union leadership. 'The first weakness that I would identify,' Race says, 'is the leadership of the TUC: it is bureaucratic, it has been incorporated totally into the apparatus of the state under a Labour Government; it was just not capable or willing to fight those Labour Government policies which needed fighting. One of the great failures of the trade union bureaucracy is that it is mainly concerned with maintaining the status quo: it is not concerned with advancing the interest of the working class in general or in advancing the frontiers of trade union control. This is deeply disturbing when these attacks are being made upon the position of the working people.'

A second weakness Race sees, is that the general council of the TUC has so little power in relation to individual affiliates. 'I think the Day of Action would have been much more successful if the TUC had called for a one-day general strike and had been able to say to its individual union executives: that is what we are calling for and we expect you to toe the line. Instead it said: do your own thing, which in fact sowed seeds of division within the movement.'

Third, Race sees the trade union movement as 'deeply divided on political and ideological questions: for example, over the legitimate role of public expenditure in the economy. At a time when the Labour Government was introducing more cuts in public expenditure, a vast argument was taking place, essentially between the public sector unions and the private sector unions (fostered I might say by Callaghan and Wilson), on the grounds that cuts in the public sector would lead to more resources for investment in the private sector manufacturing industry and so provide more jobs for the unions in that sector.

'The division of emphasis about the legitimate role of public expenditure is linked to the question of whether we have a mixed economy or a planned economy. Recently the OECD said you either have a planned economy or a market economy: Thatcher is going for the market economy; in my view we have got to go for the planned economy option. The trade union movement has neither discussed this properly nor come to any serious conclusions about it. My union is one of those which strongly favour the planned economy approach.'

Race believes there should be only one union approach to the question of wages, the position now adopted by the TUC: that is, opposition to all forms of wage control unless controls and planning are exercised over all other sections of the economy.

Eric Heffer would like to see the movement work towards one union for each industry, although he does not believe that would solve all the problems; sectional interests can still surface within a single union as, for example, in the American UAW. Even so, aiming for industrial unions would cut down the number of unions and lessen the interlacing of interests that takes place. He would also like to see greater co-ordination of the unions at the top level through the TUC. On the question of a TUC with greater power, Heffer is cautious. If the TUC were to use greater power solely for the purpose of controlling its members in a bureaucratic way, he would oppose it. But if the power could be used to lessen inter-union conflict because the TUC really had the ability to do so as well as strengthening its hand in relations with government, then he would favour a more powerful TUC.

In the end, as with so much else about the place of trade unions in British society, it becomes a question of political attitudes. Speaking of the Thatcher Government, for example, Booth says: 'This Government has broken with consensus: they are not only criticising their Labour predecessors but all their Tory predecessors as well, saying they went about things the wrong way: they were not sufficiently monetarist in their approach but dallied with Keynesian economics, and so on. They seem to be ignoring completely the experience of this country in the 1930s as well as the post-war experience of a lot of other countries. Now, therefore, I think there is going to be an argument in British politics as between a planned economy and a totally free enterprise capitalist economy and society.

'There are, however, possibilities of a middle way, although I am not necessarily advocating this. There are no simple solutions, but I think the idea of the social contract is an option which is still open. I think the TUC would respond to a government approach along the lines: we will be carrying out policies which affect your membership; you have a different policy in your economic review; so let us see how far we can do a deal. How far will you be prepared to set limits on wage claims or industrial action in return for some undertakings by government? There are possibilities for such a deal rather than head-on confrontation.

'If the response to that is a head-on confrontation, then the answer to that may have to be a straight political-industrial tie-up. In those circumstances, the trade unions would have to accept that what they could do for their membership would then depend upon whether or not they got a Labour Government into office. Now, that poses a fundamental democratic question: do the electors want to face up to this issue and accept that the TUC, which represents some twelve million people, should have a major say in policy decisions; or do they think the unions should be confined to a much narrower role, as the Tories apparently think?'

Bob Hughes is quite certain that confrontation of sorts will be with us for a long time. 'I do not see us evolving into the Swedish pattern (and that has its difficulties) or moving towards the German system: our whole historical experience is different. We may move some distance in those directions, but we are bound to get confrontation from time to time and the confrontation is sharpening. Strangely enough, the confrontation is not so much in the industrial as in the non-industrial field. The "winter of discontent", which is widely given as the reason for the Labour Party losing the 1979 election, was not really in the industrial field (although we had the lorry drivers); it was in the service industries. In Scotland, we now have something people would have said was unthinkable ten years ago: widespread industrial action by teachers who are unhappy with pay bargaining. We are getting confrontation in the health service and in the public services generally. We are getting it because they are always the ones who suffer in periods of wage restraint.'

Finally, on confrontation, Eric Heffer says: 'Well, we do live in a class society and we cannot get away from that fact. It is a class society, there is a class struggle going on, it takes place every day in factories: it is there, it is part of the industrial struggle, part of the class struggle. All I think you can ever hope for over industrial relations is to try to mitigate that struggle and keep it within reasonable bounds. You can attempt to get some order into the conflict; I think that is all you can do. I do not think one can go beyond that.

'As long as there is capitalism we shall have this kind of industrial conflict; even if you have a socialist society, provided there are free trade unions, you will still have a measure of conflict.'

71

Looking at the 1980s, which he sees as a period of mass un-employment (which in turn means that massive union-government confrontation is unlikely), Heffer says: 'What we must really face is the question of the technological advances that are being made and determine what is to be done about the people who will be thrown out of work as a consequence. We need some really radical, revolutionary ideas about how to deal with this problem, and this it seems is likely to be the most important problem of the decade rather than great confrontations between unions and government. On the other hand, if there is a stabilised industry then the unions will get stronger, so there could be some con-frontation though not along the lines which are being suggested.'

5

The Union Movement

The growth of modern trade unionism has its roots in the nineteenth-century struggles to improve the conditions of the working classes: these were long and bitter and inevitably a great deal of folklore and mythology has grown up round the movement, helping to fix attitudes in a mould which it is exceptionally difficult to break.

Depression and reaction in the years following the Napoleonic wars under the long Liverpool administration, witnessed the despairing activities of the Luddites and great misery among the working classes. A first breakthrough for trade unionism came in 1824, when on the evidence collected by Francis Place the old Combination Acts were repealed. A phenomenal if short-lived development of trade unionism followed, with strikes accompanied by violence leading to a new law in 1825 which, while allowing workers to combine to secure regulation of wages and hours, effectively forbade striking by prohibiting violence or threats and introducing summary methods of conviction.

The Great Reform Act of 1832 did little for the working classes, and their dissatisfaction led to another burst of unionism. John Doherty, at whose instigation the National Association for the Protection of Labour had been formed in 1830 (comprising about 150 unions), now joined with Robert Owen, the Utopian Socialist, to form a general union of skilled and unskilled labourers. The result was the Grand National Consolidated Trades Union of 1834, which attracted over half a million members within weeks. Its aims and leadership were confused and it achieved little except to frighten the government into repressive measures. In March 1834, six Dorchester labourers were convicted under the new legislation and sentenced to deportation to Australia, providing the trade union movement with its Tolpuddle Martyrs.

Another forty years were to pass before the trade union movement was to make significant gains in any legal sense. Then in 1875, under Disraeli, Richard Cross—the Home Secretary—was responsible for two acts which settled the labour question until the turn of the century. These were the Employers and Workmen Bill that replaced the Master and Servant Act and made breaches of contract by workers as a rule no longer liable to criminal prosecution; and the Conspiracy and Protection of Property Bill which changed the law of conspiracy in favour of the trade unions and allowed peaceful picketing.

In 1899 Richard Bell, the general secretary of the Amalgamated Society of Engineers, proposed the motion that led to the creation of the Labour Representation Committee, which later became the Labour Party. The period 1900 to 1914 was crucial to the union movement: it saw the Taff Vale judgement of 1903 make the Amalgamated Society of Railway Servants liable to damages for the actions of its members, costing the union £23,000 damages and £19,000 costs.

In December 1906, the newly formed Liberal Government passed its Trade Disputes Bill which provided that a union could not be made liable for damages on account of illegal acts committed by its members; while a Workingman's Compensation Act developed the principle of employers' liability for compensation for accidents.

In 1903, the Amalgamated Society of Railway Servants (ASRS) had launched its political levy to support the Labour Representation Committee; this was contested successfully by Walter V. Osborne in 1908, and only with the 1913 Trade Union Act could unions legally spend money for political purposes, while members had the right to contract out of the political levy.

Following the First World War, the coalminers moved into the lead as the pacemakers for trade union pressures upon government: there were two strikes in 1919, the Sankey Commission and then the great coal strike of 1921 when government control of the mines (dating back to the war) ended and proposals for nationalisation were rejected. The miners accepted a government offer of subsidies and increased wages.

1926 became the great myth year of the trade union movement: the coal strike was followed by the General Strike. Many of today's attitudes towards organised labour on both left and right in British politics relate back to the events of that year. The recession and slump of the 1930s, the hunger marches and mass unemployment which only came to an end with the Second World War, produced their own images of callous, cigar-smoking employers and downtrodden, cloth-cap workers; gave rise to the Macmillan school of thought in the Tory Party of the *Middle*

Way; and paved the way for the post-1945 bipartisan approach to full employment that was to last for thirty years.

The war itself produced the best social contract or wages policy we have yet seen. As Giles Radice says in his book, *The Industrial Democrats*:

> Perhaps the most successful of all British incomes policies was that instituted during the Second World War by the coalition government led by Churchill. As a basis for union agreement, the government stabilised the cost of living by a system of food subsidies and rationing. In return, the trade unions made only modest and infrequent pay claims at national levels and acquiesced in severe restraints on their freedom of action, including the direction of labour, the prohibition of strikes and compulsory arbitration. In terms of increases in the standard of living of British workers, trade union acceptance of incomes policy during the war was justified. Between 1938 and 1945 prices rose by only 48 per cent, while average weekly earnings increased by 80 per cent.

The 1945–51 Attlee Government could be seen as the great triumph of the Labour movement: the only government of the century to put its entire manifesto on the statute book; the peaceful revolution of the introduction of the welfare state accompanied by substantial nationalisation of key industries, which established the mixed economy we now have and ushered in the consensus politics that were to dominate the British political scene until the 1970s. The unions actually went into decline in terms of membership during the fifties; they did not pick up sharply in numbers again until the economically troubled seventies. By the middle of that decade, there were some 457 unions although only 113 were members of the TUC. While average membership of unions stood at 24,000, over 200 unions had less than 500 members while the eleven largest had a quarter of a million or more members each.* By 1980 there were 109 unions affiliated to the TUC and more than twelve million trade unionists nationwide.

The trade union movement was brought fully into the decision making process under Bevin and Churchill during the Second World War, and much union bitterness with the Thatcher Government of 1979 has been because they saw themselves being eased out of that role. The size of the movement may cause its critics to speak of its potential juggernaut powers; in fact, the

* Robert Taylor, *The Fifth Estate.*

trade union record in wage bargaining hardly measures up to these fears about such powers. The 'winter of discontent' or the Day of Action were, if anything, clear indications of trade union weakness rather than strength: if individual unions or the movement as a whole were more successful in their pursuit of wages and conditions settlements, such activities would hardly be necessary.

When compared with other union movements overseas the British movement appears conservative, lacking in new ideas and possessing insufficient influence or punch half the time to put even those ideas it does advance into practice. Part of the problem arises out of the sectional nature of the movement. Unions are essentially reactive in what they do, more geared to defend positions by safeguarding jobs than to improve pay and opportunities by pursuing more adventurous policies.

With one or two exceptions, there would appear to be little chance of industrial unionism being adopted in Britain; nor in the political climate of the early 1980s does an effective tripartite approach appear to have much prospect of success either. Instead, confrontation and defensive safeguarding of positions would appear to be the most likely way the unions proceed; such a pattern will be even more likely if the disputes within the Labour Party ensure, on the one hand, that it splits, thus enabling the Tories to dominate the decade; while world economic recession, on the other hand, means high unemployment that must greatly weaken union bargaining power anyway.

The 1970s were of great importance to the trade union movement. The developing weakness of the British economy—despite North Sea oil—was accentuated in the latter half of the decade by world recession and the abandonment of political consensus. One result was that the unions were first expected to provide too much under the social contract, and were then made into scapegoats for wider industrial failures.

The decade began with the confrontations which, sadly, became the hallmark of the Heath administration: the fiercely contested Industrial Relations Act of 1971, the arguments over the incomes policy, the three-day week and lastly the coal miners' strike, culminating in electoral defeat for the Tories who in the popular imagination—and their own—owed that defeat to the behaviour of overmighty unions. This sense of defeat at the hands of the unions undoubtedly had its reflections in a different set of Tory attitudes, when the most right wing government since the war came to power under Mrs Thatcher in 1979. Then, for example, the TUC found itself excluded from the informal discussions about the economy at Downing Street to which it had become accustomed.

The second half of the decade—1974 to 1979—was of great significance for the experiment of the social contract. In the end it failed, yet the contract did represent the first attempt of its kind and may well provide the framework for other such experiments in the future. As the Callaghan Government failed to deliver its side of the contract and the Prime Minister tried to make the unions stick to a rigid and unworkable formula of five per cent over the winter of 1978–9, having in any case made the unions look foolish over his decision not to hold an election in the autumn of 1978, the country was treated instead to the disruptions of the 'winter of discontent'. Subsequently, Labour supporters suggested that this lost them the election of May 1979. In any case, disillusionment with Labour policies of the Callaghan-Healey variety was growing in the ranks of the Party and a number of unions were becoming markedly more militant: it was NUPE's members who spearheaded the 'winter of discontent'.

A transformation had taken place in NUPE as the result of that union tackling the problem of union education. Early in the 1970s, the leadership realised that its members were, by and large, not well educated within the British system, were doing some of the worst, dirtiest jobs in the public sector, had no tradition of trade union organisation and very little of shop steward organisation, and so tended to accept whatever the leadership told them. The leadership of the union wished to change this tendency and sought ways to prevent itself dictating to members. Following NUPE's 1973 national congress, a special team was set up to examine ways of changing the organisation. The result was a report—'Organisation and Change in NUPE'—whose key recommendations were implemented in 1975. These included: first, positive discrimination in favour of women members; second, linking shop stewards to the decision making bodies in the union, which meant the formation of district committees where shop stewards could speak for their members about policy; and third, the creation of a system of workplace meetings—that is, the demise of the traditional branch meeting at 7.30 p.m. at a Labour Party hall in favour of meetings at the workplace during working hours with all workers present. The result was a transformed union which became far more truly representative of its workforce, politicised them, and besides became formidably

77

articulate not least in its production of reasoned critiques of government policies. What NUPE did in the seventies was hand back control to the rank and file, an exercise that a good many other unions would prefer not to do.

Other union developments were taking place: one of the most important was the growth of the white collar unions. Union membership during the seventies increased by more than two million. A great deal of the growth was in the membership of the two giant general unions—the TGWU and the GMWU; yet even more spectacular was the growth of NALGO, representing local government officers. In the four years 1973 to 1977, for example, the union increased from a membership of 500,000 to 683,000. There were comparable explosions of numbers in the Civil and Public Services Association, which grew from 208,000 in 1973 to 230,572 in 1977, or the Inland Revenue Staff Federation, which increased by 10,000 members over the same four years. ASTMS grew from 208,000 to 400,000, TASS from 105,000 to 161,000 while APEX added another 20,000 members.

The growth of white collar unions has changed the structure of the union movement significantly—for example, bringing in members who are unlikely to be traditional Labour supporters, and may well put status and higher pay above job security. A high proportion of them are in the civil service or other public employment.

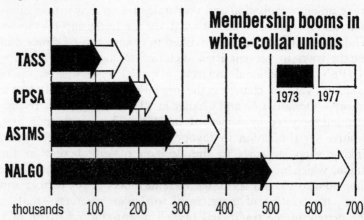

Membership booms in white-collar unions

1973   1977

TASS   CPSA   ASTMS   NALGO

thousands   100   200   300   400   500   600   700

What the social contract with all its faults achieved, was a certain recognition that the organised trade union movement had claims to be an estate of the realm. The Thatcher Government ment has clearly been determined to reverse that advance.

Differences within the trade union movement are to be expected: it is large enough and embraces an enormous range of interests. Nonetheless, the extent to which its members can co-ordinate their interests and produce joint policies will be the measure of their national impact.

The British and Scottish TUCs have little power. They are in part secretariats for the unions they represent and in part spokesmen for employed people over a wide range of national issues. The Trades Union Congress was formed in 1868. The TUC is composed of affiliated unions of which there were 109 in 1980. The structure of the TUC falls conveniently under three headings: the annual Congress; the General Council (which meets monthly) and its committees; and the main departments at Congress House, which are responsible for the day to day work. The effectiveness or otherwise of the TUC will depend on the one hand upon the personality of the general secretary, and on the other upon the General Council and the inevitable rivalries and divisions that occur within its ranks. Its members are nominated on a trade basis so as to obtain as wide a representation of trades as possible; at the same time members of the General Council are usually top union officials and therefore include the key national figures. One of the great problems of the TUC has always been the jealousy of the main unions about surrendering too much power to a central body: the TUC can only do what its members instruct it to do.

William Speirs is assistant secretary, social services, of the STUC. He is a recent style of trade union official: university educated, a trade union technocrat.

Speaking of union power, Speirs says, as do most unionists, that trade unions have too little rather than too much power. To begin with, they do not organise the entire workforce but only about half of it, while many unions operate in very weakly organised industries. Further, the powers which unions do possess are very diversified and in some industries are much greater than in others. By and large it is an economic power which can be a very blunt instrument. The STUC, for example, has policies on education, training, health, and the social services. Yet its input into the process of developing educational policy in Scotland, for example, is dependent upon the STUC's position as a very large pressure group, since in effective terms individual unions are not going to use their bargaining power to bring about changes in the educational field. Were unions to employ their power in pursuit of those kinds of change, that would represent a major development in industrial relations. The power unions have is a somewhat inflexible instrument.

On the subject of trade union political involvement, Speirs makes an interesting point about the Thatcher Government: that contrary to the arguments of its spokesmen or supporters it has gone almost as far as anyone before to make it legitimate for unions to use their power to forward political objectives: this is because, following the June budget of 1979, the Tory Government argued that in carrying out their normal wage bargaining, trade unions should take into account the tax cuts the government had introduced. That, Speirs claims, amounts to an explicit admission that in negotiating on behalf of their members the unions have to take into account more than simply the cash figure they would otherwise get at the end of the day. Other items have to be considered and these include both the tax structure and the social wage: that is, education, health, social security benefits, pensions. Once unions do this they become involved in the policy process which determines such things.

Of the social contract Speirs says: 'I think the experience, as opposed to the theory of the last five years [speaking in 1980] of Labour Government was that the trade unions did not benefit from the social contract and ultimately neither did the Labour Government or the Labour Party. I think there are real dangers of some form of corporatism being introduced and personally I would be opposed to a form of tripartite bargaining structure which met every three years or so.'

While deeply aware of the poor educational aspects of the trade union movement, Speirs is cautious about blaming lack of education for too many of the movement's shortcomings. Sections of the Labour movement—the Fabians, the Anthony Crosland strand—have often emphasised education as one of the forces that would lead to a more egalitarian society, and have put a great deal of emphasis upon this to the detriment of the question of ownership or control of the economic bases of society. The reliance upon education for the movement has not been followed through, however, into the actual training and politicisation of membership. This has probably not been a deliberate omission but rather a question of the movement failing to think things through properly, and in part results from the fragmented nature of the movement. It was only at the beginning of the sixties that the TUC decided to set up its own education service.

The Day of Action was clearly a key trade union event of 1980. It was not a resounding success; nor, however, was it the failure that government supporters and most of the media depicted it to be. Its importance lay in two things: first, the fact that the movement felt compelled to call such a day of protest against government policies because it was getting nowhere with more orthodox approaches to government that it would normally prefer to use; and secondly, because it brought out the fragmented nature of the movement. It is, of course, one thing for critics of the TUC from within the ranks of the movement to say that it should have issued firm instructions for a one-day strike which everyone would then have obeyed, thus enabling the movement to demonstrate its solidarity in face of the government. In fact, the fear that by no means everyone would have obeyed such a *diktat* was no doubt a powerful reason why instructions were vague: for unions to do 'their own thing'. The Day of Action may have been a mess, while enemies of the movement found no difficulty in suggesting that it was a failure and the trade union movement itself weak (a claim that contradicts much else that is said of the trade unions); yet how much more would these critics have been able to deride TUC effectiveness or lack of control over its members had a one-day strike been demanded which half the trade union membership had then ignored?

In the event the TUC call was for a day of action with no recommendation other than to say there might be a stoppage of work; or action might take the form of lunchtime meetings; a leaflet distribution; or whatever a particular union decided to do. Thereafter, mounting pressures from a number of areas indicated that a large number of members considered a twenty-four hour work stoppage would be the most effective action for the movement to take. Subsequently, however, some proponents of this course of action drew back. This followed the High Court judgement in favour of Express Newspapers the week before the Day of Action was due, when the print unions were ordered to desist from ordering or instructing their members to withdraw their labour. The union instruction was withdrawn; the newspapers did not appear on the Day of Action. And nothing further was done.

The way the TUC called for the Day of Action left room for vacillation and there was no real clarity as to just what was being demanded of the movement. Despite that, the fact of the choice being left open meant there had to be a considerable degree of discussion and debate at local level—at workplaces, offices and

81

factories; and while in a number of areas this meant that trade unionists decided there was no point in taking any action, they were at least forced to confront the question of what the government was doing to which the movement was opposed and what the role of unions ought to be in relation to an elected government. It also raised a more fundamental question about the democratic process: should one only take part in a vote at the general election every five years; or should there be more frequent ways in which to influence governments? At least, as a result of the call for the Day of Action trade unionists had to discuss these questions even if they then took no action.

Fundamental to any understanding of the trade union movement must be an assessment of its motivation in relation to capital: is the movement radical in a socialist sense; is it prepared to work in harmony with capital; or, in other words, does it accept the concept of both sides sitting round a table to decide how to divide the wealth between them—and working to create more? Views on this question vary widely across the spectrum of political interests in the trade union movement from fairly far right wing to extreme left wing. The way this question is regarded by officials, therefore, is of great importance since it must substantially influence their approach to their duties.

As Speirs says: 'From my point of view there is always an irreconcilable contradiction between labour and capital: ultimately I do not think there is any possibility of harmony. What you can have in a period of economic growth is employers and governments satisfying the aspirations for improved wages and conditions at the workplace and for improved social conditions in terms of education and social welfare. That is a possibility under the sort of economic conditions which existed during the 1950s and early 1960s. When those economic conditions can no longer be met, then—though there can always be discussions—I do not believe the trade union movement can effectively work with a Conservative Government unless it is a government that has ceased to represent the people that such governments have always represented. Once growth is unable to satisfy the demands of the bulk of trade union members, then the question must be posed: how is what we have got to be divided? And when that question is asked there will always be a fundamental difference between the demands of the workforce and those of the employer. If one particular government represents the employer rather than the workforce, then the latter must be in opposition not only to the employer but to the government as well.'

Such a view is opposed to tripartism: how strong it is throughout the union movement is another matter, but evidence suggests a growing number of trade unionists think along such lines, which is one explanation for the developments currently taking place in the Labour Party.

The enormous growth of civil service and white collar unions which cover employees of government, represents another major development that has occurred during the 1970s. When unions such as NUPE or NALGO carry out their traditional roles to attempt to improve the wages and conditions of their members, they at once put themselves in the position of challenging the political and economic strategy of the government of the day, since whatever they attempt to obtain must be circumscribed by government cash limits and these constitute a form of incomes policy. These unions cannot extricate themselves from such a situation; they are bound to oppose government cuts in public expenditure. A government which makes cuts in public expenditure and lays down guidelines for pay in the public sector, is imposing an incomes policy for that sector: in such circumstances the government cannot expect other than fierce union opposition.

On the subject of education and the conflict between management and labour Speirs says: 'I am not one of the people who believe that the problem of industrial relations in Britain is due to lack of communications or lack of education and that, somehow, if we all understood each other a little better we would get on better. I tend to think—and practice has shown that the more worker representatives understand precisely what employers are trying to do the more likely there is to be conflict and mistrust—that as a result of concentration of ownership and control and the development of the multinational corporations, interests are getting farther apart. This is not a personal judgement on the people who are running such corporations or for that matter those who run a huge pension fund: they have to make their judgements on the basis of what is good for the shareholders and what is best for maximising the profits of the industry. If that means shutting down a factory on Clydebank and reallocating production to Brazil, then that is what they will do: not because they have a dislike for the workforce of Clydebank but because it makes sense in their economic terms.

'Increasingly, it seems, the capitalist system can no longer sustain the growth levels it achieved for fifteen or twenty years after the Second World War that were capable of accommodating the demands which arose in a fairly peaceable period of labour relations. But when growth fails and living standards actually begin to fall then the underlying question becomes: in whose interest is the economy run; in whose interest does it actually work? Eventually, in such circumstances, if a British company is unable to provide a level of wage increases that allow its workforce to have at least a steady and preferably an increasing standard of living, then inevitably you move into a period of conflict. However, rising levels of unemployment will undoubtedly have an impact in depressing levels of wage demands among those who are concerned about job security. Today an increasing number of British companies are in that position as a result of chronic under-capitalisation.'

These are gloomy reflections which augur ill for the 1980s if, as seems likely, the decade witnesses continuing recession.

The job of general secretary of the TUC must be one of the most difficult in Britain. Len Murray has to run an organisation which has little power of its own and yet represents the interests of some twelve million trade unionists including exceptionally large, powerful unions which traditionally have always been jealous of handing over any part of their power to the TUC. A TUC with 'teeth', which various people have argued for elsewhere in this book, does not appear to be an organisation that the unions most able to provide the 'teeth' seem in any sense anxious to have.

The unions and the union movement are easy scapegoats. As Murray says: 'We are handy, we hang about in large lumps, we are very conspicuous and therefore we are natural targets.' He goes on in his dry way to tell a story of how, in the war, the union movement was outraged when the government, which wished to mount an anti-VD campaign, started by asking the TUC whether it would arrange for talks to be given to trade unionists in workers' canteens.

Opponents of the trade union movement attribute to the whole the faults of any particular section. Yet, as Murray says: 'We are a pretty good cross-section of British society with most of the virtues and as many of the defects of society as a whole: with twelve million people, half the workforce, that is to be expected and while I would not claim for our people any perfection, nor would I accept accusations of diabolism. Where we have faults,

84

of course we must recognise them and do what we can to eradicate them.'

Ever since the Second World War, although with ups and downs in the relationship, the TUC has had a growing and sometimes close relationship with governments, including Tory governments. But as Murray argues, that relationship consists essentially of bargaining: 'If we have got nothing for them [the government] they will give us nothing; if they think we have got nothing for them they will just ignore us and that is the situation at present [mid-1980]. And equally, if they cannot do anything for us, or more accurately, for those whom we represent, then there is very little we can do for them, because ultimately we can only persuade our own people to do things which the government favours if they believe the total package is in their favour.'

Moving to the social contract, Murray, who is in favour of the concept, says: 'Explicit in the social contract is a democratic bargain: I believe that in our sort of industrialised society there is no alternative to the solution of problems except by government and voluntary organisations—in our case trade unions and employers—co-operating to solve those problems.'

Murray argues without equivocation, as do virtually all trade unionists, that they are in the business of politics. 'We have always been in politics,' he says, 'ever since the first union was created by its members, and we are bound to be there.' He points out how, increasingly, governments have become involved in industrial and social affairs that affect trade union members: it is an interventionist society so that decisions about incomes, unemployment or sick benefits are affected by government decisions which unions must seek to influence. The Thatcher Government appears to take the view that unions should have no part or say in such broad decisions and that the unions should merely look after their members in a far narrower sense. Of such an attitude, Murray says: 'The two criticisms I make are, first, that if they relegate us to such a role we will have to perform that role: we will have to become introspective, we will have to consider merely the short-term interests of our members or those particular groups which are represented by unions, and the end result of that could be enormous difficulties in particular industries and difficulties in relationships between industries.

'Second, we have the dilemma about responsibility. We have a responsibility towards our members: they elect us, they sustain us in order to serve them. On the other hand, given the strengths of trade unions, we are bound to take into account the impact of our actions upon the rest of society even if only in terms of self-interest, although it may be self-interest on a longer time scale. So we have to try to balance conflicting responsibilities. One of our problems is that the government, and this Government in particular, lectures us about accepting responsibility yet at the same time denies us responsibilities. To be involved in co-operative endeavours with any government is sitting on a bed of nails: sometimes we have to go back to our members and say, we think you should take the following course of action and urge them to fight for agreements we have reached with the government, and that is a very difficult process. Governments cannot have it both ways.'

Len Murray's assessment of trade unions and their power is realistic. 'Trades unions,' he says, 'are concerned with power. And the ultimate power is with employers in the sense that if unions did not exist they could unilaterally determine matters affecting employment, the right to have a job or not to have a job, to take on, to exclude, to sack. The employers could unilaterally decide the wages for which people should work and their conditions of work. So we have always been concerned with reducing that power: or rather, sharing that power with employers, and to a large extent we have succeeded. These matters are now jointly regulated between employers and unions: we bargain, we negotiate, we establish wages, we set hours and so on. Thus we are very much about power in that sense. Then the issue becomes one of whether unions can get into a position from which in effect they can dictate to an employer what wages and conditions are going to be. Some can do this, and some do for a short time. But that can be a suicidal path. You can force wages up in some exceptional situations to a point where the whole existence of a firm, company or undertaking is threatened and employment may disappear as a consequence. There are some places in Britain today where this is happening (in the print trade for example) and this is recognised by the unions. As far as the TUC is concerned, the only power it possesses—either formally or informally—is its power to expel a union from Congress.'

Although he believes Britain to be a class society, Murray does not think there has to be confrontation. He does say: 'Frankly, the present Government have in my view shown more of a class attitude than any government since the war—and the sort of policies they have introduced smack of class attitudes. I do not believe that it is an automatic assumption by trade unionists that

86

confrontation is necessary. There are differences of interest within industry as in society, quite legitimate differences. There are bound to be arguments between employees who put in their labour and the shareholders who put in their capital about their respective shares: to deny such differences of interest is nonsensical. What is essential is to accept that these are honest differences and to devise means whereby to reconcile them. We must at least seek compromises between these interests so that always we base our attitudes upon looking for solutions.'

Len Murray's line is eminently reasonable; he then puts his finger on the nub of the problem when he continues: 'It is much more difficult to solve the problems if resources are limited and part at least of the sharpness and, on occasion, bitterness of industrial relations in this country in the years since the war compared with other countries derives from the fact that we have been a low performance country with our wealth growing very slowly indeed and sometimes not growing at all—and, as now, going right back. That accentuates the problems.

'It is in this sort of situation that zero sum bargaining emerges: my loss is your gain; your loss is my gain. We want to break such an approach, which is why we are such resolute supporters of the industrial strategy and why we react so sharply against what seem to us unnecessary and irrelevant decisions by the government to cut back the level of economic activity in this country. So although there are differences of interest and class attitudes, these can be reduced in their impact if you are arguing about something which is tangible.'

British productivity is much lower than that of her main trading partners or industrial rivals and, with variations, no one disputes this. Too often, however, the blame for such productivity, certainly in the public mind, is laid at the door of union practices: usually, indeed, people think of productivity as meaning labour productivity only, which naturally leads them to blame the unions.

Murray defines the problem of low productivity as the inadequate use of all our resources: '... investment, resources of manpower, of education, of training. And,' he says, 'politicians in particular tend to look for a single, simple reason: they are happiest when they can pin their minds on one thing and try to change that. The problem, however, is highly complex. Not just inadequate investment but inadequate use of investment; there are restrictive practices in industry, there is poor management in industry. Our people are not as well educated or trained as in

Germany or the USA and there are other historic reasons such as the post-war attempts to maintain the sterling area. Altogether we have a multiple set of problems rather than a simple equation such as labour equals productivity.'

Murray agrees that profitability in Britain is low and accepts the arguments of NEDC that it needs to be improved. He says: 'We have no objection to profits: we will have an argument about the division between dividends and wages but not on the need for profits so long as they are being ploughed back into the industry.'

One of the main sources of finance in Britain has become the big financial institutions: the banks, the insurance companies and the pension funds, and Murray would like to see an improvement in the relationship between the City and such sources of finance on the one hand and manufacturing industry on the other: how, for example, would it be possible to get the money out of the pension funds and into the new technology?

A major concern during the 1980s will be to come to terms with the effects of new technology: there must be new technology agreements to cover its effective and efficient use, but these in turn will need to be balanced by other measures which take care of the consequences upon the labour market, such as what is to be done for the labour such technology displaces. As Murray argues, all the different facets have to be put on the table between management and labour when they examine the impact of the new technology. 'You put manning on the table, hours, pay rates; you also put on the table sales possibilities, export sales, home sales; you involve both sides and make them face the consequences of their own actions. You do not allow either side to contract out and say: I am only concerned with wages; or, I am only concerned with export markets.'

On the relationship of the trade union movement and the Labour Party, Murray says: 'There is an ideological affinity between the trade unions and the Labour Party, since both broadly believe that the best way to solve problems in a society such as Britain is by combining to solve them: they should be solved collectively rather than by relying upon individual initiative and enterprise.'

Only about half the members of the trade unions in the TUC, however, are in unions affiliated to the Labour Party—some six million—while a further six million are not. The TUC as such has no relationship with the Labour Party. As Murray adds, returning to the subject of power: 'We are interested in power.

Or, more accurately, we are interested in influencing people who have got genuine power; the TUC, therefore, is primarily concerned with governments rather than with a political party.'

The trade union movement would like to see the Labour Party form a government because it believes such a government would be more likely to act sensibly (in its terms) than would a Conservative government. 'We are interested, therefore, in the Labour Party in power as the government. We are interested in a Labour Party which is capable of forming a government, while a lot of trade unions are likely to be very uninterested in a Labour Party which has no chance of forming a government but is more concerned with tearing itself to pieces.'

Despite a public opinion climate which is against the unions and asserts that they both have too much power and often misuse it as well, trade unionists point to the fact that over sixty or more years they have not greatly increased the share of the national wealth which goes to the workers they represent. On this subject, Murray says: 'The collective bargaining instrument is not in any sense an effective way of redistributing income. If it was ever thought that it would be, it has manifestly failed. We should not, therefore, pin our hopes of increasing our share of the national wealth or of making our people relatively better off in relation to other groups in society, upon this weapon. Redistribution will come more from the development of the social wage than by collective bargaining across the table with employers. The shifts will result from changes in taxation or changes in social income provisions rather than from collective bargaining.' This reasoning brings us back to the concept of the social contract: it is through some such approach to problems that redistribution of national wealth is likely to take place.

Len Murray's views are middle of the road, which is where the TUC stands at the present time. He believes in a social contract approach and tripartism. He accepts the profit motive and a mixed economy. He sees broadly the interests of organised labour being best served by the Labour Party in office.

Developments in British politics at the beginning of the 1980s, however, point to the possibility of far more extreme attitudes emerging on both sides of the political spectrum. Should this occur then the kind of reasoned stand Murray takes may become outmoded in a more bitter style of politics than those of the last thirty years, while the industrial scene could also become as bitter if unemployment continues to rise.

6

Union Powers and Attitudes

Trade unions were highly unpopular in general public opinion by the end of the 1970s: their shortcomings were highlighted by the media; they were made scapegoats for Britain's poor industrial performance. Through most of the seventies people were more likely to blame the unions for forcing up wages as the explanation for the country's industrial ills than prices, bad management, lack of investment or any other cause. And paradoxically, while union restrictive practices were often presented as a threat to individual liberty, more people than ever before joined unions: not because they were forced to do so because of closed shops, but rather because unions are seen as a form of protection or insurance in bad times. Inflation and growing unemployment have been the inducements that have persuaded people, especially in white collar occupations, to join unions which they see as a form of job guarantee. This process has been further encouraged by the demise of many small enterprises and the growth of large companies.

The close, if often troubled, alliance between the unions and the Labour Party and the fact that Labour formed the governments from 1964–70 and again from 1974–9, meant some major advances in union influence: union leaders automatically sit upon bodies such as the Manpower Services Commission, the Advisory, Conciliation and Arbitration Service (ACAS), the Health and Safety at Work Commission and, of course, the NEDC. The public has become used to the idea of 'bargains' being struck between the unions and Labour governments. In the popular imagination, Heath took on the unions in the form of the powerful NUM in 1974—and lost the election as a result.

Back in power Labour repealed the 1971 Labour Relations Act as the price of union support, and the country entered the period of the first social contract when a bargain was struck between the government of the day and an organised interest group—the unions.

Although this was the first time, historically, that such a bargain had been so openly arrived at, similar pacts of interest—between parliamentarians and the landed interests or parliamentarians and the industrial or property interests—were equally a part of eighteenth- and nineteenth-century British political history. Politics is about bargains anyway and too much should not therefore be made of a union-government pact: it certainly made sense; it also occurred in the age of an all pervasive press and television coverage and as trade unionists are quick to point out, they rarely get a fair deal from the media.

The social contract broke down in 1978 when the unions refused to accept the rigid five per cent norm Callaghan attempted to apply, but in the public mind it was the unions—especially as the 'winter of discontent' was to follow—rather than the government which broke the social contract, and as Labour Party members tended to say after May 1979, it was the 'winter of discontent' that lost the party the election—the unions again.

It was, therefore, hardly surprising that Mrs Thatcher and the Tories fought the election on a platform of union reform. The issue of union power had become highly emotive and Tories tended to be 'constitutional' in their reasoning, arguing about overmighty subjects. The union reforms introduced cautiously by James Prior in 1979 came against a background of continuing recession and rapidly rising unemployment, that together were powerful factors weakening union effectiveness and making the task of the new government easier.

The image of trade unions as monolithic supporters of some form of socialism is in any case outmoded. Many of their members in fact—whatever the public rhetoric of their leadership—believe in a private enterprise system and would prefer to operate in the sort of bargaining conditions which prevail in the USA or West Germany. They want a larger slice of the cake for themselves and in reality, therefore, are moving towards the position of partners with an enlightened industrial management. Many too—an esti-mated third of all trade unionists—now vote Conservative.

The power of shop stewards and the public estimation of that power is another facet of unions that tends to be highly ambiguous. On the one hand, trouble on the shop-floor and the inability of the union hierarchy to control its shop stewards has become a feature of modern trade unionism: many strikes start as unofficial ones on the shop-floor (although not necessarily sparked by shop stewards) and are subsequently recognised by the union as the only way of regaining control of the situation. Some Tories regard shop steward power as a potential left wing threat and Keith Wickenden MP, for example (see p. 48) thinks that possibly as many as a sixth of the country's estimated 300,000 shop stewards are what he describes as political troublemakers.

Yet many shop stewards have a difficult job to maintain any kind of control and are conciliators in their approach rather than agitators or firebrands. What does appear to have happened during the 1970s is the return of a great deal of union power to the shop-floor: decisions from factory level are passed up to the national leadership rather than the more monolithic pattern of an earlier age when the national leadership made the bargains—a result of the Second World War and the Attlee government period—and handed them down in authoritarian style to their membership. In so far as this development is a genuine increase of democracy, it ought to be welcomed; at least the more progressive managements tend to prefer a situation in which from plant to plant they know with whom they have to deal on the spot.

With all their faults, trade unions are a bastion of any free society and those who react to their excesses by wanting to break their power are short-sighted in the extreme. Tory attitudes towards the unions at the present time are ambivalent, though predominantly hostile. In April 1978, for example, a storm broke when news leaked out concerning a secret Tory report on the unions: Lord Carrington had advised Mrs Thatcher that to take on strategic unions such as the NUM could only lead to a humiliating defeat. When Mrs Thatcher became Prime Minister there were certainly plenty of Tories in the Party willing and anxious to take on the unions.

Part of the union problem arises from the fact that the movement's considerable powers are almost always used in a negative, blocking sense: reacting to members' fears of possible redundancies or the effects of new technology, while little of the power is used to initiate change. Furthermore, especially during the seventies, the centralised unions found that control was going to the shop-floor and away from the national leadership. A major result of that process has been to force the national leadership into more political positions: if they could not control the bargaining process, they could at least be seen to be influencing governments. It is in part in reaction to this development that the Thatcher Government has appeared so strongly anti-union.

The trade unions make easy scapegoats, yet they should not be blamed for an antiquated industrial system that they certainly do not and never have controlled. The trade union movement seeks to be consulted by government as well as industry: not simply on wages and conditions but on the broad sweep of social and economic policies that affect their members. This was the theory of the social contract, even if it did not work out in practice. The second part of that consultation—on the broad sweep of social and economic policies—is not an area that the Tory Party of Mrs Thatcher shows any desire to discuss with the unions, and that fact could well be at the centre of political storms through the 1980s.

In a number of areas, though aware of the nature of the problems they face, union leaders have done little or nothing to create new machinery to cope with modern developments. Thus trade unionists are only too conscious of the power of the multi-national corporations. Yet little has been done to develop co-operation with unions in other countries so as to co-ordinate responses to the cross-frontier operations of such conglomerates.

At the 1978 Tory Party Conference in Brighton, when Mrs Thatcher warned union leaders that if they used their great power irresponsibly they would only hasten a decline in jobs available for their members, she was missing part of the point: that a great deal of union power is a myth and the leadership often has little control over its members or what occurs on the factory floor. And yet of 300,000 shop stewards, only a tiny proportion—an estimated 6000 in 1978—had any real training in collective bargaining, while in any case such bargaining has become rare after years of statutory or semi-statutory incomes policies. All too often, therefore, wage bargaining becomes simply a demand for what people believe to be the 'going rate' rather than anything worked out in terms of the productivity and profitability of the plant where the men are working and actually demanding a wage increase. This is another of industry's major problems.

When he opened the CBI's second national conference at Brighton in November 1978, Sir John Greenborough, the president, said that the imbalance of power in society with the weighting totally in favour of organised labour had brought Britain to a point of dangerous disequilibrium. An article in the *Sunday Telegraph* of January 1979 began: 'Who can doubt that the greatest single obstacle to a competitive British economy today lies in the obstructive power of the unions?' In the debate on the Queen's Speech in the autumn of 1978 the Prime Minister, Mr

Callaghan, said that 'the workers' power in combination is greater today than ever before.' And in his New Year message for 1979 Callaghan said: 'Let those who possess industrial muscle or monopoly power resolve not to abuse their great strength.' Robert Taylor, no enemy of the unions, said in his book, *The Fifth Estate*: 'It is indisputable that the British unions collectively and a few by themselves have the potential power to disrupt the country's economic life through industrial action.' And he quoted Len Murray as saying: 'We are very good at stopping what we do not like, but not at starting anything.'

An endless succession of quotations from the later 1970s indicate the same general public reaction to the unions—that they are too powerful and that various sections of society would like to see that power reduced. And yet much of the reaction to union power is emotional and ill-thought out. As John Elliott pointed out in his book *Conflict or Co-operation*: opposition by management to the Bullock proposals, for example, was more in terms of the awfulness of union power than in providing viable alternatives. And yet the steel strike of 1980 did not prevent 50,000 redundancies, so despite all the talk of power where and when is it effective?

The phrase 'winter of discontent' has now gone into the language: yet when using it very few people recall that the public discontent resulted from union inability to obtain better conditions; if the general public was discontented because rubbish was not collected or corpses remained unburied, few seemed to recall that this in turn resulted from years of neglect for some of the poorest paid sections of the community, that simply no one had bothered about until their discontent took a notorious public form.

The effective use of power attains objectives; too often the unions fail in this and their power is deployed negatively to defend a position, instead of positively to achieve an improvement. The Tory election victory of May 1979 enshrined within it a union-power paradox. The Tories argue the unions have too much power. A substantial number of trade unionists clearly voted Tory in 1979 because they were disappointed by Labour's performance as far as union aspirations had been concerned. Yet by bringing in the Thatcher Government they both deprived their own allies of power and helped establish a government that was determined to lessen the union power which supposedly served their interests.

At the 1978 annual conference of the National Union of Mineworkers in Torquay, the difficulties of the union-Labour Party power relationship were brought out clearly when the conference unanimously agreed to reject any further wage restraint and voted without dissent to oppose an extension of the social contract. Emlyn Williams, the president of the South Wales miners as well as being a member of the Labour Party national executive, said: 'We do not want confrontation. We merely wish to return to free collective bargaining, and have the right to negotiate. We will negotiate responsibly, but not with the Government prepared to take cognisance of the IMF and forget socialism.' And at the same conference, Arthur Scargill, the president of the Yorkshire miners, said: 'I am sick and tired of the hypocrisy of the trade union movement, including those in our own union who are prepared to accept policies under a Labour administration that would be totally unacceptable under the Tories.'

This militant miners' mood signalled the end of the social contract which collapsed during the 'winter of discontent'. The arguments of the miners' leaders pointed up some of Labour's difficulties: as a party it has wider responsibilities and has to make many responses other than to union pressures and demands, yet it is *the union* party. When it does not satisfy union aspirations it cannot expect their automatic support. Union power over Labour, however, is also limited. When a Labour government passes measures which suit the unions, they in turn provide it with the support it seeks. But when the government puts other tasks or claims first then the unions are apt to insist upon using their power for free collective bargaining, no matter what line the government may be taking. This dilemma which emerged in 1978, highlights the importance of party constitutional changes being advanced by the Benn wing of the Labour Party: one of their effects would be to put far greater pressure upon the parliamentary party to enact policies which the unions had approved in conference. In February 1979, for example, the miners were given a pay settlement that breached the five per cent norm: they had returned to collective bargaining with impunity and the social contract was in ruins.

When the general attitude of the major union leaders is taken into account, Tory reactions to union power are hardly surprising. The GMWU is the country's third largest union and one of the most loyal to the Labour Party cause. In mid-1978 at its annual congress, the general secretary, David Basnett, found that Mrs

Thatcher was 'unimpressive'; he said that 'She appears to have a penchant for political opportunism. . . . What does not appeal is her recall of older Tory attitudes, particularly her reaction to trade unions and the collective freedom they provide for working people.'

He said further: 'We want greater involvement at all levels, from determination for figures for growth and the development of strategy for industry down to their implementation at plant level. This requires the industrial strategy to be more actively pursued and firmly implemented than at the moment, and also backed up by the introduction through statute of planning agreements and industrial democracy. Both these should be introduced by the next Labour government.'

Since on this occasion Mr Basnett also said: 'If it is an alternative between a Labour Government and a Tory government there is no danger of any advice but to help and support Labour,' it is unsurprising that general Tory reaction at the normal political level (not just in union crises) tends to be anti-union—and this despite the Tory claim that some four million unionists vote for them. There may be millions of individual trade unionists who do vote Tory; the union movement, however, throws its *power* behind the Labour Party.

Where Labour politicians might well have been less than happy was in the next statement from Mr Basnett, who went on to say: 'But we have to ensure that a Labour Government's policies are as nearly in line with our own as possible.' Basnett said what all trade unionists say: that the unions would talk to any properly elected government; but he added: 'However, there is a difference between talking and co-operation. That must depend upon policies.'

It is this commitment of the trade unions to one of the country's two major political parties which in part is responsible for some of the ills of our industrial society. The labour movement accepts the position that its interests will only be properly served by one political party. The converse, of course, is the broad commitment of employers to the Tory cause. The result is a greater degree of partisanship and political interference in the running of the country's industry than exists in any other of Britain's major trading and industrial rivals: that partisanship goes to the root of many of the country's economic problems.

The TGWU is by far the country's largest union and it, too, threw its weight behind Labour in the summer of 1978 when the

96

general anticipation was an autumn election. At the time Moss Evans said: 'Despite our differences on the five per cent, it is a stark choice facing us. In our view, our members will still support the Labour Government, and they would want them to carry out socialist policies when elected. We shall get no sympathy at all from a Tory Government, and despite the fact that we disagree with the current White Paper, our union will do everything in its power to get Labour re-elected.' At the time the union had a political fund of about £500,000 available. This certainly represented political power of a very substantial kind.

In January 1979, at the time of the lorry drivers' strike, Moss Evans said: 'I am not bothered with percentages. It's not my responsibility to manage the economy. We are concerned about getting the rate for the job.' This kind of remark, of course, is a godsend to Tory opponents of the unions. Strictly speaking, it is true: if the Thatcher style Tory approach that does not want unions involved in decisions about the economy is to be erected into policy, then such a remark becomes more apposite and must reflect the attitude which will prevail in all the unions, bringing confrontation with government and making 'irresponsibility' about the state of the economy the norm of union behaviour.

The sheer size of the TGWU is a source of both strength and weakness. The union has more than two million members and extends into an astonishing range of activities; it has eleven regional divisions and eleven trade groups each with its own national organiser and some 8000 branches. It sponsors some twenty-five MPs and pays up to half a million pounds a year to Labour Party funds. The weakness of the union results from its amorphous nature and the wide range of trades and industries it covers, so that too often the centre finds it does not control individual areas or activities and has to follow local action, making official a strike it may well have opposed to begin with, but lacked the power to prevent taking place.

Ray Buckton is the general secretary of ASLEF, currently representing about 26,000 train drivers. He is a tough, militant leader and firm supporter of the Labour Party—but a more militant party than was the case during the 1970s. He is against an incomes policy, advocating free collective bargaining; he regards ASLEF as a craft union whose differentials should be maintained.

Buckton simply does not accept that unions could be too powerful. 'If you curb union power you lead yourselves into tremendous industrial relations problems. I believe that trade unions should be strong and powerful and that their strength should be harnessed in the interests of what we are all trying to do: that is, put some life into our industrial relations and manu-facturing industries.'

Like many unionists Buckton thinks the key reason for poor British productivity is lack of investment; he finds it difficult to understand why industrialists would not invest in British industry after the war. His basic solution is to take more industry into public ownership. He believes steel should have been taken entirely into public ownership long ago: also communications equipment and the entire car industry.

Buckton is a fervent supporter of the trade union concept, but he sees the movement being weakened during the 1980s as a result of mass unemployment. As he says: 'There were two ways the government could weaken the trade union movement; the one by legislation; the other is to do what the Tory Government is doing at the present time and have mass unemployment. Of course that weakens the trade union movement for the simple reason that you now have a mass of frightened workers. They are frightened of losing their jobs, they are frightened of what will happen to their wives and children, their homes. They are *absolutely* frightened and so the trade unions are weakened. But no government can survive for any length of time with a frightened workforce and as a result the Thatcher Government will fail (unless it does something about unemployment). You cannot survive like that although you can take the power from the trade unions.' He argues that 14 May, the Day of Action, was a failure for that reason: the unions, he says, cannot instruct but may only advise their members to take action.

ASLEF insists upon free collective bargaining and Ray Buckton's views on the social contract, therefore, are interesting. As he says: 'I do not think you can run a system of that type (the social contract) with the structure of society as we have it today. It would have to be a more socialist society first for such a con-tract to work successfully. As it was (and is likely to be) the contract may run for one, two or three years but then, when the govern-ment cannot give in return and is simply taking all the time, asking workers to tighten their belts, then it is bound to run into serious trouble as was the case in 1978. A contract has to be a question of give and take.

'The Callaghan Government did not fall out with the hierarchy

98

of the trade union movement or the TUC; eventually the real pressures came from the rank and file of the movement, which told Jack Jones in the Isle of Wight, for example, that "enough is enough, we are having no more" and so he was obliged to come back and argue the absolute opposite one month to what he had said the previous month. Following that the whole trade union movement came to say "enough is enough"; in effect the movement said the contract was at an end. We told the government that the five per cent would not stick, that the workforce would not accept it and the leadership could not make it stick. But Callaghan said he was going to make it stick. We warned him: those strikes—during the "winter of discontent"—were not engineered by the officialdom of the trade union movement, they all started as unofficial strikes.

'Now in the same sort of way there is likely to be a reaction against the Thatcher Government in a few years' time—the reaction of frightened people—as there was against the Labour Government by people who felt tied by what amounted to a type of legislation. Thus there was the tanker drivers' strike. There was the strike by the lorry drivers who came out on unofficial strike: the union eventually made it official, that was the only way to get them back, the only way to gain control. And so in the "winter of discontent" there was a spate of unofficial strikes: the only ones that were official were the NUPE strikes and these had been planned for a long time.'

If there is to be an effective social contract, Buckton believes, then there has also to be far better control of prices as part of it. This he does not see as being possible while Britain is a member of the EEC. An effective contract also requires a greater degree of nationalisation. He believes there should also be a far more serious examination of the role of the City, of banking and insurance. Whilst not suggesting an end to the mixed economy or free enterprise, Buckton does believe that a Labour government should obtain control of the major industries or institutions which are the keys to the economy.

It is a doctrinaire approach not shared by all trade unionists. To the question of how the strongest unions would be prevented from always seeking a maximum pay rise under such a system, Buckton's answer is based upon his faith in the trade union movement: he cites the response at the beginning of the social contract. He argues, for example, that the influence of the TUC over the union movement as a whole is much respected and would be used in such circumstances to hold back such power plays: 'The point is,' he says, 'if you have the sort of controlled structure we are talking about, then you would not get workers in this country suddenly rearing up and going on strike.'

Prices, however, have to be controlled if any form of social contract is to work.

Speaking of the 1980 Labour Party Conference, Buckton defends measures which, he believes, would make the Party more democratic. He says of the manifesto: 'I do believe the writing of the manifesto should be widened. It should not be left to the last moment before an election: if you are going to run a country and are hoping to take the trade union movement and the socialist movement with you then I see nothing wrong in widening the basis of decision making. What Benn is really saying here is—why write a manifesto suddenly three weeks before a general election and then expect everybody to understand what you are after? Why not build it up over a period of time so that the people of the country know exactly and clearly the policies the party intends to pursue. If the electorate do not like them they will not have them.'

Mr Buckton's views are not new; he represents a wing of the trade union and Labour movement that believes in a greater dose of fairly orthodox state control as the best means of ensuring better productivity, more investment in industry and smoother industrial relations. Critics of this line will say it has already been tried and failed; its defenders will reply it has only been half tried, hence its apparent failures. Either way these arguments highlight one of the dilemmas of modern Britain as far as industry, productivity and industrial relations are concerned: the constant swing between two sides of an argument that never leaves industry alone long enough for any system to be worked out to its logical conclusions.

Moss Evans, general secretary of the TGWU, controls the largest and politically most powerful union in Britain, with very considerable resources at his back. Of the power he wields personally, Evans says: 'Of course it is not really power in that sense. Power means you can arrive at decisions and have them implemented. This particular job carries a considerable degree of influence and I happen to be principal officer of the union. Now the question is how to use that influence wisely in the interests of our members. The controlling factor is the people who really have power: those

100

who manage the economy of the country, those who literally own industry—the employers—who have not always been willing to concede to our union and unions in general the sort of aims we are trying to achieve on behalf of our members. So our power— the power of imposing economic sanctions against an employer, of refusing to co-operate with the government, has to be used very wisely. No useful purpose can be served, for example, by imposing economic sanctions upon an employer if in fact this rebounds on your membership and they lose their jobs, or their resolve is weakened while you are not able to achieve what you are aiming for very quickly. All these factors must be taken into consideration—the influence you can bring to bear on governments to effect changes in legislation or changes in economic strategies; if you decide to take action against a government by, say, having political strikes, in many cases this does not help and may have a boomerang effect. One has therefore to use a considerable degree of discretion in deploying the influence of a union the size of the TGWU.

'What we have at our disposal,' says Moss Evans, 'is the ability to talk to many people: we have access to members of the Cabinet, we have access to the Prime Minister and on top of that, of course, we have our resources to reach practically the whole public.' The TGWU does have very considerable resources.

Evans does not see great differences between the British union role in relation to government and that of unions in the USA or West Germany, although he thinks the manner is more institutionalised in Britain because of the movement's direct association with a party that is either the government or the alternative government. 'It is essential,' he says, 'that the unions retain their political associations. That does not mean they slavishly support a particular ideology: that, for example, they accept everything a Labour government wants to impose in the economic management of the country. But they will always have a political conscience: for years to come, whoever has the political management of the country's economy is bound to come into contact one way or another with the unions.

'Generally the majority of trade unions and in particular trade union leaders find the Labour Party reflects more correctly the aspirations and desires of their members than does the Conservative Party; the fact is, the trade unions formed the Labour Party in order to obtain representation within our parliamentary democracy, and people still alive today remember how difficult it was to get labour representation in parliament against tremendous opposition.'

This is not an egalitarian society and, therefore, the unions will continue to support the Labour Party. Like most trade unionists Evans thinks the media give the movement an unfair deal, although he suggests that in the last years of the 1970s newspapers had so lambasted the unions that the process was becoming counter-productive.

Unions are often made scapegoats for the ills of modern Britain, but Moss Evans has an interesting view on this question: 'People have become much less willing to accept that the unions are to blame: the reason is that the union view in relation to the Callaghan Government's attempted five per cent norm was proved right. It was an impracticable way to deal with industrial relations, to lay down rigid norms within an incomes policy.' He goes on, 'We have been proved right that there is an imbalance,' and he lists some of the groups which felt the norm should not apply to them: 'The toolmakers—and their dispute—at Longbridge: they thought they had been badly treated. The dispute amongst nurses, teachers, public service people, the disputes among professional people, the complaint by politicians about their salaries. It is difficult to blame the unions for making clear that to continue with such rigidity would mean the whole five per cent norm must collapse. We were proved correct.'

Moss Evans believes the resources of the trade union movement ought to be used far more for effective communications: he would like to see a union daily newspaper and unions having more time on television. Although he concedes that unions do have opportunities to present their views to the public, it is too often as part of the instant journalism of today: that is, outside a factory where there has been a problem or outside an employers' organisation office when there have been difficulties, usually in the form of street interviews or press conferences called immediately after a discussion with politicians.

Evans favours some form of social contract. He begins by making the point: 'The important thing when developing a social contract which involves dialogue and discussion on prices and incomes, is that one must always think in terms of incomes being progressive. So far, the history of government incomes policies has always been on the basis of restraint. The Labour approach was one of restraint. Our view is that the social contract helped the Labour Government overcome an exceptionally serious

102

crisis—the worst since 1930. Now we are experiencing an equally bad one under a Conservative Government. I believe there can be a social contract provided that it is used for progression: that is, we do not simply talk of regressive or restraining policies. We must [use it] to improve the standards of everyone and recognise that the trade union role is not merely to make general wage applications, but to deal with the problems and aspirations of members on a far wider scale.

'You must discuss job rates objectively: if you are told that the total economic demands to be allowed for a given period will only be x to cover wages, holidays, pensions, all the economic benefits which accrue to the unions' members under bargaining arrangements with employers, then I believe the process is doomed to failure. Inside the contract there has to be flexibility: you must allow people to act legitimately on behalf of their members. Many problems arise, not simply to do with work organisation, but concerning specific rewards related to the myriad different occupations which exist throughout industry.

'The trade union movement,' Evans argues, 'is not a cohesive whole. The AUEW have a different view from the TGWU, the ETU from the NUM. The four biggest unions in Britain have differing views and this can be seen according to the motions they put on the agenda for the Labour Party conference. A Labour politician will have considerable influence in persuading unions which line to take and, for example, what is termed the right in the Labour Party will influence the white collar workers. I think APEX will actively support the line taken by Shirley Williams on many issues because she is very active in APEX. I am sure the TGWU will lend support to the views expressed by Peter Shore, possibly Silkin and other members of the cabinet who happen to be sponsored members of the TGWU.'

A lot is made of trade union block votes at Labour conferences. In fact Moss Evans argues: 'The trade unions all have separate delegate meetings and many general secretaries only know the day the conference starts which way a union is likely to vote. I am not opposed to unions examining objectively their position if it is thought they exercise undue or unfair weight in terms of arriving at final Party decisions compared with other members or constituents of the Party. I have no objection to that, because I am not looking for power; what I am looking for, genuinely, is the sort of things the members are trying to achieve. We spend hours discussing how our delegation should vote at conference.'

103

Although Evans believes implicitly in sitting round the table and opposes the concept of constant confrontation, nonetheless he says: 'One of the problems we have had is the unwillingness of employers to let us know what they are about. The information we have got about companies' activities has been limited to what they are prepared to give us. This means many of our arguments can only be based upon guesstimates. There is need for far more information to be made available. Great bias appeared against the Secretary of State for Industry, Benn, when he attempted to get major companies to enter into what we termed planning agreements with the trade unions (I do not know whether that was the reason for his being moved from Industry to Energy). There was great reaction by the employers against the suggestion that there should be that sort of development—it was not something they would accept.

'Similarly, the reception by employers' organisations and politicians of the Bullock Report was another clear indication that the argument advanced by many people that the unions are always preaching *them and us* ought to be examined objectively. When governments want to introduce progressive legislation to bridge this gap so that unions can operate effectively, we find the employers vociferously and actively opposing moves in this direction.

'We have a responsibility to bargain effectively on behalf of our members and I want to be able to do this logically and sensibly. I need maximum information to do so. Government, instead of talking about picketing, should think seriously of providing both employers and trade unions with a platform where they can bargain more effectively with each other without having recourse to confrontation.'

7

Union Moderates

Four trade unionists—Sid Weighell of the NUR, Tom Jackson of the UPW, Tom Jenkins of TSSA (each the general secretary of his union) and David Buckle the district secretary of the TGWU in Oxford—may be described as moderates. As Tom Jackson says: 'I like to think I am slap bang in the middle, but most people describe me as right.' Their views are perhaps especially important at the beginning of the 1980s, because most signs in Britain point to growing political polarisation during the decade. In many circumstances these men might be expected to take a middle road, yet in 1980 they each appeared to be becoming more radical.

The growth of the road lobby and many changes of policy on transport priorities by successive governments have meant that the NUR has had its membership more than halved over the last quarter of a century. The NUR is more nearly an industrial union than most others in the country and possesses enormous power to disrupt. The union has a seat on the General Council of the TUC where Weighell is regarded as one of the leading moderates.

Tom Jackson's Union of Postal Workers (UPW) is also one of the few industrial unions: as the result of the operation of a closed shop 97 per cent of postal workers—204,000 out of 210,000—are organised in the union. The UPW has always had a seat on the General Council of the TUC except when it was debarred from sitting there by virtue of being a civil service union. In terms of numbers the UPW ranks about twentieth in the union hierarchy. Speaking of the power of his union, Tom Jackson remarks wryly: 'We can stop the letter deliveries but 1971 proves that that is not actually a winner.'

The general secretary of the TSSA, Tom Jenkins, has a white collar union of 72,000 members covering British Rail (65–70 per cent), London Transport, the National Freight Corporation, docks, Scottish transport groups, undertakings in Ulster, the travel trade (Cooks), Inland Waterways. Management staff are now joining the union in considerable numbers and, for example, these include members up to board level with salaries as high as £20,000 a year. As Jenkins says of the upper salary levels: 'To be blunt about it, they feel with the narrowing of differentials over the years that they are not being rewarded properly for their responsibilities, so they are joining us to attack for them as well as to safeguard their positions.'

David Buckle is a district secretary of the TGWU at Oxford. His brief includes the blanket industry in Witney, cement, commercial transport, food manufacturing at Banbury and the car industry—BL—at Oxford (Cowley). Buckle is what is known as a composite officer in the TGWU. He claims that 90 per cent of his work is a matter of normal negotiations which end amicably; the other ten per cent is where the constitutional machinery has been exhausted and then he could find himself dealing with a strike.

Sid Weighell's approach to the question of union power is thoughtful, though he starts by slamming the Thatcher Government. Speaking in August 1980, he says: 'If the trade unions were as powerful as some people claim, we would not for the last eighteen months have been putting up with some of the changes which are being forced down our throats.' As Weighell points out, the trade union movement has the power to stop things in the sense of industrial change, but 'What it lacks because of its own inner contradictions and faults, is the ability to mobilise its twelve million members in a more positive direction—both with government and everybody else.'

Currently there are 109 unions affiliated to the TUC, and getting that body to act for all twelve million is extremely difficult. Weighell and the NUR have for several years proposed at Congress to increase the power of the General Council, but this can only be achieved if individual unions are prepared to give up some of their powers. Weighell would like to see the TUC have greater power to negotiate on pay policy, working hours, holidays: the things which he believes should be tackled at the national level and agreed in conjunction with government. Such a process must mean more centralisation of the movement: 'The unions are not too powerful,' he claims. 'They could be more powerful if they conducted their affairs better. They could be much more powerful if there were a better trade union structure—one union for one industry more in the German or Swedish pattern. The potential is there for great power but the movement is not at present organised to exploit the power.' Relating power to economic achievement, Weighell points out that some people in his union are on a £58 minium with only £65 a week guaranteed: were his union more powerful he would have achieved £100 a week minimum.

Tom Jackson claims there is a great myth about union power: he relates this to the ascendancy of Jack Jones when it was suggested the unions ran the country. The easiest way to dispel the myth, he suggests, is to see how much of the TUC's annual economic review produced before the budget is in fact accepted by the government of the day. Even when there is a Labour Government, Jackson says, about 80 per cent of the trade union proposals are not implemented: 'It is very satisfactory to the *Daily Mail*, for instance, to be able to say Jack Jones is running the country because that way it is possible to discredit the Labour Party.' Jackson does not see the unions as having real power but only influence and, moreover, influence which is exercised at the margin.

He does however agree that the unions which are a mixture—the general unions or those with a very wide spread of membership, concentrate upon exercising political influence: for example, he says, the one subject all members of the big general unions such as the TGWU or the GMWU have in common at their conference is politics; so that is what they concentrate upon, whereas the members of the UPW all work in the same field and concentrate upon the industry's problems.

A different point about power and responsibility-sharing is made by Jenkins of the TSSA who would like to see what he calls the rights the union now has under 'consultation' transferred to 'negotiations'. He wants power as between the employer and employee sides of an industry more equally shared. The TSSA conference, for example, has said the union would be quite happy to take responsibility for decisions at board level—if the union had half the seats on the board but not otherwise.

Buckle, too, thinks that union power is negative. Like almost all trade unionists he says the same thing: that the unions constantly react to events but rarely initiate anything. As he also says, though both sides—employer and unions—take up positions, in the end it is the employer who makes the decision, while the unions either accept or reject it. Buckle further suggests that over the last fifty or sixty years, despite trade union concern to bring about a redistribution of wealth, the movement has signally

107

failed to do so. What is needed, therefore, is a redistribution of power in favour of the trade unions; only then will a redistribution of wealth be possible.

Trade unions may be committed ideologically to the Labour Party, but they all take the stand that they must deal with any government, no matter how they may dislike its policies. This has been stated frequently since the Thatcher Government came to power. As Sid Weighell says: 'You have got to bargain with them because they are there and on the thing that apparently all governments most want from us, an understanding about pay. That should be a lever for bargaining: anything the government wants from the unions they can have—at a price—those are the bargaining realities of life.' Weighell likes the concept of the NEDC as the forum in which government, management and unions get together and talk out national policies.

This is a view shared by most moderate trade unionists. As Buckle says: 'I am a great believer in the government, the CBI and the TUC sitting down together and seriously discussing what is required of industry and how we are to create new wealth.'

But as Weighell points out on the subject of a possible social contract: 'It is better with a certain type of government: you can strike an understanding quicker with a Labour government because their central objectives are similar to those of the unions. A social contract,' he says, 'is an ideal way in which trade unions can exert power on government. They enter into a deal, a discussion. I do not like the free collective bargaining in which 112 unions can decide which way they will go individually and how fast. I like the idea of twelve million from Congress House bargaining collectively with the government of the day.'

Weighell believes the unions lost a golden opportunity in 1978 when Callaghan applied his five per cent norm. The Prime Minister, he says, was literally pleading for something from the unions and the movement, instead of entering into a bargain, said 'leave it to us'; it did not use its power intelligently. 'We may have twelve million members, but then we threw away the collective power we might have exercised. If twelve million workers act together, the government would have to listen.'

Tom Jackson would like to see a proper incomes policy worked out between government and unions. He says: 'I think it is wrong that six members of the General Council and six Labour ministers should spend two days writing on the backs of envelopes what sort of incomes policy there should be and then come out of

Downing Street and tell the nation what is good for it. The process should be much more systematic: an incomes policy ought to be a single part of a total national strategy and if we do not get an agreement with the Labour Party before an election, then we will find ourselves in the usual situation of accidentally stumbling into an incomes policy.'

Jenkins's view of a social contract is somewhat different. He says of the TSSA, for example: 'We have been very unhappy with the kind of flat rate payments and agreements which came about in a certain era when that was the demand, apparently, of senior people in the trade union movement. It did not do a lot of good for management staff and supervisors who did not get the differential payments that they should have received. But we have got to bring down the cost of living and if there were a fair arrangement relative to pay, dividends and profits, I think fair discussion with the trade union movement could bring about a social deal where we could help the unemployed, improve the medical services. I see no reason why we cannot talk about a package.'

David Buckle is clear that the content of any social contract has to be all embracing. He says: 'I do not want a policy which merely says that the working people of this country, whoever they may be, can only have *x* percentage in wages while the government does nothing about taxes. I am talking about income in all forms: tax relief, dividends, every form of income if the policy is to be fair; otherwise it merely singles out wage earners, and the vast majority of these are in economic groups four and five. I want everybody to be controlled if anybody is controlled.'

Buckle admits there are difficulties about price controls and says the Prices Commission was not a success: part of the problem is that too many prices depend upon rises which take place outside Britain. But he says: 'We are not going to get any form of income control which is acceptable unless we can demonstrate to people that prices can be more reasonable.'

The power trade unions may exercise collectively depends to a great extent upon their structure and the willingness of individual unions to surrender some of their power to the TUC. Sid Weighell would like to see a far stronger, more centralised TUC with the ability to effect policies on behalf of all its members. When certain unions broke the pay guidelines of the social contract, the TUC was powerless to discipline them. The only power the TUC has is to expel a member, and that power is only exercised on the narrow front of recruiting rights—if one union infringes the recruiting area and rights of another union. Weighell would like to see a union which pursued a pay claim to the detriment of the rest of an industry being expelled. Under the social contract, he claims, ASTMS boasted that it had bust the contract and obtained 15 to 20 per cent settlements for its members. Weighell does not want to see the TUC General Council with dictatorial powers; but he would like to see it in a position to discipline members who ignore agreed policies.

He would also like to see one union to an industry but admits this to be unlikely because of the long history of the unions: reluctant to give up their powers, reluctant to change. As he says: 'Whilst numerically we are the biggest pro rata to the size of the nation of any union movement in the world, we are also the worst organized and I would suggest we are not the strongest either—the Swedish movement is more powerful, the German movement is more powerful and in the main they have industrial unions.' Ironically, it was the TUC which provided the union blueprint for West Germany after the war to build a structure in place of that which Hitler had destroyed.

Jackson wants a trade union movement that seeks social justice through negotiations with government. He does not believe individual unions can produce such a result. 'In fact,' he says, 'they are each looking after their own "patch", their own group of self-interests and in so far as the trade union movement continues to do that, we will never produce the circumstances in which we can really talk to government on the basis of what is good for the nation as a whole. So I would like to see the trade union movement less self-interested in the sense of each union just looking after its own affairs; more concerned with workers as a whole and totally concerned with the economy, which, after all, is the backdrop to all our discussions.'

Jackson would like to see organized collective bargaining by the unions as a whole working with the government—a Labour government. He is not enamoured of free collective bargaining by each union. As he says: 'Our people have insisted upon what they call free collective bargaining, the right to do their own thing, in fact to look after their own narrow self-interest in as rapacious a way as they are able to do it. That really is what free collective bargaining means. Well, they have got it and free collective bargaining is not producing the pot of gold which they felt was under every managing director's desk; free collective bargaining is leading to all sorts of troubles. So I think we are learning the lesson of the free market economy and will want to look at a more managed type of economy in which they all play a part together.'

Unlike many unions, the 1800 delegates of the UPW can spend their entire conference talking about the problems of the postal industry because every delegate works for the same employer. This is a major advantage over general unions which bring together delegates from a wide range of employers with little in common except their membership of the same union. For that reason some unions cannot spend a great deal of time discussing what is good for their industry, because in fact hundreds of industries may be represented; as a result, the one subject they have in common is the political scene. Thus such unions see a political as opposed to an industrial approach as their principal role.

Many people have commented upon the negative and reactive character of British unions: defending situations rather than creating new climates for action. Tom Jackson explains this as follows: 'We were born in circumstances where we were reacting to oppression in society. The trade union movement came into being to try to give some dignity to men who previously had had no opportunity to stand tall and, as it were, look their boss in the eye. And we were born in a negative fashion, we were born as organizations to react against this and against that—initially against repression. It is a habit we have not yet got out of: George Woodcock tried to get us out of it and I think Len Murray is trying to change the habit. The TUC Economic Review every year is an attempt to make us look at the totality of Britain and the way we fit into Britain as a group. But the habit is an old one, difficult to cure and I think it is true of most trade unions throughout the world, we are not especially unique.'

The strike weapon of course is the ultimate exercise of union power and Sid Weighell is very conscious of the impact that a railway strike has upon the public image of his union; as he says, when anything is wrong with the railways, his telephone is red hot. Part of the trouble, he claims, is that the railways are a very political industry: if anything happens, they are immediately in the public eye. They also have social obligations. Yet sometimes the union does have to decide that strike action is the only way; he controls a highly disciplined union. Despite the publicity a railway strike gets, such strikes, he says, are few and disruption caused by them is marginal, although when a strike is on it is

111

definitely on. He believes that the union could be just as effective in any argument with BR if its members were to refuse to handle freight, thus going for the most vulnerable and profitable part of the railways' business and leaving passengers alone. Passengers return once the trains are running again.

David Buckle makes the point that 98 per cent of all manufacturing industry in Britain has never had a dispute that came to a strike and suggests that British workers are no more prone to strikes than others.

There is a major contradiction between union claims that they believe in some form of socialism and in their determination to pursue free collective bargaining. As Tom Jackson argues: 'I have always said that the obverse of the free collective bargaining coin is the free market economy. Now some of our people are beginning to realise that. Remember we have had welfare governments in Britain since the end of the war: governments which have consulted with the unions and regarded social welfare and social democracy as the way the nation should be run. Many people growing up in that atmosphere which has existed for more than thirty years have then looked over the fence and thought that the free collective bargaining grass looked greener. What this Thatcher Government is proving, I think, is that this is not the case and there are better ways of doing things than by the free market economy.'

The difficulty about asking unions to relinquish free collective bargaining is that the stronger ones believe, correctly in many cases, that free collective bargaining will most favour their case. They have to be persuaded to surrender some of their power for the sake of a collective union approach. This demands the application of a socialist principle widely spoken of in the movement, but not always applied. Again to quote Jackson: 'This is a most difficult question since it means some people must give up things they could themselves get in order that other people should benefit. I believe that the trade union movement started off with a good deal of altruism and I think a lot of that has disappeared. It is my hope that the bitter lesson people are learning at the moment will bring back into the movement some of that unity and solidarity and common purpose which does not exist at the present time. It is a pity that the lesson has to be learnt in such a hard way, but perhaps it is being learned now.

'I do not want a rigid incomes policy which says all wages are frozen but everybody may get £4 extra,' Jackson continues. 'It has got to be far more sophisticated than that: there have to be safety valves, you have to be able to deal with bottlenecks in terms of labour; you must be able to retrain when old industries come to an end. I think it would be possible to develop a far more sophisticated policy if we sat down to think about it beforehand. If we simply allow ourselves to stumble accidentally into an incomes policy, then it will be discredited again. A policy which freezes wage anomalies—and every incomes policy since the war has done that—is bad because men resent the build-up. There must always be safety valves within which people can be treated specially.'

Trade unionists all claim there has not been sufficient investment in industry and advance this as the major reason—certainly as a foremost reason—for poor productivity. Tom Jenkins makes this point emphatically. 'We have not had the investment to make ourselves a modernised country. I would like to see more money being put into the basic industries and the nationalised industries: naturally I have the docks and railways in mind. For example, it would be good for London docks if we could get an underground line built into them; we have been playing about with this idea for years. We must get heavy industry invested again.'

Tom Jackson is much more reflective over the issue of low productivity. He says: 'I would like to think it was lack of investment, poor management and bloody-minded unions, because you could cure these three things. But I am not at all sure that Britain as a nation is not opting for a soft but less well endowed life. And if that is the case there is really no cure for it. If it is lack of investment, if it is bad management, if it is bloody-minded unions, all those can be changed; but if in fact as a people we are resting on our arms reversed, as it were, and saying: "that's it, we don't want to work over-hard, we value leisure, we value time-off" then I think we might have an incurable disease.'

Jackson does not attempt to explain why this should be the case in Britain rather than in any of her major industrial rivals, but simply says: 'I put this forward as a hypothesis because I cannot genuinely say that there is another reason for it. I do not understand why it should be the case, but it does appear that management prefers the golf links and workers prefer the Costa del Sol in a way which I suspect French and German workers do not. If it is true, it is a bad thing for us.'

No government since the war has attracted the ire of the unions as thoroughly as that of Mrs Thatcher: partly it is a question of attitudes—the Government will not 'talk' to the unions; and partly it is a question of measures—not so much Mr Prior's Bill, despite the rhetoric, but the monetarist policies; and, as many unionists believe, the use of the unemployment weapon to bring so-called powerful unions to heel.

As Sid Weighell says: 'It looks to us as if they are trying to find ways to restrict trade union activity on a number of fronts. I do not know whether they are doing this because of the pressures in the Tory Party or in response to what they think is public opinion. Everything they do, it seems to us, at a critical time when unemployment is two million and the prospects are for three; when inflation is still not under control (and they have now come round to the view that pay deals have got to be savagely reduced in order to make their policy work), they appear to believe that all these policies which the unions bitterly resist will be better implemented if the unions are weakened.

'Now, today, Sir Peter Parker would never dream of trying to run British Rail without attempting to reach an understanding with the NUR. If that is true of a great basic industry then it must be true of everything else about a nation. How can you govern and solve our problems in Britain unless you get an understanding with twelve million trade unionists? It will not work.'

Because of the 'hard line' the government is taking, Weighell fears that extremists of both parties will come to the fore, and he sees that as a major danger. As he says: 'If we do not learn to live together in periods when there is a government we do not particularly like, then the process of moving apart can threaten all the democratic institutions we all cherish—that is the danger at present. Sooner or later, therefore, somebody—the initiative must come from the Prime Minister—must change the tone in the Cabinet, because at the moment it is shocking. Whether that will change I do not know. There are elements in my union that would go to the barricades. Fortunately they are a minority, but for how long I do not know.'

Tom Jackson says much the same. Admitting that the trade unions are a negative force inside the economy, he argues that the only way to translate the movement into a positive force for good in Britain is for government to take the TUC into discussions about economic policy: to leave them on the outside is a mistake. But, he says, 'The present situation is that no one is talking to us at all; the Government is doing its own thing, we have very high levels of unemployment, inflation is high. I think it is absolutely

114

essential for trade unions to be consulted about the economic situation in the country.'

Quoting Sir Keith Joseph, who described the trade unions as 'one of the poisons in British society', Jackson says: 'They [the Tories] believe that the unions are bad as such and that our sole job is to negotiate pay and conditions; but you cannot do that in isolation, it is impossible.' He concludes: 'Any nation which tries to govern without taking the unions into consultation—I am not talking about unions determining government policy—but to talk, to discuss and to try to reach agreement [is being absurd] for if that does not happen, then the negative aspect of trade unionism must predominate. We will become tremendously defensive and that kind of defensive attitude inside the trade union movement is all too familiar; it has been a brake upon progress.'

Jackson also believes—and it is a harsh judgement from so normally mild a man—that unemployment is being used as it was between the wars 'as a means to discipline the trade unions and a means to produce within their ranks the fear which goes with low expectations.' Instead of the problems of the nation being solved through discussion, incomes policy, trade-offs of one kind or another, he sees them being solved in the 'most brutal of ways, which is the increase in the size of the unemployed, the wasting of the lives involved in that, the high public spending that results from paying men on the dole. All these terrible things are happening,' he says, 'because the Government believes that this is the way they will be able to solve the problems of the nation. And in a sense the free collective bargaining [of the unions] has something to answer for in relation to the present Government policies: this is a reaction to free collective bargaining.'

Concerning relations between the Labour Party and the trade unions, Jackson is not in favour of the constitutional changes being proposed in the Party, because he believes they would give too much power to the trade unions: the movement would virtually be electing the Labour leader and in his opinion the exercise of trade union power in that sense would be bad for the Labour Party. However he does not much like the present block vote system and would like to see it changed or modified so that the Party became more democratic than it is at present.*

* The constitutional changes agreed at the Wembley Labour Party Conference of January 1981, predictably caused uproar in the Party and led to members on the right of the Party and trade union movements arguing that they were determined to reverse the decision.

Unions may be committed to Labour; but a nationalised industry such as British Rail suffers as does the rest of British industry from the see-saws of policy which accompany every change of government. Sid Weighell resents the idea that the railways are subsidised or bailed out by the government. Speaking of uneconomic services, he says: 'If we were a purely commercial organization we would not carry them at all. So I resent anybody saying you are feather-bedded, you get subsidies. We do not. We get a contract to carry on uneconomic services that another firm would not carry at all if judged solely by balance sheet criteria. In the main our problems stem from government interference which changes every time a government changes. In the lifetime of nearly every parliament there is usually an appraisal—and an upheaval—in public transport. Since 1945 governments have constantly changed transport or altered terms of reference so that we have had difficulty in knowing where we are going: in this I blame Labour as much as Tory government. It would make an enormous difference if there were a common agreement between the two parties on transport policy so that the industry was not subject to change every five years or so.'

Tom Jenkins says: 'The 1947 Transport Act put together the most magnificent organization; Attlee's Government was superb. They created the British Transport Commission which was making a profit every year until 1953 when the Tory Government sold off the road side and so disintegration took place and road and rail competition started, and the merciless onslaught has continued ever since: we keep altering (according to governments) the method of funding the social (non-paying) lines which have to be kept in the rural areas that cannot be denuded of transport. The amount of money for these has been whittled down every year by both Labour and Tory Governments. Now, for example, the term "privatisation" has come in, but it means denationalisation and the present government want Sealink, Hovercraft, the Property Board and the hotels to be put into a holding company and shares floated. The British Rail chairman may have to sell these off to obtain the money he needs to keep BR afloat if government does not provide adequate funds.'

The TSSA opposed this move and wants these assets to be renationalised without compensation. Jenkins wants to see the nationalised industries refurbished: this would mean massive injections of money; profits from North Sea oil are one obvious source of such funds.

Confrontation or participation are the choices for unions and government, and according to Weighell: 'Given the right sort of government the ideal would be a form of incomes strategy within the framework of some overall economic and social policy. In that situation you may then agree what is available between government, unions and management.'

Some trade union leaders—Weighell is one—are in a much better position to deliver than are others: this depends on the nature of the unions they control. The NUR is essentially an industrial union and Weighell talks on behalf of virtually all the men in the industry to one employer—British Rail: as long as he has the support of his members he can deliver his side of a bargain in any negotiations. As he says: 'I am not going to say to BR that I am making an agreement with you before analysing the full consequences of the agreement, because once I have signed I am going to honour it and I am going to tell our people (a quarter of a million in this industry) that they have got to carry it out because I accepted it on behalf of the rank and file. If they do not like the agreement they can appeal it at the NUR annual conference.' Many unions are not in that position and the general secretary cannot speak for everybody or negotiate for them all for half the time.

All unions want maximum information from management so they can negotiate adequately. Weighell does get the information from British Rail: 'There is nothing that happens in BR that I do not know about,' he says (a claim few trade union leaders are able to make about the industries with which they are concerned), but, as Weighell adds, one result is that he also gets management problems on his plate. 'This situation can test a trade union to the limit and many do not have sufficient income from fees to provide adequate research and back-up facilities for their leadership.'

Tom Jackson believes in a similar approach and would like to see some form of industrial democracy. 'I believe the closer you can associate the workers with the enterprise the more likely you are to have better understanding of the way that enterprise is run. And I believe that working people have got something to add to management's know-how. Industrial democracy would give a union a stake in its industry and could produce circumstances in which the workforce are totally involved in the industry in which they work.'

Jenkins says the TSSA would be prepared to go half way with

117

management at every level, including board level, and take full responsibility half and half. 'But if you do not have a half and half situation,' he says, 'then it is bound to be a case of them and us.'

Buckle is a regional as opposed to national union leader and he sees great difficulties in participation. He says: 'I was never in favour of the Bullock proposals for this reason: I do not believe that there is a half way house between the present capitalist system that we have in this country and complete state ownership and worker control of all the means of production, distribution and exchange. Now I have my reservations about the second possibility as well; I think it could be just as dictatorial in some respects, but even so I do not think there is a half way house between these two positions and therefore I do not believe that there can ever be genuine participation in the sense of the trade union movement having a real role in the decision making process. Indeed, with the structure of the trade unions as they are today and the multiplicity of unions in some industries—Leyland is a good example—the conflicts of interest must present major problems.'

Buckle would like to see a wide range of problems rather than simply pay and conditions covered by collective bargaining. These would include: a company's marketing policy, the new products it intends to bring out, its promotional system, acquisitions and sales of assets, the value of depreciating stocks and stocks altogether and training programmes. The unions, moreover, should not only negotiate with management on these subjects but should be entitled to information about them as of right. If such a situation could be brought about and unions could bargain on the basis of all these subjects, then Buckle believes 'we would really have extended our power within an industry; but we should also have extended our responsibilities as well.' And he says: 'I believe that the trade union movement could accept far more management decisions and I think management could accept the role of the unions and their influence much more readily if that kind of exchange of information and therefore of influence could take place. Nothing like it operates at the present time.'

No trade unionists are easy when they look to the future. Quite apart from the immediate recession and rising unemployment there are longer-term problems, most notably those connected with advances in technology. As Sid Weighell says of the railways: 'A quarter of a million people have gone in our industry in the

118

last twenty years; not as a result of closures, but because of technological change: electric, diesel locomotives, signal boxes that
control hundreds of miles of track, permanent way sophisticated
machines which do away with the pick and shovel—these are the
biggest changes. There is no end to the process: we can operate
about 22,000 track miles from two control centres. Therefore,
unless we direct our attention to the effects of technological
changes we will have a great pool of unemployed.'

On top of this long-term worry is a sense of gloom at the policies
of the Thatcher Government, which appears to exist through most
of the leadership of the movement: not simply that her Government pursues policies the unions do not like but, more importantly,
that they are policies which trade unionists believe can only bring
about worse economic hardships: more unemployed, company
bankruptcies, short time and a divisiveness that must breed further
confrontations.

As Weighell points out: 'There is a generation coming on who
never experienced the 1930s: will they put up with being out of
work year in year out with nothing to do?'

Tom Jackson would like to see a complete reform of the trade
union movement. Because of their history, the unions are now
all mixed up and the big general unions often have little in
common with the others. He wants to see industrial unions. The
only power the TUC now possesses is that of moral persuasion:
sometimes this works, sometimes it does not. He wants to see
fewer unions based upon industries with seats on the General
Council of the TUC, and the TUC having more authority to
deal directly with government and able to strike bargains with
the government about the economy. As he says: 'We are, after
all, negotiators. We spend all our lives negotiating. There is no
reason why we should not negotiate with government. But having
said that, you have got the makings of the corporate state: therefore it is absolutely essential that in any discussion process for a
national bargain the workers in the unions should be consulted.
That means more democracy inside the trade union movement
than exists at the present time.'

Jackson sums up his ideal picture of a revamped trade union
movement as: 'Industrial unions, more authority with the TUC,
the TUC negotiating with the government over its total economic
strategy and reaching a bargain with government. But any such
bargain being arrived at through the democratic decision-making
process of the unions, which must mean both going to their con-

ferences and also allowing the branches and the people in the workplace to discuss what is being proposed.'

He is not hopeful of such a development as he does not believe enough trade unionists are interested in changing the movement's structure. And without such a change the other developments are unlikely to take place.

8

Trade Unions at Grass Roots: Shop Stewards

Trade unionists, managers, politicians all agree that in recent years the power wielded by many unions has shifted from the national leadership to the shop-floor. Some, especially politicians, hanker for a return to the days when strong union leaders issued *diktats* to their members and these were obeyed. Others, notably in management, are less bothered by the shift of power to the shop-floor if, on a factory to factory basis, that is where they have to negotiate anyway. Members of the Tory Party in particular tend to believe that there exists a substantial number of left wing political troublemakers on the shop-floor whose basic aim is disruption rather than forwarding the interests of the men they represent.

The two discussions which follow were both held with groups of shop stewards: the first, a small group of left wing shop stewards or district organisers in Ayrshire; the second a more structured meeting at Ruskin College, Oxford. The first group consisted of Willie McFall, UCATT regional organiser (Ayrshire); Jim McConochie, divisional organiser TASS (Ayr) and Jim Hendry, shop steward, TGWU, in a heavy forging steelworks, Ayr.*

There are a number of members of the Tory Party who claim the unions have too much power and that this power should be contained.

When the Tories say the unions have too much power that is nothing but a fallacy; in no way do the unions have too much power. The close relationship between the trade union movement and the Labour Party is a drawback: the more they are involved with each other so the more they restrict each other. The two bodies would be better going their separate ways. Whether the Labour Party would then become powerless I do not know; it would have to try something like Party fees.

The Labour Party would collapse without the unions.

* The author's questions are in italics.

I think in the short term there would be difficulties, but in the long term the split would make for a better Labour Party. I also think the trade union movement would be better if it ceased to be tied to the Labour Party or government.

In the past the unions always supported a Labour Government. Now I suppose it is fair to say that of any union the TGWU was responsible for the downfall of the Labour Government in 1979: it was causing strikes all over the place, unpopular strikes such as the gravediggers. And, of course, the media played up. So Mrs Thatcher and the Tories got in and the unions had a lot to do with that event.

Do you think the link between the Labour Party and the unions weakens the unions?

The tie-up between the unions and the Labour Party weakens both, since the unions feel they must not hurt the Party when it is in power, while the Party may be deterred from following certain policies because of union pressures. A break between the two could lead to greater union power: first, however, the unions would need to change their attitudes. If they were unshackled claims would go better and the movement would be more leftward in its attitudes and in every respect.

This leads to another question: what sort of trade union power are we after under what sort of system? We live under capitalism: so how do we use our power under capitalism? It is the application of strength to the maximum: that is what power means, exercising your total value at any given time. The last ten years have been crucial. For many years we (trade unionists) were told that we were involved purely and simply in wages and conditions arguments—and we stuck to that. Governments found they couldn't govern under these circumstances and so they sought a new structure whereby they could maintain the *status quo* of the system we live under; then we had to try to find a new role for the unions. We were told—and we quickly lost the argument if you like—that unions could no longer afford the luxury of being separate from the structure of British society. We could no longer hide from our responsibilities. We had to be brought into the twentieth century and into the whole process of decision making. Following the events of 1973–4 the idea of the social contract emerged and we were given a new role, some of us unwillingly, some argued against it—my own union argued against it at the TUC—but nonetheless the government of the day offered the unions powers on a plate, a role of decision making which we had

122

previously been denied. For years we had argued that governments denied unions opportunities to discuss areas of policy such as economics in any meaningful way which have enormous impact upon union members, which must also include their families and relatives. Then after the change of government in 1974 we had to face up to the question of trade union responsibilities. The left in the movement lost the argument as to whether or not we should be involved and we got involved, although unfortunately the exercise was a nonsense. The credibility of the social contract collapsed from a union point of view; I do not think the unions can achieve their true value under the present system. We got caught up in the system (under the social contract) and the exercise was a dismal failure.

We have had some influence as for example under Wilson from 1964–70. Such influence, however, is only enjoyed under Labour governments, never with Tory governments. Even so, the union movement would be better off if it broke its ties with the Labour Party: as a movement we want to be able to do as much in the way of action against a Labour government as against a Tory one. There will always be union mistrust of governments: I do not see that ever changing.

[This long discussion got bogged down on the question of a separation between the unions and the Labour Party—a line that is advanced by the Socialist Workers' Party.]

How far do you see the unions trying to work the system and how far do you see the role of the unions as attempting to change the system into something different altogether?

At present the trade union movement and the shop stewards work within the existing framework: they are not trying to change the system.

We do not see ourselves altering the system in such a way as to bring in our people politically. And I do not think that many shop stewards would abuse the democratically elected position they hold as elected members of their unions: we have to represent a broad cross section of the unions' members and, as near as possible, to put forward their aspirations. Some of us may disagree with these aspirations.

Are those aspirations merely for the best conditions shop stewards can obtain, or do they want you to work towards changing the system?

Both aspirations come through.

There are parallels between the relationship of the trade union movement and the Labour Party and the relationship of the CBI and the Tory Party. Rule Two of all unions states they are to advance the terms and conditions of employment: there are times when you cannot do that without some parliamentary protection and that is where the Labour Party comes in, why it was founded. Should the idea of a split between the trade union movement and the Labour Party come about, the Labour Party would lose its base and its heart. There must always be parliamentary representation through the Labour Party on behalf of the unions.

A lot of Labour Party MPs are trade union sponsored and most unions have periodic meetings with their sponsored members to tell them union policy: it is not a *diktat* but simply to tell them what the union sponsors are thinking so they may take that into account. The worst Secretary of State for Employment was Ray Gunter: he helped to 'deal' with 90 per cent of the members of the shipbuilding industry and battered them to death. Now, we will fight with any government if it is in the interests of our members. We are most usually fighting with a Tory government because more often that is in the interests of our members. The Labour Party was created to protect the social wage and the advances made on behalf of the trade union movement.

It is important to understand that if the majority of workers in this country were getting a fair deal and inflation were held down, then they would be reasonably content. They are conservative by nature and do not like a dog-eat-dog approach, with the big battalions getting the wage rises and the small battalions getting nothing. If a government that was responsible in terms of our interests were to be returned, it would get our support.

One of the problems with the trade union movement is that there are too many trade unionists in a position to dictate policies who are not always working for the wishes of the rank and file, and when they are trying to strike bargains with the elected government of the day it is not always for the benefit or in the interests of the majority of their members. We need a TUC with teeth, a TUC that could act on behalf of every union.

[There were mixed responses to the question of providing the TUC with teeth. On the one hand it was argued this could be done if individual unions were to surrender some of their powers to the TUC. This led to the question of fewer unions and possible amalgamations: also the question of industrial unions.]

Industrial unions could work: British workers are not less recep-

124

tive or able to adapt to changes than any others. Yet I do not ever want to see groups of workers—because of organisational structure—being deprived of their right to pursue their own aspirations. I do not want to see a TUC with such power that it tells us all exactly what to do. Trade union representatives are elected in order to forward the conditions of their members. When that spills over into politics we have to face up to it: that is what we have today. Yet I do not think we should trade off the inherent, absolute right of, say the cork makers, to pursue their claims in their own way for something else at the centre. I do not want our people being put into a structure like that of the Swedish unions where the unions, employers and government come together and decide what percentage increase they should have.

If we examine the question of trade union power, then first we have to look at trade union history. Have the trade unions more power today than they had a hundred years ago? The answer is only in terms of numbers. In terms of our position in society we are still very much a minority group as far as the media, the state and control of power and wealth are concerned. Our position has not altered over the years and yet the present [Thatcher] Government has been elected (in part) on the basis that the trade unions have too much power which has to be curbed. This is a fallacy when you look at developments of technology over the last ten years: we have put a man on the moon; there are all kinds of advances. Yet what advances have been made in terms of trade union power? Any advances are significantly difficult to define and I do not see that the unions have developed any new powers.

Everyone says the unions do not have enough power: Suppose they had more power, what would you like them to do with it?

What the unions want more power for is to influence governments. Congress represents about twelve million people who have paid up their dues, but in fact works on behalf of many more who freewheel on the movement. Congress and the Labour Party represent the aspirations of working people, and we should take our guidelines from these meetings (the annual conferences). The trade union movement should be arguing with the government of the day in terms of the aspirations of the people represented at Congress and at the Labour Party Conference. And here we come to the question of responsibility.

For years governments have said: they will deliver A or B if the unions will deliver C or D; we have delivered C or D but government has failed to deliver its part. This has happened

125

constantly. Now the trade unions are sufficiently powerful to say to government: we want certain things, such as a rise in old age pensions. At the same time we reserve the right to discuss with our employers matters concerning wages and conditions. We also want government to pass legislation to say that an employer will only be in business if he is prepared to meet certain minimum wage levels.

Thus, when we talk of influencing governments we mean across the whole gamut of their practice. There are fifty-five million people in this country and twenty-five million of them are putting in nails or drawing lines or whatever for a living and by and large the trade union movement covers those twenty-five million. Then ten million or so are above the working age; five or six million are below working age; others are infirm or unable to work for one reason or another and two million cannot work because the b------ will not give them a job. Every single action the government takes affects the people we represent, and of course we have to influence every single facet of government action on their behalf. At least we have got the structures whereby we can sound people out, get a feel and an indication of what people think should happen. Given proper television or media time and space, we could win some arguments. I do not think we have ever been treated responsibly by the media.

The trade unions have tried hard to improve pensions for those who have retired, something that is often forgotten. What seems clear is that wide-scale nationalisation is required if unions are to increase their power. I would advocate that Labour should nationalise the banks and insurance companies. It is easy to say the nationalised industries such as the railways are loss-makers, but they have only one employer—the government—and if they are loss-makers it is too often government responsibility. You will not achieve much greater power without nationalisation.

The social contract is a watershed in the history of the Labour movement: at the time we were forced by argument to accept a new role and responsibility in life. Part of the social contract was that pensions would be taken care of, unemployment would be taken care of and there would be an irreversible shift in the balance of power. The government came to the unions for concessions and said: 'In order for us to fulfil our share of the bargain, we require that you, the unions, limit wage increases—not anything else.' The unions took up the challenge of responsibility with power. Unfortunately, because we live under the present system, the

126

government could not deliver anyway, they never could. Some of us argue that they never could deliver at any stage of the game: that was a basic argument put forward in the TUC by a number of unionists. But the social contract did not die a death: it was killed off by individual unions which were unable to control their members and get them to go along with what turned out to be a one-sided agreement. Jack Jones was the architect of the whole thing and Moss Evans was the man who destroyed it.

Why did so many unions not want to go along with the social contract?

About 1·8 million votes were cast against the social contract.

I was not talking so much about the vote as about the performance.

Harold Wilson had said that 600,000 would be an unacceptable level of unemployment. We threw our hands up in horror and said: that is not on. Then before we knew where we were we had one million unemployed, so we began to talk of a social contract to deal with the problem. The government gave us a logical argument: they said with a million unemployed and inflation, the key to altering the situation is to control wages. Therefore, if you, the unions, will agree to a control on wages and so help the government get control of the economy, we will then be able to direct the economy in the way we would both like it to go. Some of us argued against that proposition and said it would not work: that the government could not deliver the goods because of the system we live under. There are arguments both for and against free, unfettered trade unionism.

Wilson certainly tried to deliver under the social contract, and he did achieve certain things. I think it true that under no government under the present set-up could you have a wages and incomes policy which could be worked to the letter of the law. Heath tried to peg prices. You can hold back wages and prices so long but then you have to start your increases and if inflation begins to creep up, you are in trouble. There is a good case for every union to have wage settlements on the same day: that would make it easier for the government to tackle inflation.

The extent to which the government—any government—can deliver its side of the bargain, is determined by circumstances. They go to borrow from the IMF: the Gnomes of Zurich give them a loan on certain conditions and the effective result is they cannot meet their side of the bargain. There may be some who want to change the system, but I do not believe that most politicians—Labour politicians—have any idea of changing the system; they are not in the 'game' for that. What I am saying is that the deal we struck under the social contract was, with the best will in the world, just not going to work.

Consciously or unconsciously, almost all trade unions are arguing for a change in the system. They all say that, but are they acting as though they want a change?

Trade union leaders are elected or appointed to satisfy the rules of their unions and the second rule of the union is to advance the conditions of the members. Every Rule Two in every union says the same. That is what they are in business to do. It is, then, the duty of the trade unions to influence the political parties for the social wage, pensions and so on. The difficulty arises from the fact that different trade union leaders come to different conclusions as to which policy satisfies that rule. Further difficulty arises from the fact that we have a multitude of unions in this country; with fewer unions we would increase the power of the movement.

I don't know if the Jewish bakers are still on the go, but there were twenty-two of them five or six years ago. Because things are of a craft nature there are many small groups; at the same time the general unions are growing fast. On the other hand, unions based entirely on a craft—railway drivers, joiners—are getting into difficulties and they have need to amalgamate. It is a mistake, however, to think in terms of trade unions wanting to change the system, and that applies to the leaders as well. They think in terms of doing the best they can for their members.

That itself begs the question: the only answer for the building workers is public control; and the only answer for the foundry workers is public control.

Some of these arguments are contradictory. I return to my question: how many trade unionists think in terms of changing the system? You first say they do not actually think in terms of changing the system, but then you at once say the only way to make things better is to bring everything under state control. Now to bring everything under public control means in fact to change the system, so how many really want to do this? How many trade unionists really think as you do and argue that the only way to get a better deal across the board for all workers is by public control, which means changing the system?

That number of people fluctuates with the fortunes of the Labour Party because the Party was created on the basis that it should change the system.

128

We have seen the Tory press take up the cry 'Who runs the country', the elected government or the trade union movement as they did during the miners' strike, and they got their answer in a sort of way because they were defeated at the election. But what would have happened if the miners had gone on strike under a Labour Government?

[A claim often advanced by trade unionists is that there is a lack of education within the trade union movement; and more generally that public education is not geared to the interests or viewpoint of the working classes.]

People understand the issues quite clearly; they might not be prepared to fight for an issue, but they understand it quite clearly. The trouble is apathy and that results from lack of education.

If this [Thatcher] Government has its way there will be less education in schools: what they will be saying is that we require 2000 technicians a year for the West of Scotland and 1000 manual workers, the rest are surplus to requirements, and education is going to be geared to that—if they have their way.

Then there is the question of research. For example, take the new technology: I mean the number of unions which have printed their union paper by means of the new technology, and they are all saying the same thing. If the TUC were to provide such a service there could be a common paper to tie the unions together. As it is, each union sees its own paper as better than that of another union; there is an element of competition for membership to get enough members to survive. One of the biggest drives for amalgamation of unions is the sheer economics of survival, and that applies to all unions. This Government's idea of providing finance for ballots is a step towards saying: you can have autonomy if you take our money—autonomy from the TGWU or the other unions.

What the government, any government, would like is an understanding that all disputes are confined to national disputes: then your right to be in a national dispute would not be gainsaid. They would like to see a situation in which the unions say: 'We will take total control of our members and there will be no local trouble'; Derek Robinson 'went down the road' for that reason. Robinson was probably the best thing that happened to Leyland over the past number of years because he controlled things on the shop-floor and brought out the real issues. Now he has served his purpose, if you like, and the object of the exercise (from a government—and management?—) point of view is to get rid of

129

people like Robinson and transfer the power from the shop-floor up the line so that the people at the 'top' decide what should happen. This is the way to alienate the authority of the trade unions as far as their rank and file are concerned. Any government, and particularly a Tory Government, would like to bring about such a situation: one in which they say let us get round the table—unions, employers and government and then we will be sympathetic to you and at this level we will agree what the increases are going to be—ten, twelve, twenty or even 120 per cent in wages if we can manage it, provided you people (the trade union leaders) can control your members. On that basis we will meet your demands, for in such circumstances things are under control.

Then we would see something along the line of the American style of unions which suits employers as well as governments?

Yes, that kind of solution means the continuation of the present system, and Rule Two of every trade union rule book in the country gets torn up because we were never instituted for that purpose. Our objective is to create the conditions in the country whereby we will all enjoy a much better standard of living.

Then there is the classic problem the press faces. When the shop stewards decide to take action the press says: Why don't you listen to the national leaders? When the national leaders decide to take action the press says: Listen to the shop stewards. It is always those who do not want to take any action that the press put forward as 'reasonable', and perhaps one of the positive aspects of the Day of Action is that the national leaders and not the shop stewards asked for it.

The shop stewards have the advantage over national leaders because they know the grass roots feelings—when it is time to go along with the employers and when it is time to fight. That is why this Government is trying to destroy the shop steward movement, because they assume the leadership when they do not get it from the top.

The TUC made a bad blunder over the Day of Action. What they ought to have done was define exactly what we were taking action against. They did not do that. Plenty of shop stewards are saying 'It is an elected government' (and therefore we should not take action). We are taking action because of the Government's attitude towards the trade union movement. The TUC should have said this clearly. Then it should have instructed members to support the Day of Action and there would have been no shop

130

steward anywhere in the country who would have argued any other way than to support the action and recommend the workforce to do so. Had the TUC put it that way, we would have achieved massive support for the Day of Action. Instead, the TUC made its instructions too broad: if they had been more precise they would have got the support.

What sort of a country do you want this to be?

A socialist country.

By which you mean what?

[There followed a discussion as to the possibility of making Britain a more socialist society: it was agreed that while inequalities will always exist, Britain is one of the most unequal countries anywhere in the world.]

What should the role of the unions be in this present context?

Whatever way you look at it, we need more power at the present time for the unions: power to force, to challenge more effectively the elected government of the day. That is why I want the TUC to have teeth. The TUC ought to be a body with enormous power. At present, however, governments are only prepared to have small dialogues with it when it suits them. Governments ought to pay attention to the TUC at all times.

Our object as trade unionists should be to say: if you want our co-operation over wage control, then you must give us something in return in terms of a social contract.

This was tried once and failed, but that does not mean it should not be tried again.

As trade unionists we can only bring about change—in the sense of achieving some form of socialist society—by welding together the forces for change within the working class movement. We have to face the common enemy: the multinationals, the IMF, and those who would influence the lifestyle of the British working people from outside. In this connection I do not think that a break-up of the TUC-Labour Party link would be a help.

But everybody is saying the same thing: change must mean altering the system, otherwise it is only cosmetic tinkering.

We must analyse what we are saying: if we accept that trade union officials are elected to satisfy the aspirations of their members, whose wages and conditions are totally dependent upon how hard the elected representatives work at their jobs, then to ask them to sacrifice an A, B, C or D for an airy-fairy something somewhere else, would be to ask the union official to do something totally outside the context of his job. When we come to the

131

question of discussion within the movement, that is a different matter. Then we can look at tactics: we offer, for example, to obtain a return for people in terms of pensions and can do a deal with the government over a public sector industry. Thus, for example, the government can say: TASS has asked for a 25 per cent money increase this year, but you are employed in a nationalised industry which made x amount of money and we intend to hive off a part of that for old age pensions, so you cannot get all the 25 per cent you are asking for.

Surely that is not the easiest way? The easiest way would be to involve every worker. The first prime minister or chancellor who has the guts to say to the workers of this country: Look, next week I am going to take an extra pound off you in national insurance and here is the breakdown of where it will go: 50p to increasing pensions as from a fortnight next Monday; 25p for A and the rest for B, then no worker in this country would object. But in the past, and as it will be in the future, they take it and you have no idea what they do with it.

Socialism frees potential; it allows people to work—there are no unemployed in socialist countries and people work to make a contribution to society and they work positively. I am opposed to the 'rat eat rat' society where the only way to advance is to make profit either at someone else's expense or for someone who is not working.

But no one on the left ever comes out and says that it stands for full socialism—the nationalisation of land, for example, or the ending of differentials.

That is not a valid thing to say. We live under capitalism which among other things brutalises human relationships and distorts the best features of humanity. It is too ambitious to try to move from capitalism to socialism in one fell swoop—

But no one even states this as an aim. If the trade unions came out and said such things, then it would be possible to sort out the people who really want to achieve socialism and those who do not.

The trade union movement is not designed to say these things.

[In the discussion about socialism there was a clear reluctance to face the fact that insistence upon the aim of socialism on the one hand clashed with the basic union insistence upon differentials upon the other hand.]

The majority of people believe in some sort of differential. So we go along with that, but we would like to see the unions aim

132

for a common structure that was based upon job evaluation so that tradesmen of one kind would be in one category, those of another kind in another category and so on. Once you had established such grades then every year when there is a wage rise it would be for everybody across the board: the result would be to narrow differentials.

Take the building industry: for years we have been saying that there should be no differential in the building industry and that we should go for a flat rate for construction workers of all kinds. That means we have to tell the workers that the really skilled man will be treated the same as the unskilled man. I argue for that, and I am supposed to be one of the few people in the west of Scotland who has established that on sites: everybody gets the same rate of pay on the sites. The labourer on the site enjoys the same level of earnings as the skilled tradesman. That took an awful lot of doing, but everybody was earning good wages so it was a good place to start. The question of differentials is very difficult to argue through and at this point, for example, we still have a two-tier structure in the industry here: the tradesman gets paid 100 per cent rate and the labourer gets 85 per cent of that. What we have said is that there should be no differential in bonuses. The differential should be in the rate.

It is not easy to get this kind of argument across to the men. There is a section within my union which is an industrial union, in fact, to whom we are now getting through and saying that if we pay the bricklayer the same as the 'brickie' it makes no difference at the other end to profits. I am convinced that industrialisation of the industry, the new technology, has gone so far that the skill level has closed: the skill differentials have closed.

Do you expect the skilled man who has done his apprenticeship to work alongside the labourer who enjoys the benefits of the money without the skill, getting the same wages?

It is a difficult propostion, but then isn't that the whole principle of socialism?

Are we saying we would like the trade unions to be more powerful and to be playing another role than they have hitherto? If the unions are to influence governments more, then they must be political. They must take political action and to do this the TUC needs more teeth than at present: political teeth and the readiness to use them. Now this in turn will depend on raising the level of the ideological argument and thrust within the Labour movement and the trade union movement. At present there is far too little education of a political nature within the trade union movement.

The thrust of the Thatcher Government and of the Tory Party at the present time is to say that in so far as the trade union movement does have political thrust, that has got to be stopped.

The Thatcher Government does not believe that the TUC has power.

No, but they pretend they do in order to emasculate even those powers that the movement does possess.

In recent years it has been said that the trade unions run the country. Now the trade unions do not run the country, the government does; yet now (at the time of the Day of Action, 14 May 1980) they are talking as though they have just discovered something unpleasant: that this is a political strike. Well, of course, if people are going to demonstrate against the government of the day, it must be political. This Tory Government is saying this as though such activity is something foreign to trade unions, and yet at the same time they talk as though the trade unions are running the country.

Every wage claim is political, because you are determining to disturb the balance. It is no use for you to get 20 per cent if the gaffer gets 20 per cent and inflation goes up 20 per cent, because then you simply keep the status quo. So every claim and the satisfaction of Rule Two, which is to *advance* and defend wages and conditions of members, is a political statement in itself. The problem we as trade unionists get into, is this: when do we say to our members this is not a wage rise for you, it is not an advance of conditions for you: it is an alteration and a challenge to the system?

The introduction of the social contract and the subsequent concept of a new political role for the unions, brought them into politics in a new way. At the beginning of the century when we decided to set up a political party, we recognised that industrial action on these questions was not enough. So we formed a party that could represent trade union interests in parliament. A point of time came when we drifted apart, but I think the social contract pulled us back together again. I look upon it as a watershed in our political life.

You are entitled to be involved in politics in this country wherever you stand. With regard to the Day of Action, we have had 10,000 meetings up and down this country on the question of government policy: we may not have won them, yet never-

134

theless, for the first time in British political life on shop-floors, on building sites where I have never seen it before, we (shop stewards) have been arguing with the men on questions of government policy—following instructions from our executives. This is the direct result of the social contract: that may have been expediency, yet it is getting in to something very tangible, and the trade union movement cannot dodge the issues raised by the social contract experiment.

That explains some of the attitudes of the present Government towards the unions: I think they are aware before some of us in the trade union movement of the significance of the social contract idea and its possible impact.

Nothing will change without education, however: that is true whether it is political education or just ordinary education to higher standards than we have at present. You have to get to people in the schools; if you wait until afterwards, it is too late. How many of our members are interested enough to come to trade union branch meetings? For example, our local TGWU branch has about 900 members; we had a meeting last Saturday morning and how many turned up? Ten stewards and one non-steward. This shows that education has been left too late.

There was further discussion about education and the impact of the forthcoming Day of Action. In relation to the latter event, the unfairness of the media was again stressed and as one person remarked: 'If the turn-out is 90 or 95 per cent the media will still portray it as a failure.'

In a more structured discussion at Ruskin College, Oxford, a number of union officials* on an advanced course in trade union studies examined the question of trade union power. One member of the group, Kenneth Castle (AUEW (TASS)), introduced the topic with a brief paper.

'The media say that the trade unions are too powerful in relation to the general public, forgetting conveniently that trade union members—twelve million of them and their wives, families

* Apart from Kenneth Castle, who introduced the discussion, they included: a civil servant (CPSA—branch secretary), a full time regional official of the AUEW, a senior shop steward (GMWU) in the food industry, a full time staff representative (BIFU) of Barclays Bank, a full time shop steward (USDAW) of the Leicestershire Co-operative Society, a Customs and Excise local branch chairman, Liverpool (CPSA), and a BALPA helicopter pilot.

and dependants making twenty million—are the ordinary people. The media never relates trade union power to the natural adversaries of the unions—the City, the IMF, the multinationals, the EEC or the media itself. The City often threatens to withdraw business confidence as they call it unless the government of the day follows certain policies. In March 1979 we saw a strike by the City about the purchase of gilt-edged securities. The City would not buy government gilt-edged securities necessary to finance the government borrowing requirement unless the rate of interest was raised: so the MLR was raised one per cent. The following day the *Financial Times* reported that the City had made a killing of some £200 million on that one decision.

'The same week the Department of Industry negotiated with the miners who are supposed to wield a lot of power. They were negotiating their wage increase for the whole year; they were offered £75 million to be divided up between 250,000 miners. If we relate these two examples of power which occurred in one week, we saw £200 million made by the City in one day and the miners offered £75 million for 250,000 for a year. So who has the greater bargaining power?

'The multinationals: in 1975 Chrysler told the government they were in difficulties. The government gave them a great deal of money without any accountability. In 1977 Chrysler came back and said—'If you do not give us more money we are going to go altogether and anyway we have sold out to the French." How many jobs have the trade union movement with all their power been able to save in Chrysler over the past five years? Who in fact has the real power?

'The trade union pamphlet *Cause for Concern* examined the media coverage of unions during January and February (1979) in the run-up to the general election: "But more serious than the attacks themselves [upon the unions] is the effect they had upon public opinion; by mid-February polls showed an almost universal cry for reform of the trade unions and what was meant by reform was clearly not strengthening. Many of the people calling for the power of the unions to be curbed had little or no experience of the disputes taking place. Their sole source of information was the media."

'The *Finniston Report* highlighted the failure of industry to invest in research and development to innovate and create commercially viable products capable of capturing export as well as

136

the home markets. So again, where is trade union power that can make employers invest in this country?'

You have mentioned the City, the IMF, multinationals, the media, and investment, and in each case your point has been that trade unions do not have as much power as these groups— although you did make the throwaway remark: that if they do have the power, they are not using it. Are you suggesting unions might have power which they are either not using or not using efficiently to obtain the ends they seek?

A general discussion followed.

Unions react rather than initiate anything themselves. They do not have an 'in' on discussions as, for example, those between the Labour Government and the IMF. They may be invited to talks after decisions have been made, but they are not there from the beginning. In any case, where you get trade unions involved inside the government, you end up with a trade union leadership which eventually gets separated from the people it is meant to represent.

The power of a union depends upon the shop-floor membership, and the leaders of the trade unions do not really know what power they have got. That is part of the problem. Other groups influence the general public against the trade unions, and in that respect the media is probably more powerful than the trade union movement.

We have an economic system that is based upon a form of development controlling inflation. What is the use of negotiating in such a system if you are trying to get better services for your members? What is the use of getting a ten per cent increase in pay if the politically dominated economy is going to increase inflation by 20 per cent because you also want improvements in the social wage and such inflation will decrease the social wage?

In my union, Rule 2a says 'to protect and promote the interests of members.' I take that interest as being wide-meaning. For instance, if this Government decides to cut back education, that affects the interests of my members; so would cuts in health or public transport—all those affect the interests of our members. So it is perfectly legitimate to fight against cuts and try to stop the Government going down a road which reduces the standard of

137

living [of members]. Cuts affect wages: for example, if school transport is cut back, that is going to cost my members perhaps £4 a week and that is economic; that, therefore, justifies unions fighting all these political battles.

But where is the trade union movement going? In the past, especially during the 1960s and early 1970s trade union power and authority was not actually used to challenge the system. In the past we have attempted to negotiate with the system and to get the best deal we could in a time of boom. But now, because we are in recession, that is no longer possible. We are now in a sense flexing our muscles to try to get better benefits, and of course the Tories, quite rightly from their point of view, come out and say the trade unions are misusing their power precisely because we are now starting in a small way to challenge the system they represent. The debate as to where the trade union movement is going will be intensified as recession sinks deeper and deeper.

[All unions have a similar clause in their membership: they are concerned with the social well-being of their members and so they have to react politically. A major question facing the unions is: to what extent do unionists want to see unions involved in the business of changing society—that is, the kind of society we have got? Broadly, there are two ways in which unions can behave: they can say they will work the capitalist system, in which case they co-operate with the employers. Then the question is what is the union share of the 'cake'. Or they can argue that the capitalist system is something they want to bring to an end, in which case a very different kind of union action must be expected.]

Our union stands for the tripartite agreement which this present government has brought to an end. Most unions affiliated to the TUC want to work within the system and seek a bigger share of the nation's wealth, if you like, for their members.

It is astonishing that the media think we have power: where and how do we use it?

This media view comes out over something like the 'winter of discontent': in other words, the unions abuse their power because people are not buried; unions can call their people out and cause discomfort to the amorphous general public. When the miners strike, electricity is cut and then sob stories appear in the press of

138

old age pensioners dying of hypothermia. These are the most obvious and emotive ways in which unions are accused of misusing their power.

But the media do not mention the old age pensioners dying of hypothermia because they cannot afford the 27 per cent increase in energy bills—it is totally one-sided.

The fat cats in industry [names] are getting fatter and fatter. What the unions should aim for is a more egalitarian society. We haven't even started: we have always been reacting. We ought to say that we will not simply go for economic advances [wages] but the conditions in which people work. There should be a more total approach in negotiations. What happens when we have a right wing government of the calibre of that which we now have, is that all the advances made in the previous three or four years— if you consider them to be advances—will be negated in the current political and economic environment.

The reasons for developments such as the 'winter of discontent' must be directly related to the growth of the informal power of the workplace; and part of that growth of power has to be seen in terms of successive governments reducing the bargaining strength and power of the formal structure of the unions. This present administration [the Thatcher Government] is unbelievable in its approach: if I were a capitalist, I would look to shore up the formal structure of the unions since they represent the only form of social control the government has over that sector of the community. Yet, instead of doing that, they are taking more and more power away, although Prior as a capitalist is a very sensible one: he recognises the score. But what I am saying is this: we are going to see more and more anarchy in industry. The 'winter of discontent' did not happen because union leadership was too powerful; it happened in spite of union leadership. If these people really want to talk about power, they must talk about how to wrest this power from various small groups. And the way you do it, I believe, is by more participatory democracy; you have to make people more careful by bringing them in, by power sharing. By going against that idea, this Administration has chopped the feet from under the formal structure of various unions, and what you are going to see—the Isle of Grain is only just a beginning—is an upsurge of what I call anarchy.

Industrial relations will get worse, but because unions are denied power: proper democracy, proper democratic control, proper participation, proper accountability all the way through the system are what are required.

One of the most persistent complaints of trade unionists is lack of information. In most factories we would like to say: tell us exactly what the decision making of this company is based upon, because we never find out. We only find out what is the directors' bargaining structure.

Comparisons are often made with the West German trade union system, but in 1967–8 when inflation went up, their workforce began to mobilise and unofficial strikes started. So that system only works when demand is good and there is an increase in production. When the gains which the workers have been led to believe are theirs by right, stop, then the system starts to come apart. So even the system in West Germany does not necessarily work well. We have to go beyond that for some form of common ownership. Yet you cannot simply have that [common ownership] in an industrial sense; it has to be a wider commitment so that it becomes part of the social pressure for a man to be part of the workforce. People have to become involved in their industry as well as in social security: it must be a total involvement.

It is one thing for activists at Ruskin to say they would like the unions to try to change the whole system, but how much support do they get from the people who simply join a union because in bad times it will look after them—a form of insurance?

There are probably only two or three per cent of the workforce in each factory who are likely to be interested in looking at a different system—and not necessarily the same different system. It is nonsense to think there is any collective unity.

Could the unions only achieve more power on the basis of changing the system? Or can they achieve greater power under the system we have got now?

That is a very dangerous line: to go for more power within the capitalist system, because there are so many inherent contradictions based on the profit motive. That way the unions could end up being the industrial police of the system. If they want more power they must first change the system.

People join unions for different reasons. A lot join for protection against a particular employer because he has the supreme right of hiring and firing, of closing down the factory and you need a collective to combat that kind of power.

I do not see that unions must wait for the system to change before they can have power. They should have power under the

140

existing system. It is nonsense to think we cannot have shared power under the present system: either at the macro level through tripartism or at the micro level in the running of an individual factory. Such power should result from collective bargaining as something we have earned as of right.

I have never been afraid to sit round a table with someone of a different ideology or philosophy if it meant I was going to gain something: if it means a gain for me I am not too worried about what the other person thinks ideologically.

But that way we could end up like American trade unions; all they do is act as labour salesmen and nothing more.

I am talking about trying to claw back some of the social wage, and we cannot do that outside the framework of the system.

If you do want to change the system, however, where do you nail your banner to the mast? Where do you start?

You work at every facet within the system and you seek power at every level within that system. You seek participation at every level with every member. It is nonsense to think that ultimately you are going to be sucked in to become part of the system: to argue that because that danger (of being sucked in) exists, you should therefore work outside the system is nonsense. The employer is only conciliatory when he is, because of the opportunity-cost involved: he is conciliatory when he has to be; when he does not have to be, he is not. That is a fact.

The question of where you start, is fundamental. Essentially, we must actually convince our membership of the need to have a fundamental change in society. The most important question that faces trade unions at the moment is that of educating their membership to understand the problems, to expose some of the lies foisted upon people by the media over the last fifty years, to explode some of the myths about trade unions.

The trade union movement ought to have had its own newspaper years ago. The media are always against the movement; if, for example, it is a dispute with low paid workers, they do not ask *why* they are low paid or why they come out on strike. Why they came out on strike in the 'winter of discontent', for example, was because they could not afford to feed their families.

One of the problems of working within the system is that you experience peaks and troughs: you make a small gain, then the political atmosphere changes and you step back again. This is particularly relevant now with this Tory Government. I think it was in 1976 that Michael Edwardes said the days are gone when someone comes in here (BL) as manager and tells the unions what to do: I believe in democracy and involving unions. Yet in 1980 he sacked Derek Robinson and imposed a wage policy. To me, working within the system just seems to shore it up until such time as *they* can get another one over and go on to the attack again. It is a defensive position for them and they muster their troops, then Thatcher gets in and we are back again and whatever we gained under a Labour Government—which was not a lot, the Employment Protection Act for example—is now being eroded away again. That is the problem.

We have to create our own common sense if you like: so that people say: yes, it is common sense to have a strong trade union movement and have people involved in their firm and not necessarily working for profit to the extent of social damage.

Some unions believe there is too much power at the branch level. They want the power at the top. We have found that you have got to strengthen the branch system, because the more people you get involved at the botom end then the more people there are who actually want to change the system. When we started, most of us took on our union jobs because no one else wanted them. Yet once you get involved in the business and start seeing the problems, you then begin to get educated—and you start moving to the left. I find that most people who get involved in the union movement start moving to the left. I have seen people come into the movement who are really right wing reactionaries; yet as they start to get involved and begin to understand the problems, they go to weekend schools, meetings and get educated, then they begin to move—and move to the left. It is essential to get more people involved at the bottom end of the movement.

Why do people at the top end of the unions start moving back to the right again?

Because they want power. Also, I think it is because of lack of confidence in the people on the shop-floor because that is where the power is, although it has not been sufficiently harnessed through training, education and good communications. But the power is there. At the present time, I do not believe that the leaders of the trade union movement have got the confidence of the people on the shop-floor. That is their dilemma.

Do the shop-floor unionists, in reverse, have confidence in the people at the top?

The problem of the trade unions is that they do not explain to their members why they take certain actions. People are not

142

involved as they should be. To my mind a good branch secretary should welcome somebody looking over his shoulder all the time, because that means they are interested and then the branch secretary works twice as hard to keep the job and the members get good service.

Len Murray himself said on 14 May (the Day of Action) that if we had power we would not know what to do with it. From that point of view he was honest. We would not know what to do with the power we say we would like to have. That is why Murray worked within the confines of the system: the TUC leadership does that because we do not actually know what to do with our power.

Perhaps we should change—or try to change—our fundamental role in society and cease to be merely a reactionary pressure group, a radical pressure group stemming from the failures of liberalism. We ought to look at our role for the 1980s.

We trade unionists all have different policies and approaches. We pull against each other. The present Government has got one basic policy. That policy is stated, the lines are drawn; but ours are spread all across the field in groups of ones and twos, that is our basic problem. We know where we are going, but we do not have a train in which to get there.

[There followed a discussion of trade union rules and rule books and whether these needed to be changed.]

Rule books can be used in a number of different ways. What is important is why there is not more reaction within the unions to keep abreast of the changes taking place in capitalism.

One reason is that union officials are overworked and underpaid without sufficient back-up in research or anything else.

That is a major problem. Union members resent having to pay 30 or 35 pence a week: as a result there is lack of cash and facilities, while officers are so snowed under with the vast amounts of work they have to do for any negotiating procedures that they cannot go through all this and then say the next socialist millenium will start on 1 January 1981 . . .

There are conflicts between the day to day business of running union affairs and trying to change the system. We face a situation in which things act against each other like water and oil and it is very difficult to say to someone: pay £4 a week and we will give you a better society, when they have got the kids to feed, the cutback in education and school meals to meet and so on. People learn in different ways: schools being closed, teachers cut back, increases in the cost of school meals. Such experiences are reflected in their union aspirations and activity. Such experiences can culminate in major frustration. The 'winter of discontent' was not just a single issue; it was a culmination of things and another such build-up is taking place now. Trade unions will look to the Labour Party for answers and the Labour Party leadership presents another fundamental question: how to make those people more representative.

Instead of talking about unions changing the system, it might be more realistic to ask how many people join unions simply because they know it is the only way for them, that there is no alternative? I would say that most people are in the unions for that reason.

The only way ordinary members are going to follow the trade union leadership if it tries to take them out of the present system—a system in which you are educated to be avaricious, to be greedy, to be self-centred and self-interested—is if they make it rationally viable for the members to follow the collective: people will join a collective not because they love it as such, but because there is a bigger return for them in being a part of it.

The British working class in particular are very slow to change. Talk of socialism, therefore, must be a matter of demonstrating that socialism will actually improve the material needs of the working people: that as an option it is better than what we now have.

In terms of the Labour Party I am not pro-Callaghan, yet I do not blame him or anyone else on the right or centre of the Party if they come to power under the present so-called representative democratic system. I blame the system itself: the nature of the parties, Conservative, Labour, Liberal. The manner whereby the elected leadership is totally undemocratic and unfair means they are put into oligarchic positions. It is not a conspiracy thing: the politicians get themselves there (to the top), they find themselves in the driving seat and find they are accountable to no one, so they get on with the job. Now it is easy to blame Callaghan and say such behaviour is inherent in his nature. But I do not see that it would matter what Callaghan (or any other leader) was like if we had a properly structured democratic Labour Party. So it is unfair really to blame the leadership for how things go under the present system.

144

9

Management: The CBI

In Britain employers look to the Tory Party if not quite as the trade union movement looks to Labour, then at least in the expectation that a Tory Government will pursue policies broadly acceptable to its aspirations. The party slogan 'Conservative freedom works' hardly appeared to be the case when members of the CBI assembled at Brighton in November 1980: unemployment was rising, mighty ICI had done the unthinkable and begun to lay off workers, firms small and large were laying off and in some cases facing bankruptcy, export orders were getting smaller and Japanese and other rivals appeared to be penetrating ever more deeply into the British market. Monetarism and high interest rates did not appear to be working at all.

The CBI does not have the close organic links with the Tory Party that the trade union movement has with the Labour Party, but its members, overwhelmingly, support the Tories and provide the Party with the bulk of its funds. This business loyalty to the Tories is the other half of the divide in the British industrial scene: workers vote left, employers vote right and between them they ensure an endless political see-saw which effectively prevents industry working as one.

In many respects the CBI and the TUC find themselves in comparable positions: both try to express the wishes and aspirations of their members; both have little real power; both may find that their members say no to what they propound. The members of the two organisations meet and sit together on a number of bodies, most notably the NEDC, but also the Manpower Services Commission, the Health and Safety Commission and the Advisory Conciliation and Arbitration Service (ACAS). Yet they are hardly close, and suspicion each way is deep. David Lea, assistant general secretary at the TUC, said of the CBI in 1978 that it did not try to look at things from a trade union perspective: 'It has never seemed to us that they have looked at questions in terms designed to elicit a positive approach from the trade union movement.' He went on: 'All our endeavours are towards having a constructive role in industrial and national economic policy. We still look in vain for a recognition by the CBI of the positive role of the trade union movement. If you look through the references to trade unions in recent CBI publications, they are always expressed in terms of redressing the balance of power in industry, and so on.'

This may well be true. It does highlight a CBI obsession that too much power in bargaining terms is all on the one side. It is, perhaps, possible to divide employers into two broad groups as far as attitudes towards the unions are concerned: those who simply want to curb union powers; and those who accept union existence as a fact unlikely to be much changed and consequently seek ways of working with the unions. Employer feelings about trade union power came out clearly in 1978 at the second national conference of the CBI at Brighton, when there was a debate about industrial democracy: delegates then unanimously endorsed a policy of opposition to the government's proposals to legislate for union nominated worker directors. Participants in that debate stressed there should first be union reforms before they would be prepared to accept such legislation. Yet as one member told the conference: 'It is time employers stopped wishing that trade unions would go away.'

The theme of the imbalance of industrial power in Britain was given a further emphasis by the 'winter of discontent', so that by February 1979, the president of the CBI, Sir John Greenborough, was telling European Parliament MPs in Luxembourg: 'The biggest challenge now facing Britain is correcting the imbalance of power in the nation's industrial relations. We in Britain are now talking openly about the way strikes are financed, about picketing, about the way closed shops operate and the desirability of secret ballots.'

In the run-up to the 1979 election, the CBI was looking at a new plan to reform the country's wage bargaining system. The CBI's director-general, Sir John Methven, said that 'The economic forum should have a very wide membership including, for example, the Government, other political parties, unions, trade and industry, consumer groups and academics.' At the same time the CBI proposed a new bargaining calendar (set out below). The forum was to be public and would take evidence from both sides of industry as well as other interested groups.

146

The CBI envisaged the following 'bargaining calendar'.

May–June: Economic forum takes evidence after the Budget and experience of the previous pay round.

July–August: Publication of annual economic review. Possible Green Paper. Parliamentary debate.

September–October: CBI, TUC and party conferences consider the review.

November–December: Main bargaining begins, with the first settlements operating from 1 November. Government decides cash limits for public sector and outlines links between pay developments and the next Budget.

February: Budget representations by CBI, TUC and others, as at present.

March: Tax-dependent public services bargain. April settlement date to coincide with start of financial year.

April: Budget, taking full account of pay developments.

May: Work on next annual review begins.

In an article which appeared in the *Sunday Times* of 1 June 1980, the new CBI president, Sir Raymond Pennock, began with the statement: 'Wealth creation is a state of mind, a state of mind that, unfortunately, we in Britain, for all our many admirable qualities, have not had for many years.' This surely is the crux of much of Britain's industrial malaise: both employers and unions talk endlessly of equity, of redistributing wealth, of shares of the cake, of government interference from either side in politics, of the imbalance of power or redressing wrongs. In every case the problems enumerated could be better tackled from a larger wealth base and yet it seems that the creation of wealth, which is just as important for a left-inclined as opposed to a right-inclined political ideology, comes very low on the list of priorities. If more wealth were being created, half the problems under discussion in this book would fall away. As Sir Raymond also says in the same article: 'The diagnosis remains the same: workers seek and employers concede increases they have not earned and have no way of earning . . . I am a great believer in the intelligence and quality of the British worker. I also know, from personal experience, that given the chance and the right environment, British management can be as good as any in the world.'

Sir Raymond argues that the failure to marry these two ingredients of workers and managers so that Britain competes successfully with her principal industrial rivals, has perhaps two

147

main causes: first, a dangerous tilt in power balance between unions and management in favour of the former; second and more fundamental, he believes, is the fact that alone of industrial powers the two sides of industry in Britain are confrontationalist in their attitudes, whereas wealth creation has to be a co-operative process. Not only is the *them* and *us* mentality part of the industrial scene, but it is reinforced by the two-party system which sees Labour supporting the unions and the Tories supporting the management. Such political allegiance to one or other side in industry must perpetuate a *them* and *us* attitude which is destructive and retards wealth creation. Everyone, as a result, suffers.

In February 1980, the CBI published a discussion document, 'Trade unions in a changing world: the challenge for management.' It had been prepared at the request of a CBI steering group chaired by Sir Alex Jarrett 'to assist in its review of employers' relationships with trade unions and government.' The document is detailed and wide-ranging, bringing out a number of developments in the trade union movement which are of crucial importance to management.

The study, for example, emphasises how the authority of full time union officials has been diminished, while this diminution has been matched by a rise in power and authority of work group representatives or shop stewards. A figure of 300,000 shop stewards in 1975 is expected to double during the 1980s. As the document argues: 'This shift in effective power from the full-time official to the shop steward or more recently to the convenor has brought with it a number of real problems.' That may be true, but as employers argue elsewhere in this book, they would prefer to deal with a strong shop-floor movement within their industry than with union officials coming from outside.

One of the fundamental changes affecting British industry in recent years—a change that goes to the root of many of its problems—is that of education and attitudes among the workforce. One sub-heading in the study is 'The Alienated Employee', and the section begins by listing those factors which have undermined authoritarian leadership: 'greater individual self-confidence, a rejection of deference, emphasis on rights rather than obligations, encouragement to question and criticise.' These factors, it is suggested, have led to a greater readiness to use shop-floor power, especially when this is coupled with the frustration of working people who have had their economic expectations raised to unrealistic levels by the period of post-war economic

148

stability and prosperity. One suggested result of economic stagnation, coupled with policies of pay restraint, has been to make many employees lose faith in their companies.

A great failing of large sectors of British industry would appear to be their inability to secure the allegiance of the workforce to the company. As this study suggests, there are two major tasks for management: first, 'to secure the primary allegiance of employees to the company'; and second, 'management must be prepared to manage'. The mere statement of these two aims would seem to indicate that at present they are often not being achieved. It is vital that companies make explicit to their workforces, for example, their long-term common interests; equally they must be prepared to check unreasonable and irresponsible behaviour at source—the problem of management.

A number of businessmen have suggested that in the relatively easy economic climate of the fifties and early sixties, management abnegated some of its responsibilities: it was often easier to give way to union demands since rising economic conditions made it possible for the companies to carry the extra burdens. Yet, by so doing, they created a constant norm of expectations and in the harder times of the late sixties and seventies, these could not be met. From this comes at least part of the present difficult climate of unrealistic expectations and the assumption that if it comes to the crunch then, somehow, management will always come across with the means to meet the demands of the workforce.

According to a Gallup Poll of 1979 (*Daily Telegraph*, 18 September), 78 per cent of trade unionists gave priority to their unions for safeguarding jobs and only 15 per cent for seeking higher pay. This may well contradict the popular image of aggressive unions demanding money 'on the table', but it indicates both the reactive motivation which is a powerful trend in all unions and the fears of workers in a time of high unemployment. Against such a background the key problem for management is how to induce higher productivity from which both sides of industry can properly benefit.

Two key management figures in 1980 were Sir Raymond Pennock, successor to Sir John Greenborough as president of the CBI and L. J. Tolley, of Renold Ltd, Manchester, the retiring chairman of the British Institute of Management (BIM).

The role of the CBI is to ensure that the views and interests of its members—employers and managers—are constantly brought to the attention of the government, the trade union movement and the community generally and to see that those views have an impact upon decisions which affect members of the CBI before they are made. The CBI is similar to the TUC in its objectives on behalf of the employers, although organised in a different way. Sir Raymond Pennock believes it is more effective than the TUC because it seeks its director-general, as it did in 1980 for Ford's Sir Terence Beckett, from the business world rather than, as in the case of the TUC, promoting to the post a general secretary from within the organisation who, whatever his qualifications, will have had little or no direct experience on the shop-floor. Although really big businesses can operate on their own, more and more have come to see the value of working through the CBI in an era when governments tend increasingly to interfere in the running of industry.

On the subject of union power, Sir Raymond says it is important to define the sort of power under discussion. He argues that half the time top leaders do not have the power to control their own unions; this goes back to the early 1970s when Jack Jones of the TGWU and Hugh Scanlon of the AUEW changed their organisations so as to build-up shop-floor control of their unions. Both these men had strong personalities and were therefore able to control the process, at least until the end of their respective periods of office when each got 'a bloody nose'—Jones from the dockers and Scanlon from the Leyland tool room operators. Increasingly since then, power has moved to the shop-floor and the ability of the national leaders to control their unions has been much more problematic.

'But there is another power,' Sir Raymond claims: 'the power to control the Labour Party and decide the politics of the Party, and that does remain with the unions. One of the sad things today,' he says, 'is that the union leaders, because they are failing to lead their own unions and have difficulty in representing their own members adequately, are instead sublimating themselves by getting more and more involved in the Labour Party, its constitution and the election of its leaders.'

Debates about the state of British industry can easily enough degenerate into a competition to blame the 'other' side. On this question of where blame lies between management and unions, Sir Raymond says: 'I think both are responsible; it would be silly to say one is to blame and not the other. On the one hand the unions have pursued very short-sighted, short-term views of more

150

money. The phrase "we must have the money on the table" sums up where they hold responsibility: "we don't give a damn about the business, we must have the money on the table." And management must share the responsibility for the failure: first, it failed to fill the vacuum when Jack Jones and Hugh Scanlon abnegated that responsibility; second, and of wider significance, management has failed to recognise that if you live in a political democracy—and in Britain we have the most advanced political democracy in the world in the sense that the rights of the individual in this country are more strongly preserved than in any other society—then management has failed if it imagines that once a man is within the factory fence he can be told what to do, as opposed to being given reasons for proposed courses of action. So the unions have failed in their short-term bleeding of profits for quick gains; and management has failed in getting the economic facts of life over on the shop-floor.'

Although he does not believe any changes in this situation are likely to be dramatic, Sir Raymond does think that the country's present economic plight is forcing management to be more efficient, as well as making it ensure that economic realities are better understood on the shop-floor. As he says, the power there is now so strong that 'if they (management) do not get these messages over, they go out of business.' Further, Sir Raymond thinks that if union power has returned to the shop stewards from the national leaders this could well stimulate management to manage better.

Much of Sir Raymond's industrial experience was with ICI, whose reputation for good industrial relations has long stood high. Such relations, he claims, require constant hard work and in ICI, for example, there are very sophisticated procedures starting on the shop-floor where there are some 500 committees which meet every month to go through the economic performance of the business, and to assess the part the particular plant is playing in that performance. Sir Raymond sees such an approach as of paramount importance to any successful industrial relationship, but unfortunately such procedures are not practised in many British companies. Some managements do not give this aspect of the business high enough priority, despite the advance of democracy in Britain which makes such communication essential. Managers argue that they have got to run their business, achieve a certain level of financial return, master new technological developments and make sure their products sell: these activities

151

are full time. Surveys carried out by ICI, for example, show that in West Germany, where the company employs 8000 people, the manager may spend 15 per cent of his time on works councils, industrial relations, communication, participation and other similar activities, whereas in Britain his counterpart may spend 45 per cent of his time on such matters. It may be argued that one reason why the British are not competitive is because management has to spend so much time on such matters, but Sir Raymond's answer is that living in our society (as opposed to West Germany, for example), there is no alternative.

A great part of the time spent upon industrial relations should not be taken up solving problems, but rather in ensuring that the workforce is properly involved, understands what the company is doing and their own part in the operation. While he claims that ICI is particularly advanced in this respect, Sir Raymond says such procedures simply do not take place in much of British industry.

Low productivity is at the root of much British industrial failure. Sir Raymond cites the ability of the trade union movement to exercise brakes upon developments which threaten job security and says: 'Every time I visit a new factory I say to the manager: if you had a completely free hand—no union restraints, no restraints of money for new technology—and you wanted to make this plant more efficient, what would your manning be compared with what it is now? And almost without exception I get the answer: "about 25 or 30 per cent fewer people could be employed in this place tomorrow and it would not interefere with production." '

Sir Raymond also claims that, on average, workshop fitters in many plants work four or five hours in an eight-hour day because for the rest of the time they are waiting for things to happen: 'and one of the basic reasons for that is restrictive practices. The ingrained habit has grown up that a job and the particular exercise of a function belongs to one man: no other man can do it. That practice has become absolutely ingrained over 100 years and is easily the most difficult thing to remove. This, I believe,' Sir Raymond says, 'is at the root of our industrial problem.'

Speaking in 1980, Sir Raymond says of productivity: 'Until 1977 we were paying people about 55 or 60 per cent of what we paid our German opposite numbers, so that the unit cost per ton was in effect the same. But by 1980, when for three years we had been paying ourselves between 15 and 20 per cent increases

152

a year for no more production while the Germans had been paying themselves increases of only four or five per cent, we ended with a 45 per cent increase in wages in three years as opposed to a German increase of 12 to 15 per cent, so that Britain had achieved a 30 per cent increase in wages (above the Germans) without any increase in productivity: thus, while coming close to the Germans in wages, we are no longer competitive with them per unit ton.'

Sir Raymond is unequivocal on the reasons for low investment in industry: lack of profit. In 1980, he says, real profitability was only at the level of two or three per cent and through the seventies profitability was less than half what it had been in the sixties. The primary reason for this, he claims, was that we carried on paying ourselves 15 to 20 per cent increases every year, certainly for the last five years of the seventies, while we produced little or no more. The effect of that on profits was catastrophic: consequently money was not ploughed back into industry.

In his job as president of the CBI, Sir Raymond Pennock must spend a good deal of time dealing with the government. It is his belief that the problems of industry are in considerable measure the result of changing government policy. Far more than in France or West Germany, industry in Britain suffers because we do not have a bi-partisan industrial policy. So when one party comes into power, there follow developments such as the establishment of price commissions, incomes policies, programmes of massive government expenditure, the approaches to industry that are believed in by Labour. Immediately they go out of office we have the opposite kind of approach. Problems in industry result less from detailed interference than from reversals of policy; in consequence, management is never sure for how long it may pursue a particular line of development. Constant changes of policy have a major effect upon industrialists: the approach to industry of the two major parties is so polarised that the results can only be harmful to industrial performance.

The British Institute of Management has as its main function the pursuit of excellence in the art and science of management. This involves education, information, training, co-ordination, co-operation with universities and so on. There are both company and individual members and, while it is expected that finance comes mainly from the companies or corporate bodies, output goes mainly to individual members.

153

In recent years, responding to pressures from its members who felt that the voice of management (as opposed to the company or trade union voice) was not being heard sufficiently, BIM adopted a representational role, putting the case of management to government. There is a certain inevitable overlap of the BIM representational role with that of the CBI, though management views do not necessarily always coincide with company views. BIM membership includes middle management so that some of the Institute's representations may differ from those of the CBI, although generally they reinforce each other.

L. J. Tolley, the chairman of Renold Ltd, retired as chairman of the BIM in the autumn of 1980. Renold is a traditional engineering business making power transmission products such as chains, gears, hydraulics, couplings and speed control mechanisms. The business has been in existence since 1879 and has grown steadily until the present period of recession, and is now contracting in Britain for the first time in its history. The company employs 15,000 people round the world, 11,000 in Britain: it is completely trade-unionised and always has been, the unions having been encouraged by management. The founder of the company, Hans Renold, and his son Sir Charles Renold were liberals who believed in trade unionism and wanted to encourage it. Joint consultation in the Renold works dates back to 1919 and is still carried on according to the constitution drawn up by Sir Charles Renold at that time.

Management must take a good deal of the blame for the state of British industry and Tolley accepts that, judging by results, there are plenty of examples of bad management in Britain. In any case, he says, management must always take responsibility. Tolley makes an important case when he argues: 'It is always surprising how successful British management is when it goes overseas. There the most outstanding advantage is that managing ability and opportunity are not impaired or frustrated. Managers do not face the difficulties they have to face in Britain. Trade union power is one of these difficulties; continual policy changes by governments, particularly of economic policy every time there is a new government, are another. These constant political changes do not happen in other countries: there economic policies have a continuity despite changes of government, whereas in Britain that is not the case and in consequence amounts to a constant extra burden for management. Another problem arises out of the way companies are financed in Britain (by institutional shareholders): this often means that instead of being able to take long-term decisions companies are obliged to look over their shoulders at their institutional shareholders. Now there are many restraints of this kind in Britain upon management that do not exist—or not to the same extent—elsewhere.'

It is a major trade union complaint that there is not enough investment going into industry; it is also a complaint of the left, including trade unions, that too much power resides in the hands of the institutional shareholders, such as the great insurance companies. A difficulty for industry is that investment by institutional shareholders will usually be short-term and non-risk, while the placing of such investment is governed by a fund manager who operates in the interest of his clients and has no commitment to his investment as such or to the creation of national wealth. This pattern represents another inhibition for management.

On the subject of investment, Tolley says: 'I do not believe there has ever been a shortage of funds for investment in industry in this country. There have been two major deterrents to investment: the first is the ability to utilise the investment when it is made. You can find many examples of very expensive investment being written off as a result of lack of co-operation by the trade unions to use the investment as it was intended to be used. A classic example would be the Hunterston iron ore terminal, but there are many others; container ports, automated transfer lines in the car industry, new electronic industries where the resistance, the inbuilt suspicion of anything new comes out, and this, un-fortunately, is encouraged by the unions whereas they ought to encourage a willingness to respond. If the unions were more responsive to such developments they would get investment and jobs; by resisting they prevent such developments. That is the first deterrent.

'The second deterrent is the cost of money: if you study this over the last fifteen or twenty years, then compared with the cost in our competitor nations—the USA, France, West Germany or Japan—here it has always been exorbitant. This is mainly because we have been paying ourselves without producing the efficiency that has warranted the payment; as a result we have had inflation and with it the high cost of money. An investment of £1 million for new machinery is much more justifiable if the borrowing costs seven per cent to service rather than seventeen per cent. Industry, therefore, must see the cost of money come down and stay down consistently.

'In summary then, the problem of lack of investment in industry results first from trade union resistance to making new investment work efficiently and second from the high cost of money.'

Tolley is precise in enumerating the drawbacks that he sees operating within the trade union structure: 'The biggest drawback is trade union organisation and their constitutions. There are too many trade unions originating from the craft unions and they are organised with constitutions that are a hundred years old, have never been brought up to date, are open to abuse, prevent control within a union and—a result of their history and links with the Labour Party—they are involved in politics. They do not always have power in the industrial field but they do have political power. The corporate body of trade unionism has very little power; rather, the power nowadays resides in the hands of various, usually militant leaders on the shop-floor who have been elected by very doubtful methods.'

On the subject of low productivity, Tolley hammers away at union resistance to change: both trade unions as corporate bodies and perhaps even more at the shop steward level. He says: 'If you put a new machine in an English factory, long negotiations have to take place as to how the machine is to be manned, what possible speed of production may be obtained from it, what is to be the floor to floor time of the individual products, how many units will be produced from it in a day and all this will take up a long period of negotiating. The same machine can be installed in an American factory and twenty-four hours later it is either working at the speed intended or the operator comes back to say that he can only get say 380 instead of 400 units an hour out of it. That is the difference of approach in Britain and elsewhere.'

Explaining this phenomenon, Tolley says that in part it is a question of politics. There are, he believes, throughout industry people who have engineered their way into certain places in trade unions who are not interested in the success of the enterprise but only in changing society. Conceding that the same thing may happen in other industrial societies, though he believes to a lesser extent, Tolley says that the main reason for the difference is that in Britain workers are politically motivated, while in the USA, Japan and West Germany, where it does not happen, workers are essentially enterprise motivated.

The malaise in British industry, or a great part of it, results from attitudes which, whatever their reasons, inhibit industrial co-operation as between management and labour and result in suspicion on one or both sides. As Tolley says: 'There is a general attitude which has grown mainly as a result of trade union thinking, that the pot is bigger than it is and that you can distribute wealth before you create it. There is the attitude which has grown in this country that you do as little for as much as possible rather than a fair day's work. That attitude exists, though why it is difficult to say. It may be the welfare state; it may be that the safety net is too close to the working reward; yet these attitudes persist in this country, whereas you do not find them in those countries wedded to the success of the enterprise.'

As Tolley sees it, one of the most dangerous of prevalent attitudes is the belief that wealth is already there rather than that it must be created before it is distributed. This, he thinks, is an essential aspect of some trade union thinking. There is envy and the *them* and *us* attitude to contend with, but whereas in the USA or West Germany those who are envious of people who are better off than themselves, tend to think in terms of working harder so as to earn the rewards they at present lack, in Britain the approach is different: 'With our socialist history and our thinking that there must be free and fair play for everybody, we find instead that people take the view that if *they* can have it then so can *we*.'

Speaking of the Conservative Government's approach to economic problems, Tolley says: 'We are going through a period of confrontation with reality. It is being forced on us by a very determined government: not necessarily the best government and not necessarily the one that ultimately will make things work, but a government which is determined that the nation shall face reality and that people who do not play the game shall suffer as a result of their actions. If we respond to that approach, and I see quite a lot of evidence that we are responding, then we might pull out of the present phase. People are accepting the need for higher productivity, are trying to make investment work, are trying to become profitable, are trying to ensure that their companies do not go under and so are accepting lower wage increases and recognising the forces of inflation. All these recognitions and responses must be good for the nation: my doubt is the determination of the British people to see them through. Such a state of affairs cannot be put right in one term of office by any government, but if people see what is being attempted and re-elect this same determined government for a second term, then I see the 1980s offering something to look forward to. On the other hand, if we do not have the courage to support such harsh measures and

157

are blinded by the blandishments of the left, then I see nothing but disaster.'

Tolley's views—and after two years as president of BIM he should be close to the thinking of a great deal of management—are surely representative of a large slice of managers and employers: that is one side of the industrial spectrum.

When the CBI assembled at Brighton in November 1980 for its fourth annual conference, it did so in crisis conditions for British industry. Its new director-general, Sir Terence Beckett, came to his appointment just in time for the conference. He enjoys considerably more powers of initiation in his job than, for example, does the general secretary of the TUC. He and his president, Sir Raymond Pennock, will need all their resources if they are to reconcile the traditional business support for a Tory government with the effects of the Thatcher Government's monetarist policies upon industry.

The difficulty of the relationship with government was brought out in October 1980 on the BBC's *Today* programme when in answer to a plea that the government should do something to lessen the impact upon industrial competitiveness of high interest rates and the high pound, Sir Keith Joseph, Secretary of State for Industry, replied that industry had been uncompetitive long before the Thatcher Government came into office. As Sir Raymond Pennock said in October 1980: 'It is important to leave the government in no doubt that the idea of the present situation simply being one of a shake-out to distinguish the efficient from the inefficient is now wearing very thin indeed. Competent, proven companies are now finding it impossible to compete in world markets.'

At the end of October 1980, as a prelude to its Brighton conference, the CBI published the results of a survey and the trends reported were described by the CBI as 'the blackest ever issued'. They showed that nearly 70 per cent of 1,927 senior industrialists surveyed expected to cut their workforces during the succeeding four months (compared with 56 per cent in a previous survey of July 1980). The CBI estimated that 360,000 jobs would be lost in manufacturing industry in eight months to December 1980. Further, the survey revealed that output was at an all-time low, with factory capacity more under-utilised than at any time since records had been started in 1958: 84 per cent of British manufacturers were operating below capacity. Sir Terence Beckett commented on the survey: 'There is no doubt that it is the blackest survey the CBI has ever issued. We are now in a much more serious recession than that experienced in 1974–5. We would have to go back to before the war to find industry in comparable difficulties.' And in what could only be taken as a direct attack upon the Government's monetarist policies, Sir Terence said: 'Have we got to go through the next three or four years destroying great tracts of British industry to convince the world that sterling is overvalued?'

On the other hand, some business leaders who attended the Tory Party conference at Brighton (including the chairman of Babcock and Wilcox, Sir John King, and Leslie Fisher of Glynwed) came out in opposition to the growing CBI demand for a cut of at least four per cent in the MLR. Clearly the CBI itself faces the possibility of a split in its ranks between those who see the continuation of an inflexible monetarist line, which includes high interest rates and a strong pound, pricing their goods out of world markets, and those who support such a line whatever the immediate costs.

When the CBI did meet for its Brighton conference, Sir Raymond Pennock repeated his call of the previous September for an immediate cut of four per cent in the MLR. Reminding his audience of the results of the CBI survey (mentioned above), he called upon the government 'to take notice of the figures, respect the numeracy and take action accordingly before it is too late.'

Sir Raymond also reminded his CBI audience that the real malignancy in the British system was the prevailing 'them and us' attitude. He said: 'There are those of us who believe that the consequences of 250,000 young people out of work from the day they leave school—which could rise still further to 400,000 in next year's peak for school leavers—are that the "them" society and the "us" society will be prolonged and even more pronounced well into the next century.' He went on to say that one of the results of the monetarist policies and the world recession was that for many months thousands of people had lived in fear.

Although industrialists were at pains to express general support for the Tory Government, they demanded again and again an easing of interest rates. Sir Michael Edwardes of BL, for example, referred to possible uses of North Sea oil revenues and suggested that these should be applied to help industry become more competitive, rather than to pay for the results of industrial decay. As he said in his South African manner: 'If the Cabinet does not have the wit or imagination to do this, if they cannot cope with North Sea oil, then leave the bloody stuff in the ground. The talk is of risks. Well, from where I sit looking at overseas markets waving us goodbye, there is only one risk that matters; a massive withdrawal of United Kingdom products, a break-up of distribution networks abroad which cannot be rebuilt when the better times return.'

Never in the CBI's history could so much dissatisfaction with an incumbent Tory Government have been expressed as on this occasion. Sir Raymond Pennock summed up much of the general feeling when he said: 'The working of the economy starts with the people in this room. We pay the bills, we pay the wages, we pay the taxes and are the people who go bust. It is right, therefore, that our views should be known.' There was, however, little indication that those views were influencing the government of the day.

At the end of the conference the new director general of the CBI, Sir Terence Beckett, launched a further and even stronger attack upon the Government's policies. He said: 'You had better face the brutal fact that the Conservative Party is in some ways a rather narrow alliance. How many of them in Parliament or the Cabinet have actually run a business? This matters. They do not all understand you. They think they do, but they do not.' Sir Terence made clear what were industry's short-term needs: 'We have got to have a lower pound, lower interest rates and a reduction in the National Insurance surcharge. This surcharge is a tax on domestically produced goods versus imports and it discourages exports. . . .'

The consensus of the CBI conference was that the government should change its monetarist policies. Yet in the same speech Sir Terence also said: 'We are 100 per cent in support of government policy to bring down inflation. We are 100 per cent in support of Sir Geoffrey Howe's aim, declared in his first budget sixteen months ago, to achieve a profitable and flourishing company sector.'

The CBI and the Tory Party are not unlike the TUC and the Labour Party: CBI members in the main are ideologically wedded to the Party and what they believe it will do for business interests; they sometimes find it pursues aims not at all to their liking. In this case an apt if harsh comment was made upon CBI attitudes by Keith Wickenden, a Tory backbencher and chairman of

European Ferries. The company resigned from the CBI and Wickenden said: 'I take exception to the double standards being promulgated by the CBI, namely, "We are wholly behind the Government in all it does, so long as it does not hurt us. It can hurt handicapped children and local authorities but don't let it hurt us." '

10

Some Industrialists' Views

Leaders from four major industrial concerns—two unionised and two not—and the owner of a very small business employing only eighty people, provide a wide range of reactions to the problems both of union power and its uses; and, more generally, to some of the reasons for the present difficult and declining state of the British economy. Sir Alex Jarrett is chairman of Reed International; Sir Hector Laing is chairman of United Biscuits; Lord Sieff, chairman of Marks and Spencer; L. H. Peach, director of personnel and corporate affairs of IBM (UK) and Ian Pirie, the managing director of a small company.

Sir Alex Jarrett came into industry from a civil service background and, for example, was concerned with setting up the first incomes policy under George Brown in 1964–5; he was the first secretary of the Prices and Incomes Board. Later he spent two years at the Department of Employment under Barbara Castle through the 'In Place of Strife' period. He joined Reed International at the beginning of the 1970s. The company deals with thirty-eight trade unions and has 486 bargaining units and a workforce of about 50,000 in Britain. The two most important unions from Reed's point of view are SOGAT and the TGWU. The company is an industrial conglomerate and, according to Sir Alex, 95 per cent of its relations with the unions work well, although in the print section they have their 'punch-ups', as he puts it.

Sir Hector Laing, chairman of United Biscuits, explains that his company resulted from the merger of a number of family companies, although for a time after the merger these operated as individual companies under the umbrella of United Biscuits. Then in 1964, the companies were brought together under one direction which involved taking family directors away from individual factories so that 'almost literally overnight the people who had been quite happy without unions before that time then said:

162

"who is to look after us now?" and some joined unions. Soon after that we had trouble between unionised and non-unionised members and so we went to very nearly 100 per cent unionisation.' This was a conscious management decision.

Since then relations with the unions have been good. The company employs 36,000 people of whom 24,000 are in factories, the rest in offices and the sales side of the business. As Sir Hector says: 'Having decided to become fully unionised we set out to make a success of the relationship because a lot of the problems this country has experienced in the human relations field over the last twenty-five years have been because top management has divorced itself both from the workforce and from the unions, so that there has developed a gulf of mistrust and misunderstanding which has been disastrous.'

Marks and Spencer is not unionised. Lord Sieff says: 'We are not unionised because over fifty years we have had a policy, in fact a basic philosophy, that we have to be caring for our staff and establish what we call good human relations with our staff, our suppliers, our customers and play a socially responsible role in the areas where we are represented. It is a very practical policy: we have a personnel department of 700 people of whom 500 spread throughout the stores and head office are concerned with staff management: primarily that is with the well-being and progress of groups of individuals for whom they are responsible. This means we can treat people as individuals.'

Marks and Spencer provide facilities for unions to hold meetings in their stores, but few people turn up at these occasions.

Marks and Spencer employ 40,000 and according to Lord Sieff on two occasions when there were reports that staff were joining unions, it was found that the management of particular stores were not adequately implementing company policy. 'Policy,' Lord Sieff says, 'must not only be based upon good human relations, but it has also to be practically implemented.' The main benefits provided for the staff are: decent meals at nominal cost; considerable medical and dental facilities; a system of cancer prevention which is fully utilised, especially cervical and breast cancer (since a majority of the staff are women); and very generous non-contributory pensions. The cost of these services in 1979 came to £35 million. As a result, says Lord Sieff, 'The staff appreciate that they are being looked after well and that they have benefits; because of this they equally accept their responsibilities and there is a very considerable discipline in the business which is largely self-discipline. This is very rewarding.'

On whether the company should become unionised in the future, Lord Sieff says simply he would be quite happy if that were the wish of his employees. But he believes they are content not to be unionised because of the way the company operates. 'I have been nearly fifty years in the business and the unions have had their opportunities to recruit. Our employees feel they are part of the business, they have considerable motivation even today and they regard it as their own business, right down to the most junior grades of staff. Many of them get quite upset if anything goes wrong. They are concerned with the progress and well-being of the business. Further, management from the top downwards gets round all the stores and talks with all levels of employee. This happens constantly.'

IBM (UK) is not unionised: explaining this fact Mr Peach says: 'We set up in this country in 1951 and we brought with us a set of values and they have served us very well over thirty years. If one wanted to change those values, therefore, one would have to ask what the alternative system offered. Since our own values work very well for us and we have a very good system of personnel relations, the question is: why should we change?'

When ACAS carried out a survey of IBM in 1977 to see whether its employees wished to be unionised (four unions were hoping to organise its workforce) an overwhelming 95 per cent voted against the unions coming into the company. And Peach explains this result by saying: 'If you pay people well, if you have good benefits, if you operate on a single status basis, if you have good appeal systems, if you have full employment, then one questions what a union can offer. And if in fact you have a very good system of communications which enables people to speak their mind to management and get a response from management, then I think you probably have all the essentials for good personnel relations.'

One of the unique aspects of IBM is that management decisions can be queried by staff and on occasion are reversed as a result. The company has an average of forty 'open doors' or appeals against management decisions a year and of these, thirty will be settled in Britain, five will go to the regional headquarters in Paris and another five will eventually go to the top in the USA.

All businesses have to face one or other form of collective bargaining with their workforces: the form this takes will depend only in part upon their business approach; in part upon the union structure among their workers—one or several unions; and in part upon the current political approach to economics—whether there is a wages policy in force, whether that is voluntary or statutory and so on.

Sir Alex Jarrett had considerable experience of operating the government side of such policies as a civil servant before switching to industry and has become disenchanted with such an approach. As he claims: 'I suppose I have had more to do with running incomes policies than almost anybody else in the country; and at that time I was quite dedicated to them.' Now, however, he has come to the conclusion that they create more inconsistencies and anomalies than they solve because of the structure of business and the trade unions, because of people's different expectations and because of the shifts that are constantly occurring in terms of bargaining power and bargaining ability between the public and the private sectors. As a result he concluded that despite its many faults, collective bargaining presented a more workable alternative.

Sir Alex says: 'I dislike intensely many of the forms it takes, but it is a more natural way of determining pay than a super-imposed solution. The trick, therefore, is to try to improve the way it is done.' The social contract idea—a deal—falls between an incomes policy and collective bargaining, and against the contract Sir Alex advances two main objections: the first, that there can be no justification for a government to do a deal with one particular institution (either a trade union or an employer) which in effect masterminds what happens to the rest of the economy. Secondly, he believes that neither the TUC nor the CBI can in fact deliver: they do not have the power to commit their members and are no more than representative bodies. The result, therefore, is some form of specious agreement which lulls people into a sense of security that their problems have been resolved, when this is not the case.

Labour costs are a fixed aspect of any business like other capital costs, so that any negotiations about wages are a question of dealing with a major cost component; but, more than that, wages also determine how the business is conducted and how people work within it. Yet, as Sir Alex Jarrett maintains, the two sides to a bargain are ill-equipped to do what they are supposed to do. 'They sit across the table from each other: on the one side the employers who say they cannot afford it; on the other side

165

the employees who say the going rate is 20 per cent or whatever it may be at the time and that a neighbouring concern is paying 21 per cent and they want the same. Thus, there is a lack of sophistication in a negotiation of this nature. Moreover, the negotiators on both sides if they are national negotiators are unlikely to know the exact details of the local business they are discussing, since this knowledge can only lie with the manager of the company and those who are in it.

'Second comes the framework for the negotiation: all too often that consists—it has been a marked feature of recent years—of the claim, the offer, the strike. This is not negotiation as people normally understand that word but a set-piece battle that develops into trench warfare.

'Third is the problem of whether in fact you are negotiating with the right people. Are they able to commit? If it is a national employers' federation, for example, is it backed up by the membership? And if it is a trade union, are the officials out of touch with the rank and file so they, too, fail as negotiators? What is needed is more sophistication in negotiations, a sensible framework within which to negotiate and people who can commit on that about which they are negotiating.'

Consultation, the provision of information and procedure are stressed by all good management as essentials for properly functioning industrial relations. Sir Hector Laing, for example, speaks to up to half his total labour force of 36,000 every year in groups of 200 or less. In most of United Biscuits' factories there are briefing groups so that everyone has the chance to know what the business is doing. On the other hand far too few companies do anything of the sort.

IBM have probably gone further than any company in Britain in the sense of providing information and consulting with their employees—again the question of procedure. Speaking of consultation as the key to better industrial relations, Peach says: 'It is the provision of information about the company's results, about individual division and department successes and failures; it is the first-line manager's ability to sit with a group of people every month and talk to them about the department—and be talked to about the department—and also to be supplied with information about what is happening in the company, which creates the feeling that management is genuinely interested in every department of the company. And we are also genuinely interested in the viewpoints which employees express. An informa-

166

tion structure is essential; it is also expensive.' (If done on the IBM scale, for example, it means that of the 4000 people in the manufacturing sector of the company who meet in groups of between ten and twenty for two hours once a month, a total of nearly 100,000 hours a year will be taken out of their manufacturing activities for these information sessions: therein lies the expense, yet as IBM claims, the company is as productive as its American or German counterparts, so this approach clearly pays.)

Further, however, the managers themselves have to be trained to hold such meetings, for if these are badly structured and poorly conducted they are liable to be counter-productive, raising more questions than they solve. What IBM especially prides itself upon is the two-way exchange of information, with members of staff saying what they want and management doing the same in return.

On the long-term view of management Sir Alex Jarrett believes that the country is in for a period of economic uncertainty and therefore that there is no easy, automatically acceptable way to run anything. Management must be prepared to change all the time, which means it must be more ready to open up and say to its workforce: 'Share my problem with me so that we both understand what I am trying to achieve with your help on your behalf.' A good deal of management, he says, will find such an approach very hard to adopt. It is far harder to manage by consensus than by the older method of saying do this or do that. Today, management has to win the argument as opposed to giving the order. It is a major barrier for older management to get through, though younger men find it less difficult. At the same time, Sir Alex says, those on the other side of the equation, the employees, must also try to overcome their attitudinal barriers: there are many hurdles to overcome both ways.

Sir Hector Laing says he blames management for most of the problems, although the situation has got far worse in relation to the unions because of the immunities allowed them under the laws.

Surveying industrial relations over the last twenty-five to thirty years, Lord Sieff believes that management failed to understand its social responsibilities in relation to its staff and did not co-operate adequately with moderate union leaders. As a result, he says, tougher union leaders moved to the fore in a number of cases and some of them, such as Scargill or McGahey, are very definitely to the left and do not like the present economic system

167

as a system—they do not want it to work but wish to change the whole economic structure.

Although he believes an improvement has taken place in managements' co-operation with staff, he still thinks that management generally has a long way to go. He also says that management must be prepared to stand up to unions; too many managements took the easy way out of problems during boom times and that has created part of the problem which now exists.

The secret of the IBM management relationship with employees lies in the fact, Peach claims, that the company effectively offers its employees a contract for life in return for their flexibility and willingness to relocate geographically and in terms of skills (being retrained for a different job). The company qualifies this slightly, he says, because they cannot guarantee 'for life' since there may occur an economic cataclysm beyond their control; but they do make their best efforts and in return need the co-operation of their employees.

A typical IBM employee may move round Britain four or five times in his working life with the company—from Havant to Greenock and back to Havant and so on. A key to the operation of this policy resides effectively with the director of personnel for Britain (Peach himself) since no one can hire for IBM from outside the company without his agreement. As a result, although the various divisions of IBM have hiring plans, there is a central resource manpower committee which may direct how people within the company are to be redeployed. Moreover, the director of personnel has the authority for transferring people from one part of the company to another. This is an important power which simply does not exist in most other personnel departments. Such unique power requires exact planning. Peach admits that IBM enjoys certain advantages which other companies do not have: their product cycle, for example, tends to be longer than that of other companies so that IBM is actually selling this year what it manufactures and installs next year—that is, six to nine months later—whereas a company that may be affected twenty-four hours after a decision by a slump does not have the same flexibility. On the other hand IBM labour turnover is only four per cent whereas average labour turnover in the computer industry is 20 per cent.

The message of each of these managers is the same: the need for participation. This in turn highlights what is all too often a

168

part of British industrial life—the *them* and *us* attitudes which prevail.

Sir Alex Jarrett is convinced this is a major bar to progress and cites worker suspicion of management despite the fact that nowadays most management is salaried and has the same interests as the workforce as a whole. 'Mind you,' he adds, speaking of himself, 'I had a different sort of education though I went to state schools, but I also went to university and I have made it, as you might say, I have got to the top of the company. But actually my background is almost identical—I was born in the East End of London—with that of most of the workmen. But I am sure they regard me as being in a different class.' As he says, there is a vast amount of folklore wrapped up in the *them* and *us* relationship. It is precisely this divide which makes the process of participation so important.

Sir Hector Laing explains much of that divide in terms of a failure of management after the Second World War. Then, he says, 'The post-war generation of leaders in industry had been officers or non-commissioned officers in the forces who had learnt and understood the importance of communication leadership. Yet when they returned to industry they went back to the methods of dealing with people which had proved so damaging in the 1930s. There was a lack of leadership and I blame most of the problems on management because I think management dropped the "ball" after the war, having had it in their hands in the 1930s, because of fear. And that fear's coming back now. The unions picked the ball up, held it for some time and then ran with it in a direction they found increasingly attractive since no one tried to stop them.

'The other thing that has made the *them* and *us* gulf wider has been the very high level of personal taxation: 98 per cent on unearned income (investment income) and 83 per cent on earned income. Because people were not being rewarded properly at the top of business or in the management stream, companies started giving them cars and perks of various sorts and different facilities in the factories and this created a greater divide.'

The excesses of capitalism in the 1930s allied to Britain's class structure have perpetuated a class division of *them* and *us* into the present era that remains in patterns of behaviour despite all sorts of other changes and new, high standards of living. As Sir Hector says: 'There is a sort of stultification of class attitudes which holds people back.' And he tells how one of his own shop

169

stewards remarked to him: 'You know, when I am agreeing with you I have this terrible tension inside me that I am letting down my class.' As long as such attitudes prevail, the difficulties facing both sides in industry are clearly enormous.

On the same subject, Lord Sieff says: 'I think such attitudes are decreasing, but not fast enough: there is still far too much of we and they. I like to think in this business that anybody can rise to any job. Most of the directors of Marks and Spencer started in the warehouses, stockrooms or on the counter in the stores, including members of the family, and if members of the family were not good enough they got kicked out.'

From the viewpoint of an IBM man whose distinctive industrial practices among other things include a single status approach, Peach says: 'It is ridiculous in this day and age that we have companies which are quite so splintered in providing different kinds of benefits at the various levels throughout the organisation. In this way you stratify industrial society so as to produce conflict by treating people with a good deal less than respect, by laying down that the blue collar workers will get this, the white collar workers that, the managers something else and so on. Such an approach has to change: it demands an effort from both sides, employers' organisations and trade unions.'

Peach suggests that such differences may be emphasised where more than one union operates within an industry, since a union representing white collar workers would seek other compensations if differentials between white and blue collar workers were to disappear.

One of the problems about British productivity, according to Sir Alex Jarrett, is the desire to avoid risk rather than take it. He suggests the growth of the big company in the sixties and early seventies is part of that process: 'Do not grow yourself but pinch somebody else's growth by acquisition. Then you become so big that you cannot manage the enterprise at the end, anyway, and so compound your problems. Management confidence and ability is a part of this process.'

Trade union demarcation practices are another part of the problem and for much of industry a whole series of demarcations are simply accepted as the norm. On the question of new investment leading to new machinery or technology, Sir Alex says this has to be talked through with the men first: there is no point unless management gets the workers' agreement since they must work whatever new machinery is installed and make it earn the returns of which it is capable. An aspect of this problem, Sir Alex believes, is that although the TUC shows understanding of the technological changes which must be taken into account, down the line it is far more difficult. There is likely to be lack of understanding by the officially appointed representatives of the men on the shop-floor, and this may well produce the greatest hurdles which have to be overcome.

Sir Hector Laing sees two things at the root of Britain's productivity crisis: 'First of all a failure by management to get over to their workforce what productivity is all about. And second, the fear of unemployment so that new machinery to increase productivity is seen as a threat to jobs.' Yet when reaction against new machinery prevents its use this, in the long run, may destroy jobs permanently: to explain this and so make acceptable the use of new machinery is the task of management.

Speaking of his own United Biscuits, Sir Hector says: 'It is unrealistic to say to men who have served the company ten or twenty years that new machinery is to be installed, and although it will make the company more productive, they may lose their jobs.' United Biscuits said that if its workforce would accept that 70 per cent of added value was their share (while the remaining 30 per cent is divided between reinvestment at 20 per cent, dividends and pension funds at five per cent and tax at five per cent) and be prepared to work new investment efficiently and flexibly, then the company would guarantee job security after five years for five years and after ten years until retirement. Sir Hector claims there is nothing novel in such an approach, which is common in Japan, but he adds, 'because of a general mistrust in the country people react by assuming there must be a catch in such an offer.'

In order to achieve an improved standard of living we require greater productivity, and here Lord Sieff goes at once to the nub of the problem when he says: 'Greater productivity is often accomplished with fewer people—in fact it is almost a corollary. Therefore the question is how do management, capital, government and unions encourage the development of new industries? For example, over the last twenty years the greatest developments have been in the electronic industries; in the next twenty years one of the major developments is going to be in the bio-technological industries. It is, therefore, a question of looking now to improving productivity, which may initially mean more being produced by fewer people and so it is essential to decide what new industries to go into. Thus bio-technology should first be encouraged by management and by government and discussed with the unions to see how it can be implemented.'

On present performance, Lord Sieff says: 'We are poor in many areas in terms of productivity because we stick to outmoded methods, partly due to lack of investment by management and partly due to unions sticking to outmoded practices. There exist many examples of areas where the introduction of new machinery would increase productivity enormously but result in fewer people being employed. The unions argue that if new machinery is to be introduced, employment should remain at the old level: the newspaper world is an example of the working of this process. Such attitudes preserve jobs initially; in the end, however, they make the enterprise uncompetitive and the whole organisation closes down.'

Productivity comparisons are difficult, but to the question whether the same kind of motivations work in Britain's main competitors Lord Sieff does not think they do. 'In the USA anybody reckons he has got the chairman's job in his knapsack if he has the capacity; in West Germany there is a much simpler union structure. In Japan, which is now outstripping all the others, there is enormous personal motivation: much greater care of quality; their production costs are low—they are a low cost country.'

The popular image of over-powerful unions is one often not held by industrialists themselves, although they may well complain about abuses of power in particular situations. Sir Alex Jarrett, for example, argues that the unions wish to exercise political influence in part as a substitute for their lack of industrial power. Further, he suggests that given they are very slow at reforming themselves so as to be better able to control and commit their own membership, he considers them to be too weak.

Sir Alex believes there are two possible ways for unions to develop. The first, that the unions at national level try to reform themselves and then recapture the authority over their members which they enjoyed formerly. That way they could begin to deal on behalf of their members much as do the American unions. Alternately, development will take another direction: rationalisation of the unions will not occur, but instead the shop-floor will become the permanent centre of power: the power will not simply reside with the shop steward, but beyond him with the individual member. Should this development occur, it would no longer be possible to know from day to day how that power would be exercised. Should that be the trend, and Sir Alex thinks it will be, then management will have to learn how to deal with a new situation. Then at least everyone in a plant—those on the shop-floor and the management—would be talking about the same thing: what they had in common at that plant and with luck, instead of *them* and *us*, there might develop simply *us*. Such a development represents a huge challenge to management.

Sir Alex Jarrett also believes that union political power in the sense of consultation with government has come to stay. 'Trade unions are about negotiations and trade-offs and governments almost inevitably look to them for things to happen such as wage restraint.' The social contract, he believes, was more about the institutional power of the union movement than the interests of its members. In a sense in recent years the unions have been digging themselves in politically, saying as it were: 'If we cannot have power on the shop-floor, then we will hold on to what is left, by being so important as a body to be consulted to help control government and other developments in society, that we become a major part of the establishment.'

Sir Hector Laing takes a different view. He says of the unions: 'I think they are too powerful. The unions that are not in the industries which can bring the country to a halt use their power reasonably well. But those which are in monopoly industries and can use straight brute force to get what they want, have misused their power and I think that one of the main reasons why we have a Conservative Government today [1980] is because the unions were quite clearly seen to abuse their power: their members not minding people dying in hospital or patients not getting to hospital just as long as they get their money.'

On the political issue, Sir Hector says it is not to be expected that unions should not involve themselves in politics—the chairmen of companies do—both sides of industry in fact work at pressuring governments. It is the quality of life in society that matters and the wealth to provide it must come from profitable industry. 'As long as both sides are trying to press governments to institute procedures, laws or climates of opinion which create additional wealth, then it seems right for both management and unions to try to influence government.'

Peach, on the other hand, makes a point that is vital to any understanding of union power: that in much of British industry the workforce identifies with its union first and the company

173

second. That presents industry a major problem. The workforce ought to identify first with its company, then with its union. The fact that, too often, it is the other way round is an indication both of union strength or attraction and an indictment of past managements.

Commenting upon the Thatcher Government, Sir Hector Laing says: 'I support the strategy of the Government totally. Where I think the Government has to be careful, however, is to make greater efforts to show that it cares and that there is no alternative policy. Otherwise, with very high unemployment, we shall build up this mistrust again between the two sides, because people will argue that it is the fault of the Conservatives. It is not the Conservatives: Callaghan said five per cent, but the answer he got was that he did not know what he was talking about and the workforce, or a large part of it, was going to have 20 per cent. Also there is a whole accumulation of attitudes to contend with. If there is no self-discipline, there has got to be fear and we do not have much self-discipline as a nation. We have to have a caring society but it must also be an efficient society.'

Ian Pirie runs a small company employing eighty workers which services manufacturing industries. He has spent one third of his working life in management consultancy and another third as managing director of a fairly large company. His present company is not unionised and since its eighty members are divided between three sites, it seems unilkely they will be. He says: 'I believe very firmly that to be unionised would produce absolutely no benefit at all and might in fact be a retrograde step as far as the employees are concerned.'

Pirie defends his forthright attitude as follows: 'We have extremely full consultation on matters of any importance at all; we have a formal joint consultation committee which has its constitution in the formation of which the employees played a very full part; we have monthly meetings to discuss how the business is progressing and to look into the future.'

Everybody is involved through the company's briefing groups. There is a profit sharing scheme and employees know they can and do influence the direction of the business, although that in no way detracts from the responsibility of management. Essentially, Pirie is arguing that he renders union involvement in his company unnecessary by the way he runs it.

Applying this approach to the broader canvas of British industry, Pirie believes that if similar consultation and participation by their workforces were a major feature of their activities, then many industries would also render union participation in their affairs largely unnecessary.

Having made this point, Pirie insists that he is not ideologically opposed to unions. He recalls a childhood in a depressed area with high unemployment, so that he both understands and sympathises with the reasons for trade unionism. But what he objects to, he says, is the abuse of the power which trade unions now have: such power is often used and abused by militants rather than the union at the official level. He does not believe the militants understand, or alternately they deliberately misunderstand the long-term damage they do to the companies in which they operate, to the employment prospects of the employees and to the total British economy. 'Striking or stoppage of work,' he says, 'seems to be the first shot in the locker today rather than the last resort. Militants use the term negotiate to mean management must give concessions.'

Pirie is emphatic that management has to earn the respect and win the trust of employees: he emphasises the words 'earn and win' because he says it is no longer possible to award authority in British industry—it can only be earned. While accepting that a major fault of management has been its assumption that it has respect which it has not earned, Pirie also argues that British society does not accord adequate respect to industry and to the manufacturing industry in particular. Industry, he says, has become a poor relation in our society, and in manufacturing industry the production function has become a poor relation, and it is the production function that brings management face to face with the broad mass of employees.

Apart from North Sea oil Britain is totally dependent upon its ingenuity and manufacturing capacity, so that society ought to esteem manufacturing and encourage some of its best people to go into that sector of activity. Yet, at present, public service is far more highly esteemed; a long-standing left-over, he suggests, of the ethics taught by Dr Arnold of Rugby.

On the attitude of *them* and *us* Pirie is unusual in saying: 'What I am clear about is that the *them* and *us* attitude stems entirely from the trade unions.' He does not believe it comes from the management side because 'No manager in his right mind thinks in such terms. He thinks of *us*, for the only *them* is the competition. Any manager who thinks *them* and *us* will not

175

succeed.' He ascribes such union thinking to the depression years of the 1930s.

Pirie sees only drawbacks should his company be unionised as a result of expansion. First, the introduction of restrictive practices and, for example, being obliged to keep people on when no job exists for them as a result of union pressure. 'I can think of nothing worse,' he says, 'than condemning a man to do nothing for years on end: I regard that as almost criminal because people only derive satisfaction from being useful and knowing they are useful and have a job to do.'

Pirie believes it should usually be possible to redeploy labour without trouble, provided that management recognises the problems involved: that he is breaking up social groups; that adjustments of earnings need to be made; and as long as sensitivity is displayed in dealing with these personal problems.

Unions would be much better employed using their energies to get people retrained who are made redundant than exerting pressure to keep them in non-jobs. Industries can usually carry a small surplus of labour and most have got into the habit of doing so. Now it has become a question of small surpluses becoming substantial parts of the workforce. Where there is surplus labour Pirie thinks the unions ought to adopt an attitude which in effect says: 'Here is a surplus of labour, we will put a six-month time limit upon it and there must be a measured, predetermined plan for redeployment, adjustment or financial compensation and this must be implemented.'

Like other industrialists Pirie sees a vital distinction between the representatives of the shop-floor and union leaders who come from outside to negotiate. 'It is the difference,' he says, 'between knowing the people you work with and therefore planning something with them, or dealing with an outsider who may know very little of the way in which a particular plant operates.'

Pirie's basic argument is that where management constantly communicates with its workforce, unions become largely redundant. A further union problem, he believes, arises out of the fact that a full-time union official will be judged by his members, his superiors and probably himself according to how much he is able to increase the nominal wages of his members year by year. The fact he may price them out of employment five or ten years ahead is too long a time scale for him to judge or be judged by. Pirie is a great believer in bonus incentives and, for example, thinks these should be paid certainly quarterly and perhaps monthly and

176

depend not simply upon the performance of the company, but also upon that of particular sections in it.

Pirie's is an essentially individualistic approach to industry, admittedly from the standpoint of a very small company: his main feeling is that industrial progress and therefore the interests of those working in industry have been restricted rather than advanced by union activities of the type predominant throughout the 1970s.

The consensus of management opinion represented here is that unions are negative in their actions and most especially over restrictive practices and in defence of jobs; that where management is really doing its job unions are rendered largely redundant; that the prime responsibility for industrial developments must lie with management and too often, unfortunately, this has been found wanting; that it is unrealistic to expect unions to refrain from exercising political power where they can; and that a great deal of union power has returned to the shop-floor, away from the national leadership, but often into the hands of militants. As Sir Hector Laing says: 'In the 1930s capital or management abused its power; in the last part of the 1970s the unions abused their power. Now let us look forward and not back.'

11

The Motor Industry

Confrontation, strikes, misunderstandings, bad industrial relations, union irresponsibility, militancy, low productivity, accusations and counter-accusations: those appear to be a not unrepresentative series of words and phrases to describe Britain's car industry, which in the 1950s had something like half the world's export markets. An outsider witnessing yet another unofficial strike, yet another clash between 'bitter' workers and 'tough' management may be forgiven for wondering whether the collective of all those who work in the industry from top management downwards, are not possessed of an almost morbid determination to work themselves out of jobs and Britain out of any car producing capacity whatever. None of the industry's problems are made easier by a press which always presents any situation as a war with winners and losers. The partisan nature of most press presentations about the industry is deeply resented in union circles.*

1980 was possibly a crunch year for the industry although there have been other crunch years. So often have the two sides come to the brink—unions threatening and then striking for more pay, management insisting it has made a final offer which then turns out to be one of a series—that it has become immensely difficult to accept the credibility of either side any more.

In mid-November 1980, Ford introduced a tough new disciplinary code under which the company will deduct pay from workers who indulge in unofficial stoppages. Ford had experienced 254 disputes in the first 198 days of the year. Leyland, whose troubles seem endless, made a loss of £180 million in the first half of the year. In any case Leyland had rendered 30,000 workers redundant over a two-year period, so perhaps unsurprisingly in 1980 its employees were on edge.

* Speaking with a trade union official I fell into the trap of using current press jargon and asked a question about 'Red' Robbo; his response was an angry demand: 'Why did I talk of "Red" Robbo and not of "Fascist" Edwardes?' He had a point.

178

Following the 1980 August holidays, Ford experienced seventy unofficial disputes within three months in its seventeen plants across the country, an average of twenty a month, which is an appalling record. Both Ford and BL launched new models during the year, the new Ford Escort and the BL Metro, and both companies hope that with these models they will recapture part of the home and world markets they have lost. Yet the auspices are not encouraging.

The Secretary of Trade, John Nott, told the Japanese government in November 1980 that he expected Japan's share of the British car market to be kept below the previously agreed 11 per cent limit, when it appeared that for 1980 Japan would take at least 12 per cent of the British market. His concern reflected the poor performance of the British motor industry, yet such demands come oddly from a minister of Mrs Thatcher's Government whose much vaunted belief in freedom and private enterprise appears in this instance to stand on somewhat shaky ground.

The tough managerial style of BL's Sir Michael Edwardes has made a substantial impact upon the industry. In April 1980 he took a major gamble—and won—when he said that workers returning for work after Easter would be deemed to have accepted the proposed pay increase (between five and ten per cent) as well as a series of sweeping changes in working practices. Edwardes has certainly had his confrontations: over his recovery plan; over the sacking of Derek Robinson, the convenor. His pay and conditions package presented in April 1980 was the key to his strategy, since he believes that he must get improved productivity if Leyland is to survive. Edwardes has appealed to his employees over the heads of union officials, which has not added to his popularity with the unions.

The plant at Longbridge, which is producing the Metro, is one of the most modern in Europe; yet by October 1980 BL was once more on the brink of yet further confrontation. For the third year running Edwardes made a pay offer of single figures (when half British industry was going for doubles) and the workforce was debating whether to reject the 6·8 per cent offer and come out on strike. Sir Michael made plain that a final offer meant just that and a strike would not only endanger the Metro, but also the possibility of the government putting a further £400 million into the industry for the new LC 10 medium range car and the new lightweight Jaguar, both deemed essential to the company's future. In April, Edwardes had won his battle when he not only imposed his retrospective five per cent increase (dating back to November 1979) but broke the strike with his threat of dismissals if workers did not return to work.

When the shop stewards called for a strike against the 6·8 per cent offer in November 1980, this was called off when the leader of the AUEW, the moderate Terence Duffy, intervened. He certainly put his own position at risk, yet in doing so he took the kind of action that industrialists often lament has been absent in recent years: that of the national union leader exerting his authority to control a local situation rather than this being left to the 'militant' shop stewards. Duffy's intervention worked. As *The Times* of 11 November put it: 'The last minute reprieve will be seen as another victory for Sir Michael Edwardes, BL chairman, and Mr Terence Duffy, president of the Amalgamated Union of Engineering Workers.' The trouble about such language —a victory—is the implication of a defeat for the other side, and too much of Britain's industrial relations are presented in such terms.

Some of the more militant shop stewards were upset by the Duffy intervention, and one remarked: 'What in God's name is the use of having a formally constituted BL Cars negotiating body? We might just as well leave it to Edwardes and Duffy.' There are plenty of both industrialists and trade union leaders who would happily echo that sentiment. Yet a week after Duffy's intervention, 9000 Cowley workers voted to reject the 6·8 per cent offer. Terence Duffy commented: 'We understand how frustrated the workers feel, but to obtain good wages we must sell the products.'

Sir Michael Edwardes insisted that the pay offer could not be improved and that a strike would lead to a permanent closure of operations within five days. By mid-November, when it was still touch and go as to whether there would be a strike over the 6·8 per cent offer, sales figures for the Metro were reported to be rising (ironically it had then captured 6·8 per cent of the market as opposed to 6·4 per cent going to the new Ford Escort).

A shop stewards' meeting on 18 November, representing all thirty-four BL car plants, voted to accept the 6·8 per cent offer and reject the call for a strike. Stewards said the deciding factor was the tough stance taken by Edwardes and his threat to close plants if the strike took place. Commenting upon the outcome of one more BL war Mr Grenville Hawley, the national automotive officer of the TGWU who chaired the shop stewards' meeting in

180

Coventry, said that BL management was 'storing up a great deal of trouble and bitterness by forcing workers to take a single figure increase for the third successive year.' He went on: 'In the interest of preserving jobs and keeping a viable BL we have had to take another totally unacceptable offer, but it cannot go on like this year after year.'

In Tokyo, where European car makers for once working in concert were discussing with the Japanese ways of curtailing the latter's penetration of European markets, Sir Michael Edwardes congratulated both workers and management for allowing commonsense to prevail and said he was proud of them. Three days later, angry Metro workers went on a rampage through the Longbridge plant in protest at management stopping production of the car after 500 assembly workers were laid off for the second time in a week because of a shortage of car seats. And so the troubled saga of embattled and embittered relations continued.

Ford's reputation is perhaps better, but only marginally. In 1977 Ford made a profit of £1593 for every worker employed, a fact which ensured that in 1978 Ford broke the five per cent norm in a pay settlement of nearly 17 per cent, though not until after a long and damaging strike. Despite a record of success, profits dropped right down in the second half of 1980, although the company had made a pre-tax profit of £386 million for 1979. Nonetheless, in November 1980, the unions put in a pay claim in the region of 20 per cent. The TGWU national organiser, Ronald Todd, the chief negotiator, argued that the company was well able to pay the claim on its performance over a number of years. Whenever the unions have argued their pay claims on a single year's performance, he said, they were told one year could not be taken in isolation: 'By no stretch of the imagination can it be argued that they are not among the leading companies in the motor industry. There is no way we are going to accept any further erosion of living standards.' Thus one more set-piece battle was under way.

Ford then told its 57,000 workers that it would introduce a new tough plan to discipline unofficial strikers as a way to protect the company from the effects of stoppages which threatened its survival. Then Ford made a 7·5 per cent pay offer and Mr Paul Roots, director of labour relations, said: 'If Ford Britain continues to perform as badly as it has done in the 1960s and 1970s it will not survive the next few years.' To this, Mr Ronald Todd said: 'The company was talking about commercial suicide fifteen

181

years ago.' The management argued that the workers showed a total unawareness of the crisis confronting the company and that profits were not enough to enable reinvestment on the scale needed to ward off Japanese competition: 'Productivity in the Japanese motor industry is far ahead of Ford Britain. Either we get efficient and employ fewer people or we will end up employing nobody. . . . Our labour costs are far too high for what we produce. We have to reverse our disastrous performance or we shall go under. That is why we had to act to stop unconstitutional strikes and why attitudes have got to change.'

According to Ford management it is cheaper to produce Cortinas in Belgium and Fiestas in Spain and ship them to Britain than make them at Dagenham. Toyota produce five times more vehicles an employee than do Ford Britain. Yet such arguments are unlikely to make much impression on Ford workers when set against the figure of £1593 profit for every employee in 1977 or the pre-tax profit of £386 million for 1979. So many of the arguments in the troubled car industry depend upon the standpoint of the individual who advances them.

In March 1978 the *Sunday Times* ran a major article about the car industry and then published a number of letters about it from various car workers. Two are worth quoting here. The first is from Brian Stringer, of Llanelli, South Wales:

For the past thirteen years I have worked as a toolmaker in Leyland radiator factory in Llanelli. Your article points out, when new investment takes places there is union opposition. The reason for this is our appalling industrial relations record. For almost three centuries the working class have been used as cheap labour during booms and thrown on the scrapheap during slumps.

There is no point in telling the worker these days are over when we have 1,500,000 people on the dole. The union attitude is therefore protectionist. I would love to see Leyland efficient, but I am not going on the dole to help it.

After almost three hundred years of performing mundane, menial tasks our people have had enough. There are people in my factory who perform the same operation day in, day out, 600 times an hour. A stoppage of work is the only way to break the hellish boredom. Until you have worked in a car factory you have no idea the excitement a spider can cause, just by crawling up a wall.

The second is from D. L. Starves, of Brandon, Suffolk:

As a 55-year-old engineering tradesman I'd like to say a few words about the role of union power. I worked at Fords, Dagenham, a couple of times in the 1950s. The second spell was on the assembly line making the Mark I Consul. I would imagine it to have been one of the most soul destroying jobs going. The factory environment was atrocious—low ceilings hung with equipment, air polluted with foundry fumes and the work line going so fast that as a welder I could not do my job properly because I would have taken too long and missed some bodies, therefore the job was fast and botched.

It is stated in the article that the Germans are convinced that British managers are too distant from their workers. I think that more often than not this is entirely correct, and I would suggest this goes for the whole of staff-worker relationship. It is as if the workers were a different race of people with a much lower requirement of life fulfilment.

At fifty-five I'm completely disillusioned with work and the need to feel any responsibilities towards the nation's efficiency. It cannot be otherwise when one sees the relative affluence of white collar workers, and others on the commercial perimeters of British life.

I therefore think the following points are important:

Promotion into management must not mean getting into ever more select clubs, and even remoter from the shop-floor where the dirty work is done.

Shop-floor workers must have the same opportunities as staff. The same sick pay entitlements, length of work day, annual salary increments from starting pay to maximum must be provided. Opportunities for promotion also are a must, and perhaps most important, the rate of pay must reflect the skill and experience required for the job.

As far as I'm concerned taking up a trade is putting oneself in a dead-end and my own son will certainly not do it!

The industry suffers from years of appalling industrial relations so that suspicion and 'bitterness'—a much used trade union word —go deep on the labour side while management appears, if not to have lost touch, certainly not to possess any common touch. The complaints of dreary monotonous work are true enough, yet this applies also to the industry in other parts of the world where it is more productive and less strike prone. It is important, therefore, to look for some other cause for the troubles which for years have beset both BL and Ford. The answer would seem to lie in the confrontation mentality that persists: much industry in Britain, certainly not just this sector, appears to assume that it is and must be a war between management and labour: it is always 'I win, you lose', rather than a joint approach to greater productivity and therefore greater wealth for everybody. How this may be changed lies at the root of half the country's industrial problems.

Pat Lowry moved to what was then BLMC in 1970 from the Engineering Employers' Federation where he was director of industrial relations. He is director of personnel and external affairs for BL.*

Trying to answer the question of what lies at the root of BL's apparently endless industrial problems, Lowry starts by pointing to the background: 'BLMC resulted from the merger of a number of companies in the late 1960s to form the new conglomerate in 1969. Each of these companies had had their own autonomous managements, Rover, Standard Triumph, Jaguar etc., and when they were combined they brought together a wide variety of wage levels and conditions of employment which caused problems. Further, during the 1950s and 1960s the need to maintain ordinary discipline in the factories had been sacrificed for the more urgent need for the product, which was then demanded by a British market which had been starved of cars during the war. At the same time, the export business was thriving. As a result of this situation, a number of management indisciplines also developed while strikes became almost a way of life rather than other procedures being used first.'

Lowry argues that industrial relations in the company are now more right than they have ever been. He splits industrial relations reforms into three: the need to reform collective bargaining institutions; to ensure that the pay and conditions package is equitable; and to change built-in attitudes. Speaking in September 1980—before the near-strike at the time of the Metro's launch and the company's offer of a 6·8 per cent increase—Lowry said that employee attitudes seemed to have changed and that there appeared to be a greater element of reality and common sense.

Like a good many industrialists Lowry does not find it easy

* Mr Lowry's appointment as chairman of ACAS was announced on 24 November 1980.

184

to explain why, for example, there appears to be greater industrial unrest, in BL than in its overseas equivalents. Partly it is a question of trade union structure—seventeen unions for the management of BL to deal with—although he does not believe this is a primary cause. Partly it is because Britain industrialised first and some problems persist from those early days: for example, British trade unions were nurtured on a voluntary basis whereas overseas contracts are normally enforceable at law. Partly, perhaps, it relates to national character—better discipline among the Germans or a different approach to work in Japan. 'In Britain this is absent: we are an undisciplined people by and large and I think the national indiscipline which comes out in many facets of our life is reflected also in the workplace.'

On productivity, Lowry makes the point that too often like is not compared with like and that, for example, some Japanese car manufacturers are in fact no more than assemblers. Yet, having made the point, he admits that British productivity is often exceptionally low in comparison with its main competitors. This in part results from low investment, although he says: 'With the new Metro facility at Longbridge we are able at long last partly, if not wholly, to redress the balance with Japan. We would be very fortunate if we could wholly redress the balance; but this is undoubtedly the level of investment that is needed.' That is one side of the question; another concerns work practices.

'One of the reasons for productivity differences is not that people work harder overseas compared with their British counterparts—when these are working—but the fact that the intervals between work in Britain are longer: the amount of relaxation time which is necessary in any mass production system—employees get so many minutes of relaxation time an hour—tend to be greater in Britain than in Europe. Similarly, the amount of "down" time to change tools, the amount of "stop" time in order to rectify breakdowns and so on also tend to be greater, and that is the main reason why British productivity suffers. Thus over the last decade we have talked about productivity, but not about people working harder while they work. We talk about continuity of production, which is why the emphasis has been upon reducing the number of strikes. You get more quantum leaps with improvements if you are getting forty hours of work out of your employees than by getting them to work harder when they are at work.'

These longer rest periods, the fact that British workers take more time off, rather than work less hard when at work, are the result of trade union pressures or managerial weakness over the years. As Lowry points out: 'Times which by any objective standard are known to be accurate times, or levels of manning which again by any accurate standards are known to be the right levels have in fact been diluted as a result of union pressure either for more time (to do the job) or more men (on the job); or as a result of weak managements giving way to such union pressures—it always takes two to make a bargain. Thus, although unions can say forcefully and forcibly at times that the time to do a job is not enough or manning is inadequate, it is the response of management which has been as much responsible for overmanning as have been the initial demands for it by the unions. It is always open to a company to say: "No, we are certain this level of manning (or whatever) is right and we are not going to move from it." Historically, however, that has not been done.'

On the recurring question of lack of investment, Lowry says two things: first, that during the seventies the company was simply not producing enough cash in order to invest adequately in new factories and new facilities. Second: 'It has been alleged, and I don't know how true it is, that historically the company has paid out more in dividends when proper commercial prudence would have dictated more being ploughed back into the company. But I do know that in the past ten or eleven years in a market which by and large has boomed, BL failed to produce the goods in either the right quantity or in the mixture of quantity and quality and this has led to a situation in which profits were inadequate and investment was inadequate as well.

'It was only with the Ryder Report of 1975 when BLMC was to all intents nationalised that the Ryder Plan led to £1000 million of investment over five years. Then we got the investment money in something like the right amounts; yet even that figure is small compared with the amounts being ploughed into the industries in the USA, West Germany and Japan.'

Confrontation and strikes appear endemic to the motor industry, yet as Lowry points out, British industrial practice is adversary based to a greater extent than that in many of our main competitor countries, while the only aspect of industrial relations that is news consists of confrontation: the ability to sit together and talk does not make news. Further, Lowry is scathing about the politicians and argues that 'developments such as employee participation or industrial democracy have been badly set back because the politicians have interfered with the process and polarised the two sides. Otherwise this is potentially one of the most fruitful ways of eliminating some of the adversary based nature of the country's industrial relations. Now, for the time being, such an approach is in limbo.'

The return of power from national union leaders to the shop-floor has been a marked aspect of industrial development during the 1970s. It has certainly had its repercussions in the motor industry. Pat Lowry says: 'It was easier, more comfortable and tended to be more authoritarian when all dealings were with the national centre—management preferred it.' Now he believes the pendulum is swinging back towards the centre after this devolution right down to the shop-floor. He sees the development of a new series of bargaining arrangements which combine national officials, local officials and shop stewards, that he thinks will be both more authoritative and more responsible.

Like others in industry Lowry sees part of our industrial problems stemming from the *them* and *us* attitudes in society; these in turn arise out of inadequacies in the educational system. Of every 100 young men who enter the motor industry at the age of eighteen or nineteen he reckons that as many as ninety have reached their career maximum by the age of twenty except for the economic increments the unions may get for them. 'They have been denied a system of education which would enable many of them to make that leap from semi-skilled or even skilled shop-floor status to something more senior. To that extent,' he says, 'I think the barriers which the social system of this country has erected do mean that the "aggro" at industry level is that much greater. I do not believe that people remove their prejudices and their frustrations with their overcoats when they come to work. If they are dissatisfied with the place society has allotted them, they will take their grievances to the workplace and there it is possible to express oneself collectively rather than as an individual. This fact—the ability to express themselves collectively in the workplace—enhances the problems created by the social stratification of this country.'

Lowry thinks that a failure of management has been in its over-concentration upon the need to find short-term solutions to problems often at the expense of long-term needs. He adds: 'We have almost been brought up to believe that if the unions want something strongly enough, then management perforce has no option but to concede. Management has made this problem more difficult by not being consistent in its reactions to problems—the whole question of discipline, for example. I could apply all this to BL and our critics would say: "you are in such a bad way you ought to have done these things years ago," which is fair criticism. Nonetheless, it would still be easy for BL to be inconsistent and not face problems when they arise because we believe that peace is necessary if we are to survive. We have been more consistent, however, in the last few years.'

Management in recent years has fallen into the habit of expecting some outside body, either government or unions, to do part of its job for it. Says Lowry: 'Managements have demanded a framework of industrial law, for example, to cover industrial relations, yet when they had it they did not use it. Or management demands a sense of responsibility from the trade unions, forgetting that that is not what the unions are in business for. Trade unions are not there to be "responsible"; they exist to improve or maintain the living standards of their members. It is when we ask trade unions to do things which they are not in business to do that relations go wrong, since we shout "irresponsible" if they do not do what we ask.'

What Lowry would like to see is companies returning to an older tradition of taking greater responsibility themselves and managing; a point made by other industrialists in relation to the present British scene.

Finally, Lowry would like to see new employee commitment to the company for which he works. 'There is a tremendous task to be achieved in securing employee commitment to the business. We have not yet done it and this lies very much in the hands of management. It is not the job of the trade unions to teach our employees about BL and its problems; they have got their view of BL and of events in the company and they have a right to ensure that their members know what those views are. But we and many other companies have got a massive job to do to change employee attitudes so as to secure their commitment to the company.'

Bob Ramsey is director of industrial relations for Ford in Britain. Ford deal with some eleven manual unions and three salaried unions and Ramsey says management has worked very hard during the 1970s at getting the institutions for bargaining right. Today the bargaining unit is the entire company, which he believes is a crucial development. There is only one bargaining table for all employees and only one negotiating committee representing the eleven manual unions. This structure means the eleven unions have first to agree a strategy before they bargain with management: then they enshrine what is said in a written agreement, the company obligations and employee obligations. Since each union has to sign the agreement this means each has the right of veto; it also means that if one union holds back, none gets anything and so creates a sense of inter-union responsibility. Such agreements are normally for one year, though they may be for longer. Ramsey argues that the system works well when there is no government incomes policy, no doubt with 1978 in mind. Then Ford broke the five per cent norm and the employees broke their agreement with the company a month before it was due to expire, the men arguing 'we agreed not to strike for twelve months but you are not bargaining freely, you have made an offer which is dictated by the government, therefore we are not bound by our agreement.'

Britain is notorious for unofficial stoppages. Ramsey argues that the habit has become ingrained: 'put on the pressure and you will get a quick answer'. 'What is not understood in this situation,' he says, 'is that the use of such tactics means you become an unreliable organisation and fail to impress the customer and so eventually lose your markets.' Such behaviour, he believes, is part of the reason why Britain has got its present unemployment problems; why we have our present standard of living compared with that enjoyed by our main competitors. Ramsey argues that the undisciplined approach to bargaining that is so prominent a feature of union behaviour, especially in the motor industry, lies at the root of many British productivity problems: 'If you look at companies abroad—I see their results every day—they always make their schedules, they never fail; they might once in a blue moon have a wage dispute, although they do not even have that in Germany—but they may in Belgium or Spain and these can be quite bitter while they last—but once settled, then the following day the schedule is met and this continues month after month thereafter.' In Ford Britain, however, the schedule is not met very often.

In the last few years Ford has done better with its programmes and can compete very well in Britain, where it is a highly successful company. Yet translate this performance overseas and it is not at all the same success story. Ramsey points out that if there are a number of production centres and all but one complete their schedules, it is obvious where the customers will go and which will attract the investment.

Much of Ford's production problem results from stoppages by possibly no more than fifteen or twenty workers: these disputes concern employees required to work more effectively, the introduction of new processes, employees who do not wish to be moved from one job to another and a variety of other causes. Overseas, Ramsey says, unions would not permit stoppages about such problems nor would the workers walk out over them; rather, they would use existing procedures to solve whatever the problem might be. This does not happen in Britain: instead, there is a walkout (the reason for the tough disciplinary code introduced by Ford in November 1980). Like many others Ramsey sees industrial relations in Britain (habits which date back to the Industrial Revolution) as essentially adversary based, trade unions against management.

Today, however, the position of the work people is immensely strong, more so than that of management, yet the adversary approach continues. Workers can in fact ruin a company any time they choose. As Ramsey argues, modern society has become so interdependent with everyone relying upon the efforts of everyone else that any small group, sewage workers, airline pilots, computer operators, is in a position to stop vast areas of activity. And since people know they possess such power, they tend at times to want to use it. Thus the problem is greater than simply union-management relations: it is a question of diffuse power. The power to disrupt exists and is being used more: in the civil service and the National Health Service, for example, and the trade union movement is often too weak to prevent such disruptions. Moreover, the movement is unused to disciplining its members or telling them to stick by agreements they have made.

What Ramsey would like to see in industry is a return to customer orientation. 'It is all about the customer,' he says. 'Without the customer there is nothing. The customer is the boss and it is up to us to please the customer so that whatever we do, however much management and employees may disagree, we do not behave in such a fashion as to alienate the customer, which is what we have done.'

A major problem for British industry is government interference: or rather, the changes of industrial policy which come with every change of government. It is a factor which on the whole Britain's industrial rivals do not have to contend with. 'Getting British industry efficient is as important as trying to solve the

Ulster problem; there are some things which are serious enough to warrant a bit of working together,' says Ramsey.

Looking for the ideal relationship with a huge workforce in an industry which has seen more than its share of industrial problems over the years, Ramsey contends that the basis for such a relationship exists. 'The only relationship management wants with its workforce is one where, since we have set up the requisite institutions to transact business, they use them. If, for example, one of the unions says "why don't you alter this or that" we look at it; the institutions are there and I think we are communicating about as much as we can.

'We want two things: we want the unions to accept that the procedures are adequate, that they really should be used and that we should not have any disputes unless we both consciously embark upon them. And second, we want the unions to discipline their members so that these daily disputes do not take place and disrupt the works. We want the unions to discipline their members, not because we say so, but because they should know that unless they do, if agreements are broken there is no way that we shall change the attitudes of the customer towards us, which is what we have to do: and most particularly the attitude of the overseas customer.'

For any automated production industry such as Ford, a key to productivity and success lies in continuity of production and it is the wildcat strikes which so often disrupt that process and hence lead to low productivity. Ramsey says: 'If we could keep continuity of production and make the schedule every day as does Ford in other countries, we would still be left with big problems: overmanning, inadequate preventive maintenance and so on. But once we were making the volume then at least we would be giving the customer what he wants the day we promised it and we would be getting the cash flow. Then there would be a management that was not constantly dealing with a crisis in industrial relations and instead could look more constructively at its normal problems.'

Bob Ramsey's final word upon management-union relations reflects the mood of much other management in industry. 'Many years ago, I used to say management has got to do a great deal to set its house in order; but now, speaking for Ford and I think for large areas of British industry, a great deal has been done to put management's house in order and we have learnt the lessons of the past. We listened very intently to the unions and many of the things we have done were what they suggested. They said:

191

"If you do this or that everything will be better; if you give us a shorter procedure arrangement, if you introduce status quo, if you give us 100 per cent membership agreement, if you give us a better appeals procedure when you discipline people, (if government gives better protection to people when they are thrown out of work), if you introduce lay-off pay for those laid off through no fault of their own; if you do all these things everything will come right." Well, we have done all these things and everything has not come right. In some respects it has got more difficult. So I think we are at the point where we are entitled to say: "We have done quite a bit and now we require a response." '

Some final comments on the motor industry come from David Buckle, TGWU district secretary in Oxford, who looks at the industry from the viewpoint of both a trade union official within whose area the Cowley works fall and as someone who worked for years on the shop-floor at BL.

On the question of declining productivity, Buckle says: 'The figures are there and we cannot escape them. In 1968 BL had 42 per cent of the British market and at the present moment [July 1980] it has 14 per cent. There are a wide range of reasons for this fall in the market share and I do not for one moment exclude the fact that the trade unions have their share of the blame. Though just what the proportion should be I find difficult to calculate.

'I think the British car industry is a victim of a number of circumstances. First, if one looks at Germany, France, Italy and Japan in the immediate post-war years, their industries enjoyed massive government aid in terms of investment. In Britain, on the other hand, the industry was owned by several manufacturers who were each competing within a single market, which meant that none could be very efficient. They were concerned with looking after the shareholders and the industry suffered from lack of real capital investment. BL was formed in 1968 and in the Ryder Report it was shown that in the period 1968 to 1974, while the company made a net profit of £74 million, only £4 million of that was ploughed back into the industry and £70 million went to the shareholders. Now that is a classic example of the problem facing British car manufacturers: the serious lack of capital investment.

'Further, for political reasons, governments have been afraid to put money into the company because of possible reactions either from the opposition or the public. The Labour Government of

1974 did put money into the company but did not give this to the company as is popularly believed but lent it at severe interest rates. So the industry has suffered from lack of capital investment.'

On the question of the attitude of car workers—even when they have comparable machinery to their overseas counterparts, they often produce less—Buckle can speak from personal experience. He says: 'I tell you my attitude when I worked in the industry for fourteen years and I do not think it varies much from everybody else's. In the 1950s and 1960s the car industry was used as an economic regulator by successive governments. If the economy was going well then the industry was left alone; if the economy got into difficulties then the industry was hit—hire purchase controls or other instruments were used—either to contain or to expand the industry so that the workforce found they were on short time one week and then were asked to work excessive overtime the next, and this sort of thing happened overnight. It was not something that came after several weeks' notice. You could arrive at work on a Monday morning and be told: "Sorry, the market has collapsed over the weekend, there is no work, come back in a fortnight." It used to happen just like that and in the early 1960s many thousands of workers were sacked. At one time, for example, BLMC announced 12,000 redundancies overnight; as a result the attitude which developed among car workers was as follows: "If this industry is going to be used as an economic regulator; if we are going to be sacked one day or told we have got to work excessive overtime another day, then we will try to pace our work over a long period of time so that there is not this job insecurity which we have experienced over the past years." That feeling of pacing the work and so of ensuring job security runs very deep in British car factories.

'Another reason why attitudes are so bad at BL, results from the fact that up to 1971 there had been a long experience of piece work so that although workers were "pacing" their work they could also maximise their earnings if they wished: there was an incentive for those who wanted to use it. In 1971 Pat Lowry, the personnel director of Leyland, said: "We are not going to have any more piece work in these factories, it is degrading for workers to have incentive schemes, they can simply work the normal eight hours." We warned the company of the dangers of such a policy, but they rejected our advice: we told them they would have substantially to increase the labour force to obtain the same production under a measured day work system to produce the same

193

output as they did under piece work. At Cowley the average increase in manpower to produce the same output under the measured day work system (instead of the piece work system) was 25 per cent. That policy ran for nine years and then in October 1979 Pat Lowry said on television that "the only way we can encourage the workers to produce more in Leyland is to offer them an incentive scheme." I heard him say it and it took him—and the company—nine years to learn the lesson.'

Buckle would like to see the company being run with a real system of consultation between management and workers, so that decisions about such matters as piece work are arrived at by management and unions sitting down together to see jointly how they may improve the viability of the company. He does not believe there is any chance of that happening under the present BL management regime.

Public Sector Views

The British economy is mixed and though the greater part is still private the public sector contains vast industries of crucial national importance as well as covering hundreds of thousands of employees in the civil service and local government. Public sector or nationalised industries include coal, gas, electricity, telecommunications, railways, ports and harbours, steel and water, as well as border line industries such as BL, which, though not technically nationalised, depend upon government for their investment income.

Kenneth Young is board member for personnel and industrial relations in the Post Office and has functional responsibility across the corporation for manpower resources and utilisation, and for collective bargaining. The Post Office employs 400,000 people and deals with eight unions, the largest of which is the UCW.

Sir Peter Parker is chairman of British Rail. He came to the industry after wide experience in the private sector and presides over British Rail at a time when inflation, cutbacks in public spending and massive competition from road transport for both freight and passenger custom make it exceptionally difficult to ensure a profitable railway system.

The views of these two men clearly reflect a different approach to industry from those of industrialists in the private sector; in both cases, too, they face a more compact situation with regard to trade unions which are nearer to being industrial unions in the Post Office and British Rail than is the case across most of the rest of British industry.

On the subject of union power, Kenneth Young believes that although abuses are found in relation to disputes, a more general form of abuse is union resistance to desirable change: it is often extremely difficult to win union support for changes which are required for the future of a business and its customers and, therefore, for those who work in that business. Such resistance to changes which threaten traditional and entrenched positions is no different among unions than in other institutions, but it is there. Secondly, he believes union power is misused when unions, or groups of their members, unofficially take industrial action too precipitately in pursuit of a particular claim.

As far as the Post Office is concerned, Kenneth Young claims that the history of industrial relations has not included frequent outbreaks of industrial action of a disruptive kind. He believes that unions are probably too powerful in relation to society as a whole and argues in this respect that within the Post Office industrial relations are fairly advanced: there is a history of union recognition so that over a long period of time both management and unions have been able to develop and refine a fairly sophisticated framework for collective bargaining.

'In industries such as this,' Young says, 'I am not normally conscious of our unions being too powerful—except in the sense of slowing down the pace of change.' On the wider national scene, however, Young says that the 'winter of discontent' was an extreme case and that 'I find it impossible to believe that what happened then can be described in terms other than an abuse of union power.'

Young is both ideologically and pragmatically in favour of unions. He says: 'I do not believe that management is free to deal unilaterally with issues that we now regard as being legitimate trade union interests; that management devoid of trade union pressures would in fact do as good a job of resolving the human problems which arise.'

Sir Peter Parker believes the unions are too powerful in a special sense: 'They possess considerable power and are an estate of the realm. The problem,' he says, 'is how that power is used. I think they have too much power in one sense: that if they wish to be an estate of the realm they must assume the responsibility of an estate of the realm. Before the First World War the employer had too much power and when left simply to pursue his own ends, these were likely to unbalance the general common wealth of society. When his *raison d'être* was no more than to satisfy his shareholders or maximise his profits, then he had too much power. Modern managers, I think, now admit to their basic social responsibility and must try to see their role within a wider social purpose.'

'Now the unions face a similar problem: they have very considerable power, but if they only use it to protect the interests of their members that would seem a failure in terms of their social responsibility. Just as the employers had social responsibility and now admit it, so the unions have social responsibility beyond their membership, but at present do not admit it. In summary, then, power which is exclusive power is too much in a democracy; second, the unions can be tempted to assert this power of theirs in an anti-democratic way.'

Sir Peter describes how trade union leaders sometimes talk in terms reminiscent of the Duke of Newcastle in the eighteenth century: ' "I have got eleven members, I know J—— has twenty-four"—and they mean members of parliament. So we are really talking of people who are exercising power as a corporate force in a corporate state way outside the parliamentary processes,' he says, 'and that could be highly dangerous in the long run.'

Looking at union action during the much publicised and, as he describes it, 'humiliating' 'winter of discontent', Sir Peter says: 'It seems to me it is not good enough trade unions saying they are there simply to protect the interests of their members if that means inflicting intolerable harm on standards of decency in the society. The strike weapon must be one of last resort, not first resort; and there is also the question of self-control. A trade union leader cannot just look after the interests of his members in our inter-linking modern society; that is not enough. If you are the leader of any of the estates of the realm you have to balance your own, necessarily selfish purposes with a wider purpose.'

Union power grew as a result of economic conditions in the boom years of the fifties and sixties when management could 'buy' its way out of problems. Fleet Street, Sir Peter suggests, is a perfect example of this process: it has 'bought' its way out of industrial problems to such an extent that today the trade unions are almost invulnerable.

After the Second World War better management, often with some sense of guilt from the past, felt it had to get its relationship with its workforce right. There grew up a new feeling that management and labour between them had 'to rely upon education, better communications, better consultation and then in the old liberal spirit they would come to see the logic of a situation: the two sides of industry would come round to sensible conclusions and moderate ways and see that they were interdependent. Thus, if management dared to share its problems, perhaps this would induce the unions to dare to listen and then both would dare to sort things out together and there would follow a declaration of interdependence.

'But the really frightening development has been that while more consultation and more communication has taken place, the unions have said, in effect: "Right, if we have that much power we shall use it." And the test is simply: "it's in the interests of my members." There is a sense of "now it is our turn".'

A wide range of reasons have been advanced to explain low British productivity. Kenneth Young does not believe this has anything to do with the inherent quality of British workers. He does think that union structure plays a part: there are too many unions; demarcations between them in particular industries are not clear; and employer-union procedures in Britain, unlike on the Continent, have always been conducted on a voluntary basis as opposed to having a strongly supportive legal framework.

However, Young believes that low productivity is less to do with unions than with management and levels of investment and the vacillations of government policies. He argues that the most noticeable disparities of performance, as between British and overseas productivity, are positively correlated with the degree of capital investment in support of the workers. There has been less capital investment in some sectors of British industry than in those of other countries.

The Post Office itself now has the biggest investment programme of perhaps any British industry, running at the rate of £1,500 million a year, mainly for modernising what is now an antiquated telecommunications system. The cost is enormous, yet essential to make the system more reliable, more versatile and more saleable in export terms. The Post Office is doing this out of profits, out of depreciation and borrowing. But until the British system has been modernised, Young does not believe that it is easy to make true productivity comparisons with systems such as those in the USA or Canada.

Sir Peter Parker enumerates the usual reasons for low productivity first: Britain's apparently strong position after the Second World War while her main rivals in fact were revamping their industries from scratch; what he calls her 'imperial size hangover' —the assumption that the markets were there for us and that we did not have to try very hard: British complacency. One of the reasons why Britain did not compete effectively over the last thirty years was because we were not fighting in world markets so much as operating reasonably well in traditional markets. But huge changes were taking place and many of Britain's traditional markets have dwindled or disappeared.

Much more important, however, are attitudes to management and productivity. Thus, Sir Peter says, it is only in the last ten to fifteen years that Britain has looked seriously at business schools to produce professionalism in management. Further, 'the trade unions have hardly bothered about the problems of productivity— the whole tradition of the Labour movement and indeed of the Labour Party has been to take productivity for granted. The problem (from the viewpoint of Labour) has been one of distribution of wealth. And, for example, in the works of such Labour "gods" as Tawney and Cole, management is not mentioned in the indices. Indeed, it is regarded as something rather feeble, the lackey of capitalism. The tradition of the political left in Britain has been to assume that production would somehow emerge anyway. The trade union movement has taken production for granted; it has also taken its own professionalism for granted and only recently has it gone in for proper training for itself.'

Sir Peter makes the point that the trade unions do not yet take seriously the importance of education and training of their own people, so that in collaboration with management they may face problems together. Everything is compartmentalised: business schools for management and other schools for trade unions. 'We have lacked the common social basis of common ground and common sense that exist in this area in the other great trading nations of the world. Too often still the trade unions are fighting old battles and securing positions which had been denied to them in our earlier industrial society when their comparative position was different.'

There is an assumption that the trade union movement favours the nationalised industries for ideological reasons and because it is considered to be easier to obtain what they want in terms and conditions from a state industry than from private enterprise. Kenneth Young certainly accepts that the unions like the concept of nationalised industries. 'This has,' he says, 'much more to do with the kind of political link between unions generally and the Labour Party than perhaps anything else. The unions tend to subscribe to the philosophy of public ownership; and they tend to be suspicious of private enterprise and profit. And here let me make another point: one of Britain's problems is that we regard profit as a dirty word. The concept of profit is still insufficiently understood. Too many people associate it with shareholders' dividends and think of it in terms of an unearned handout to the rich. There are massive misconceptions on this score among trade union rank and file, so a major educational task needs to be undertaken. Profit is not dirty: it is earned in Iron Curtain countries and needs to be earned here.

'Now this misconception can more easily be overcome in the case of a nationalised industry where it is assumed all profits are ploughed back.'

Young, however, disputes the assumption that trade unions can more easily exploit nationalised industries than they can private ones. 'If you examine what happens to pay across the whole of British industry over a reasonable period of five or ten years, then in times of relative boom and buoyancy, earnings in the private sector have tended marginally to outstrip those in the public sector. Moreover, for this purpose, it does not matter whether you look at the public sector as a whole or only the trading nationalised industries. Conversely, in times of relative recession earnings in the public sector tend to outstrip those in the private sector. Over a period of ten years it is difficult to conclude that pay increases are more easily obtained in the nationalised industries than in private companies.'

Sir Peter stresses the importance of demonstrating that a national enterprise can be successful: 'There is the feeling that nationalised industries have got a reputation for failure, otherwise they would not be nationalised. There is a kind of permanent smog over the public enterprises.' Because the trade unions concerned with British Rail support the concept of nationalisation, Sir Peter believes they are more likely to back a chairman who also clearly believes in the concept. The relations with the unions are somewhat different to those with unions in the private sector: they feel the unions are statutorily placed in the consultative process.

Sir Peter assumes that we belong to a corporate society: 'Initiatives are with various corporate groups—private or public giants, employers or unions. They are all key components in a corporate society and I begin from the undodgeable fact that we are in a corporate society. The whole philosophy, therefore, must be to find the right balance between the conflicting pressures. In such a corporate society—if you want to keep it democratic and prevent it becoming a corporate state—you have to say that there exist a set of competing claims on the country's attention and that in the balance of these corporate powers there is a competitive relationship. This means facing the trade unions, for

200

example, as one of the key powers in society with their responsibilities which must be bigger in purpose than simply their own more limited goals. At the same time corporate relationships are also adversary relationships and it is the adversary aspect of these relationships which ensures the continuation of democracy.'

On the subject of union involvement beyond pay and conditions Young says: 'I believe it is inescapable in practice that unions should express an interest beyond the pay and conditions which they negotiate. That I think is their prime responsibility. But it is unrealistic to expect the unions to discharge their responsibility without attempting to influence other elements in the total social wage. It is unrealistic for an employer—whether government or in the private sector—to expect to determine pay without regard to prices. Once you accept that fact it is only a short step to saying that unions have an interest in general government policy and from that follows their interest in the quality of life, the standard of living and the use of taxation for desirable social ends. The reality is that governments must expect unions to argue about how the economy is managed.'

Many of the discussions about British unions and industrial performance come back to education—or lack of it—and British class attitudes. Sir Peter says that one thing which is urgently required is to 'deodorise' the management-trade union relationship in terms of class. It should not be a class adversary position, although sadly and all too often this in fact is what it develops into. Britain still has class problems of a kind which are not to be found in the USA or other countries. Looking at West Germany, he says: 'If you take the German scene, which is particuarly important to us, there was a basic defeat shared by the whole common man in Germany and arising out of this common defeat and humiliation there are now very strong unions and very strong employers, but there is not the class relationship in that corporate struggle.' In Britain, on the other hand, 'we drag attitudes round behind us like a ball and chain the whole time and they slow up everything. This, for example, is the problem of the unions in that so many of them have become closed orders, worlds within themselves. They are welfare states within a welfare state; it is the ambition of a strong union to look after its own and this has produced almost separate breeding in the industrial community. These attitudes spring from the whole educational old-fashionedness in Britain. We have not invested enough in public education as the Americans and Germans have: there, any family, whatever its wealth, can *trust* its children to the public system. We, on the other hand, have allowed our educational system to be pickled: it perpetuates class differences and these reflect themselves in the *haves* and *have-nots* in terms of power in the industrial community. Thus there exist very galling conditions for those who are on the wrong side of the class or educational barriers in our society, and in an egalitarian world we seem still to be clanking about with old-fashioned attitudes on both sides of the negotiating table.

'The situation is becoming more class-militant, not less, more split, less coherent. The class struggle has revived, misbegotten by our mismanagement of the post-war economy. Class warriors are to be found in both Parliament and industry, and with them you are fighting a different battle.'

The Middle Ground

Harold Macmillan, eighty-six years old, was interviewed on BBC television by Robert Mackenzie during October 1980.* He argued persuasively that any solution to Britain's problems of recession, low productivity and unemployment required a middle approach, a consensus. At the present time, he said, the British disease was 'really the apparent determination of everybody to take more out of the pot than they are putting in. . . . It isn't really a wage problem, British wages are rather low compared to German and Continental wages. It's because of the lack of productivity, modern plants, modern methods and modern usage.' Harold Macmillan believes reflation to be the answer: 'Not to make more people out of work, hanging about doing nothing, but to use the plant and machinery to make more wealth.'

Macmillan is opposed to dogma from either side and he argued on this occasion: 'Both sides now seem to want confrontation. . . . They want to have a row, they want to fight. . . . You have got to get people to have a reasonable degree of argument about where we are going.'

That thought could well be applied to the British industrial scene.

Many people on the political and industrial right and left in Britain dislike the so-called middle ground: tripartism or reliance upon such bodies as the NEDC; they dislike such approaches because they are committed to a full-blooded dogma—either of free enterprise and its latest manifestation, monetarism; or of further state intervention and nationalisation. The result is intense partisanship which produces violent swings first in one direction and then another as governments change, thus ensuring a lack of industrial policy continuity which is responsible for a good many of the country's problems.

There are a number of institutions which occupy the middle

* Quotations from this broadcast are reproduced by courtesy of the BBC.

ground. It is their function in a variety of ways to bring the two sides of industry together and encourage joint approaches and a search for joint solutions.

John Garnett is the director of the Industrial Society, a practical body concerned with communication in industrial relations—agreements, leadership, structures—anything concerned with people. The society is ruled by a council, which draws its members from leaders in both industry and the trade unions. It is, Garnett claims, a totally practical body entirely concerned with those factors which involve people at their work.

William Daniel, an industrial sociologist, works for the Policy Studies Institute (PSI) on projects covering the unemployed and industrial relations and has spent a great deal of time studying employment, labour relations and, therefore, the unions.

Sir Richard O'Brien is the chairman of the Manpower Services Commission, which was established in 1974 to run the public employment and training services; in his job he is accountable to the Secretary of State for Employment as well as the Secretaries of State for Scotland and Wales. Members of the commission are appointed after consultation with the TUC, the CBI and associations which represent local authority and education interests. Sir Richard's previous experience has been in the engineering industry.

Jim Mortimer is the chairman of the Advisory, Conciliation and Arbitration Service (ACAS), which was set up in 1974 and whose principal roles are to help good industrial relations, to encourage the extension of collective bargaining and to help in the development and, where necessary, the reform of collective bargaining machinery. Mortimer came to ACAS from a mixed union and management background: the draughtsmen's union, DATA; and as board member for personnel and industrial relations at London Transport. He had also served as a full-time member of the National Board for Prices and Incomes.

Geoffrey Chandler is the director-general of the National Economic Development Office. The NEDC was set up at the beginning of the 1960s under the Macmillan Government and includes ministers, trade unionists and employer representatives. It is the chief of the tripartite bodies. Geoffrey Chandler came to it from Shell.

Michael Shanks is chairman of the National Consumer Council, a government body with relatively little power. The council's terms of reference are broad and vague: to identify and represent the consumer interests. The theory is to provide a counter weight for consumers to the pressures of the TUC and CBI. Michael Shanks made a major impact with his book *The Stagnant Society* published at the beginning of the 1960s, in which he argued that class barriers and traditional values combined to produce the stagnant society.

Drawing from a wide range of experience in the industrial field, these men are talking here in their personal capacities.

Union power is the theme of this book, yet the more it is examined, the more complex do its ramifications appear. John Garnett says that the old idea of unions with the general secretary at the top and the members below whom he instructed and if necessary disciplined, has totally changed. Nowadays, 'A union is an inverted pyramid where the members are at the top and the general secretary is at the bottom and it is the members who instruct the general secretary, not the other way round. Until one understands that union power is not about the role of officials at the top, but about how one begins to win the hearts and minds of the membership, one does not begin to understand what it is all about.'

What people have failed to see over the last ten or more years, Garnett argues, is that the problem concerns creating more wealth: arguments about distribution are pointless unless there is something to distribute.

William Daniel differentiates between the positive and negative aspects of union power: the power to do things and the power to prevent things being done. In economic and management terms he sees union power as being mainly negative: the unions, he says, tend to fill the role of a permanent opposition. 'Management proposes and unions oppose until their consent is won. When management proposes changes the unions look for snags; they will not accept a change until satisfied it will not damage the interests of their members.' On the positive side unions work towards creating a social structure and distribution of income that are equitable in social rather than economic terms. The trade unions take the view that people should be paid according to the work they do rather than market circumstances. As Daniel says: 'I find it difficult in relation to the British trade union movement to see examples of positive use of power. I have the impression that Continental unions are much more active in terms of themselves initiating change in relation to industrial democracy, work sharing, reducing unemployment, in relation to the organisation of work and job enrichment, in relation to the use of manpower and investment. The European unions have been much more inclined than the British unions to say: "These are the things we have to promote positively in order to serve the interests of our members." '

Sir Richard O'Brien would like to see the unions reorganise themselves in order to be able to exercise legitimate power more effectively. The unions are in competition with each other in Britain. As a result, he believes, this weakens effective union power as well as the opportunity for it to be wielded responsibly. At the same time such weakness encourages the positive fragmentation of power which may, therefore, be used in ways that do not in fact promote the interests of the membership and are damaging to both employers and other people.

Speaking of union power's general drift back to the shop-floor in recent years, Sir Richard says: 'I do not regard this as necessarily unfortunate at all; what I am concerned about is creating at the individual firm level a clear bargaining structure which locates power where it ought to be.'

Jim Mortimer does not believe unions have too much power and he argues that in relation to other union movements, Sweden for example, the British movement has less formal power than they do. He sees the basic British problem as being economic and that has a symptomatic effect upon industrial relations.

Michael Shanks says: 'My own ideal has always been to move towards the Scandinavian or West German situation where undoubtedly the unions do exercise more influence than in this country: in that sense they are more powerful. But they are also more powerful in the sense of being better disciplined: they have more internal power, with the leadership more able to commit members. The problem with the British trade unions is that they have a considerable degree of external power through their influence upon the Labour Party and therefore on Labour Governments, but they have relatively little internal power in the sense that they have great difficulty in committing their members to policies. It is this discrepancy between their external power and their internal lack of power or lack of discipline which causes the problems.'

Perhaps of greater interest are Michael Shanks's reflections upon the direction of union growth and development. 'At present,' he says, 'not only are they very unpopular—all public opinion polls reveal the same message—but they have been unable to prevent massive rises in unemployment, while in many ways technology is working against them because, with the advent of the silicon chip, the possibility becomes increasingly likely that operations may be decentralised. There could be a move back almost to cottage industries and should that be the case it would create a situation where it becomes very difficult for the unions to break in: for example, in the computer software business where the degree of unionisation is still very low.

'Thus it seems that already union strength is being restricted to the declining sectors of the economy and the public sector, while in the new expanding areas of the economy the unions are weak. It is possible that in the 1980s we shall move nearer to the American pattern—in contrast to Europe during the 1970s—where the unions have lost power and membership very sharply. Such a development will not necessarily be to the advantage of society: a declining and bitter trade union movement fighting hard to protect its positions (which could be the pattern of the eighties) would as a consequence be less amenable to the interests of the broad public since their own interests were becoming more and more those of a minority. What we are now seeing in the printing industry in *The Times*, could be an example of what we may well see in other industries during the 1980s. In other words the country is moving away from the possibility of the Swedish or German union pattern to one where the unions have less influence.'

Industrial relations in Britain are certainly cause for enough expressions of concern. John Garnett says, 'It is primarily the job of those who manage industry and commerce to get people to co-operate and if people do not give of their best it is not the fault of the unions or the government or anybody else, but those who manage: that is what they are there for.' Britain, Garnett argues, is ahead of the world in problems in industry because it was the first country to industrialise. Thus, he says: 'If you are the first country which has given unto each according to his need or somewhere near this, you will also be the first country to run into problems: of how you get from each according to his ability. It is only when you have achieved the first that you have problems with the second. When you can earn as much money lying in bed as coming to work you have some real problems of persuading people with high expectations to come and do the kind of work that has to be done if we are to create the wherewithal to meet the expectations.'

On this theme, Sir Richard O'Brien believes in a precisely

defined relationship between management and labour so that each side knows the legitimate role of the other. He does not believe that such a relationship between management and unions should be confined solely to money; it should in addition embrace the whole economic strategy of the company and there should be a continual exchange between the two sides based upon the developing facts of the situation in which they find themselves.

Jim Mortimer claims that because of a long period of slow economic growth, industrial relations have suffered since there is less margin to share between the competing claims of different groups in society. Today, he says, 'We are actually in a declining economy and that does not provide a basis for good industrial relations; it may provide the basis for fear, but that is not good industrial relations.'

The Industrial Society teaches aspects of management communication. John Garnett argues the need for management to ensure that there must be supervisors ready to spend twenty minutes once a month bringing their immediate teams round them to inform them about what the company or their part of it achieved during the previous month. In 1980, about 500 companies in Britain had adopted some such method of communications downwards.

Sir Richard O'Brien is somewhat sceptical of union complaints that they do not get enough information from management. Some companies go to great lengths to operate works committees and these often face great difficulties: apathy, the difficulty of reaching the shop stewards or of interesting the membership. Management has many other things to do, he says, and suggests it may spend too much rather than too little time these days on industrial relations. Multinational firms, for example, claim that it is extraordinary how much time management in Britain has to spend on industrial relations compared with overseas and that this is to the detriment of the business. 'Therefore,' says Sir Richard, 'while it is, of course, correct that too little information is often provided, it is also correct to say that there is far too little interest in receiving the information when it is provided. There is need for a formal structure for passing on information and the information then passed must be genuine. It cannot be a question of merely talking to shop stewards or producing glossy accounts.'

Michael Shanks thinks that half the problem depends not upon whether you consult, but with whom you do it. 'A difficulty with our trade unions,' he says, 'which you do not find to the same extent in Scandinavia or Germany, is that a power struggle is going on all the time within the unions, between the officials and the shop stewards. This does not apply to all unions, but where it does the officials are often being left increasingly on the side because, certainly in the private sector, the people who actually wield the power and influence are the shop stewards. If as management you are going to consult, therefore, the people you need to consult with and bring along with you are the shop stewards. There is little point talking to the general secretary in some trade unions because he is too remote. Even his local officials are often remote as well and not trusted by the shop stewards. Thus in the private sector at least, power is moving steadily away from the union officials to the shop stewards.'

The search for an explanation which can adequately cover Britain's low productivity performance is endless and circular: few people pretend there is any simple or easy solution. John Garnett, for example, thinks there is an element of overprotection which derives from our former possession of the old imperial markets and the ideas their possession induced. There is, he says, the need to understand the economic facts of life instead of being protected from them. The fact that Britain is the most socially advanced country in terms of the protection it accords to the rights of the individual, also means a higher degree of expectation of rights without, necessarily, an accompanying sense of obligation.

Sir Richard O'Brien says we all know that productivity in Britain is low. He goes on: 'This is deplorable because there is no reason why it should be low. In fact it is very high in certain parts of industry compared with others: thus in particular factories our production is as high or higher than that of rivals overseas. Such examples are too few, yet they show it can be done.'

Having stated his belief that we have the capacity to produce as well as anyone else, Sir Richard looks for causes. 'In part it is a cultural phenomenon and there is no one answer to the problem. In part it lies with our inability as a nation since the Second World War to agree upon long-term policies for both industry and for our overall economic approach which could command general support so as to have been pursued all the time, no matter which party was in power, although there would no doubt have been different emphases. This failure has been very damaging to industry.

'It is very difficult to be clear about management competence: there is evidence that when managers go overseas and start managing factories abroad they do as well if not better than their counterparts from other countries, while back in Britain they tend to blame inadequacies upon the trade unions or the government. In the past Britain's management has been too unprofessional. It is dangerous to generalise, but we have had too much emphasis upon virtues connected with public school leadership qualities and too little emphasis upon the technicalities of the job.'

To support his contention about professionalism, Sir Richard says: 'I think you can say that the very dominance of the accountant in the boardrooms of British industry is a commentary upon the other functions that are represented there because the accountant has to be professional, he has to go through certain accountancy hoops; furthermore, he has to produce precise figures. If other people are equally on top of their disciplines the accountant is put in his proper place.'

Jim Mortimer thinks Britain is now suffering from low productivity in especially acute form because we were the first nation to industrialise and so have a heritage of old industry and old-fashioned industry. So when problems arise, they do so in more acute form than in other countries which developed their industrial bases later. 'Further,' he says, 'we have suffered for many years from a low level of industrial investment: this is also part of the price we paid for being an imperial power with heavy overseas investment. It is an ironic fact that ever since World War Two Britain's rate of investment has been much lower than that of Germany; but our rate of overseas investment has been considerably higher.'

The investment circle is one of the keys to British productivity failures. As Mortimer goes on to argue, there has not been enough investment because the returns on capital in British industry have been insufficient and this results from the heritage of old industries. At the same time many potential investors have long felt it to be more profitable to invest overseas and so he sees British imperialism as historically having imposed a tragic burden on British industry, because it focused the direction of our investments outwards instead of inwards.

Geoffrey Chandler sees no single cause for British productivity and industrial failures. He says: 'First and foremost there is no single cause, there is no single villain for the comparative failure of the British economy over the last hundred or so years. It is a very complex matter indeed: it involves government, management, trade unions, the educational system and our inherited culture. Therefore simplistic explanations that the trade unions, government policy, or lack of investment are the cause are just not sustained by analysis. They are all part of the cause. If, for example, you take productivity which simplistically is interpreted to be labour practices, this is a false diagnosis of a very complex chain of failure which involves choice of markets, design of product, quality of product—all of which are management responsibilities—in addition to labour practices to which the word productivity is generally applied.'

On the investment question, Chandler makes the point that while investment per man is less in Britain than among our main industrial competitors, output per unit of investment is also much lower, so that the incentive to invest is diminished: the two elements cannot be taken separately. From this low investment and its possible causes it is natural to move to the subject of restrictive practices, and here Chandler argues that productivity is primarily a management responsibility although requiring trade union co-operation. 'Now the significant thing about the British economy,' he says, 'is not that it is one great disaster area or a number of disaster sectors; it is relative failure compared with our competitors: even in the worst-hit sectors you find individual companies which are internationally competitive. In other words, despite all the factors making for poor performance, good management can achieve good industrial relations, a good product, and there we are capable of leading the world. In almost every sector there are first class companies which are internationally competitive, so we can do it.'

According to Michael Shanks there are two basic reasons for low British productivity: the low rate of capital investment in most British industry since the war; and second, even given the rate of investment, the poor utilisation of labour. The first of these shortcomings is essentially one of management; the second of management and the trade unions, because even when investment has been made the unions have not always co-operated and allowed their skills to be used flexibly. These two reasons interact in a circular fashion: because of inflexibility of labour management has been less ready to invest; and because there has been low investment and therefore low productivity unions have become defensive.

'There are other reasons, however,' Shanks says: 'Behind the failure to invest lies the stop-go policies which have characterised the management of the British economy for most of the post-war period; where government policies have been continually changing, firms have been reluctant to undertake long-term investments because they have not known what their marketing conditions were going to be. In turn the stop-go policies were related to a series of other factors: the attempt to maintain sterling as an international currency when clearly we did not have the resources to do it, the heavy investment in defence spending; now we have the problem of North Sea oil pushing up the exchange rate and so making our goods expensive abroad while imports into Britain are cheap.'

Trade unions are inextricably bound up with British politics: this is the case at present and will be likely to continue despite any arguments to the contrary—that unions confine their activities to the wages and conditions of their members. William Daniel says, 'Given that I see no answers to the problems of managing the economy other than through incomes policy, then I see an overwhelming case for the power of the trade unions freely to negotiate over rates of pay to be reduced. A necessary corollary of that would be that their power in other areas needs to be enhanced.' The other areas where he would see more power go to the unions would be across the entire area of management decision-making in relation to an industrial operation: in other words he sees an overwhelming case for increasing industrial democracy.

Daniel goes on to argue: 'The trade unions are about power; they are about ensuring that people who are deprived of power in terms of formal position and authority have a mechanism through which they can exercise influence on those who are in positions of authority and influence and have formally assigned to them the powers of decision-making.' The argument against trade unions exercising 'power' outside their formal role of looking after wages and conditions of their members—an argument advanced by a number of both Tories and management—is no more than an argument, Daniel says, for the maintenance of the status quo or of conserving the power of those who now possess it anyway.

The question of a social contract in some form is bound to recur during the 1980s. Jim Mortimer believes a contract is possible in an expanding economy in which other steps are also being taken to improve living standards. 'If the purpose of the contract is to reduce living standards it will not work anyway; that is why the last one came unstuck. But the idea that the government of the day and the trade unions should have an

212

understanding—not solely about wages but also about the entire economic environment and the distribution of income in society as well as protecting workers' employment rights—is sensible as a concept.' A social contract, however, has to be about a wide range of subjects: first, incomes which must be expected to rise faster than prices; then the cost of living; taxation policy; the social services; and the distribution of wealth. Such a contract may be acceptable to trade unions.

If on the other hand you try to run the country according to market forces, he argues, then labour is part of those market forces and it is a philosophical contradiction to argue for a market economy and at the same time suggest that unions should restrain themselves: 'If you believe, as I do, that it is not in the interests of the community for the trade unions in all circumstances to secure for themselves the maximum that they can, then you have to accept that restraints and interference with the market will apply in many other areas of the economy.'

Mortimer argues that a form of consensus would only produce a colourless middle. 'You either believe,' he says, 'that you need a sharp turn to the right (which we are getting at the present time) or you believe that you have got to have a stronger social contract policy. What is absolutely vital for the long term is less the politics than the economic issue of increasing the proportion of our resources which are devoted to investment in the community: for economic expansion, creating jobs through an expansion of the public sector. There must be a reversal of the present trend which is to close down plants. What is vital is to increase the level of investment in industry. And not only industry, but the whole range of economic activity.'

Michael Shanks is against Bullock and thinks the time is not ripe for worker directors. He believes the first stage has to be works committees and one of the problems, he suggests, is that Britain did have joint consultative committees during the war, but afterwards they tended to fall into disrepute. Nonetheless, Shanks thinks the starting point for industrial democracy would be to build up shop-floor committees with power to influence the decisions affecting the people they represent. 'My great worry is that industry will move too slowly in this direction and we might, therefore, have Bullock foisted on us out of sheer frustration.'

Many people across the spectrum of politics and industry agree that confrontations arise as a result of the *them* and *us* syndrome which, they think, exacerbates industry's problems.

213

Britain suffers enormously from a certain kind of trade union structure which has grown up because of the way industrial evolution developed and the way the trade unions were formed in the nineteenth century. At the same time Britain is immensely harmed by its class structure in regard to both different classes and different forms of education. Thus management is separated out from the workforce because it is so often public school educated; and even when it is not it adopts the airs of the public schools while the shop-floor never is and so has different assumptions and certain differences of outlook. Even when this is not as true as it may appear to be it seems to be true because of the different ways people speak or act.

There is the further problem of the elaborate difference between basic conditions on the shop-floor and for staff and management and the excessive developement of 'perks': privilege should be related to function although this does not mean that everybody should be paid the same.

Sir Richard O'Brien says: 'You cannot make any sense of British industrial relations unless you know the history and the social structure of the period when industrial relations were set in their present institutional mould round the beginning of the century.'

Geoffrey Chandler also sees *them* and *us* divisions as a factor in the industrial scene, but in a rather different fashion. He says: 'There are two types of division in this country. There are horizontal divisions, which are social divisions that in fact are changing. There are vertical divisions which mean the world of academe, the world of government; the world of industry; the world of journalism and these are far more constipated in their ability to change. There is very little cross-movement between these various divisions. How to change this must be a question of education, yet not simply education at primary, secondary and tertiary levels although those are important. There is also the system of education within industry: we have a particular problem to confront in that we have a stream of trade union education and a stream of management education and they are completely separate, so that there is no testing of the shibboleths of either management or trade unions against a hard debate with the other side. There should be common training for management and trade unions. I should say that there should be no management course without trade union representation and vice versa. They both have their own skills to learn and the negotiating

214

skills of trade unionists must be taught; but these two separate streams, which either implicitly or explicitly appear to be kept deliberately separate, constitute an enormous handicap.'

In a sense this book is about a consensus, or the lack of any such consensus, of what is needed to make British industry perform better. The NEDO is, of course, a consensus body and it is natural that Geoffrey Chandler has some precise things to say about consensus politics: 'Let me define consensus: I do not mean the fudging of policies; I mean an achievement of agreement about what the nature of the economic problem is. And we have to face the fact that one problem in this country is an absence of consensus about productive activity, about the creation of wealth, about profit. If there is doubt about these things that is a powerful reason for joint management-union education so that the prejudices of the one side can be tested against the prejudices of the other and the truth may emerge. Fundamentally, therefore, NEDO is providing a means of getting agreement first on the nature of the problems and second on the nature of the necessary solutions so that ultimately we can provide a better basis for decision-making by the three parties involved, management, unions and government.'

Geoffrey Chandler makes the fundamental point that industrial policy must be essentially bi-partisan. 'If a man from Mars came down and saw how the two sides of industry were allied with two opposing political parties he would think we were mad. The logical alliance is that of management and trade unions. This area of industry has been hag-ridden by changes of government and changes of industrial policy and I believe it is vital that managers, the CBI and the TUC try to take industrial policy out of the political arena. It is fatal to industry that the trade unions are very closely allied to one political party and the CBI and management less closely yet still allied to the other party.'

Asked whether he sees any prospect of industry being left alone by governments in the sense that foreign policy used to be treated as bi-partisan, Michael Shanks answers rather discouragingly: 'Success breeds success and failure breeds failure: in part the choppings and changings of British policy in contrast with those of West Germany result from the fact that while West German policies have manifestly succeeded so that nobody wants to change them, British policies have manifestly failed so every new government tries something new. Thus, if the policies of the present [1980] Government appear to work then it will be much more difficult for a new govement to change or want to change them. Therefore, in one sense everything depends upon how things develop during the term of this Government. The other factor is what kind of Labour Party will emerge from the present party maelstrom. If the Labour Party goes left there is virtually no single plank in the Benn policy which is identical with either the "Healey" policy or the Tory policy and there would be a radical change. There is a need for continuity for almost any policy and almost any policy pursued for long enough is going to be better than a series of changes of policy.'

Discussion of the British malaise can be endless and at least the Thatcher Government has concentrated attention in a wonderful way upon the economic-industrial problems the country faces, whatever one's views of its approach to those problems. The British do not lack the ability to run an advanced industrial society; they produced more per capita in war materials during the Second World War than did any other country including Germany; they are perfectly capable of competing effectively; while currently there are at least signs that people are beginning to realise that competition from abroad is genuine and we cannot continue with a system under which five people produce what elsewhere is produced by three people. Whether these signs of awareness will be translated into something more positive remains to be seen.

There are a variety of ways in which British industry may develop during the 1980s. To a great extent those possibilities depend upon how the unions behave. The stronger unions may, for example, say in effect to their colleagues: we are not interested in you or the aspirations of a wider union movement, we are only concerned to protect our own interests; we are in a strong bargaining position and we are going to exploit it. Such a development could well take place during the eighties. Michael Shanks suggests there is a rising generation of union leaders now operating in areas where in the past there has not been a strong tradition of trade unionism and these leaders have got to justify their existence to their members. It is possible they may behave much more like American trade union leaders than British ones. Should this occur they will go for marked differentials and the argument about comparability will disappear.

Present indications suggest that the world is entering a period of relative stagnation and high unemployment, which could last until the 1990s. Thereafter, as the new technology comes on

216

stream and China emerges as a major trading nation, there could be an improvement and the nineties might be another period of high growth. But as Michael Shanks says: 'It is difficult to be optimistic about the 1980s: it will be a decade of high unemployment and stagnation with Britain perhaps suffering more than most because of its basic weaknesses. The question is whether this period also produces a major shake-out of ideas. I would be very surprised if the trade union movement emerges from this in anything like its present form or with its present philosophy. The unions have got to rethink a great deal of their approach because at the moment all the trends are working against them. I believe we are going to move into a much more decentralised situation where small is beautiful. There is likely to be a return to entrepreneurship simply because the difficulties of managing large centralised organisations are becoming so great. So I believe a new pattern is developing: the trade unions will adjust to this, but I very much doubt whether the TUC as a major force is going to exercise the kind of influence that it did in the 1960s and 1970s.'

Consensus views are always tempting in a situation where manifestly there is a great deal wrong, no matter which political party is in power and what remedies it applies. This is certainly the case as far as the British industrial scene is concerned. Trade unionists, politicians, employers and others all testify to the damage to industry resulting from stop-go policies which depend upon the political party in power. The lesson they draw from such failures leads them to plead for a bi-partisan industrial policy, which in essence asks something that at present appears inherently politically unrealistic: that unions will cut their close bonds with the Labour Party; that employers and the CBI will do the same in relation to the Tory Party; and that—the obverse of this operation—the two political parties will treat industry which is central to the progress and development of the country as outside politics. If this is not to be the case then where do the answers lie?

217

Out of the Impasse

The British are extrovert in their introspection: we have great capacity for analysing our weaknesses; we discuss them at length; we parade our faults as though to do so itself constitutes a virtue. We seem remarkably weak at the present stage in our history in arriving at solutions. Our productivity is low; our industrial relations are bad; the political approach to industry is unbelievably partisan; the unions are negatively reactive; failures are the result of poor management; too little is invested. The list can be extended almost indefinitely and every accusation contains part of the explanation for Britain's current malaise: we are still, to use Michael Shanks's phrase, a stagnant society.

No one anywhere in the pages of this book has suggested that there is anything fundamentally wrong with the British people as people: indeed the contrary is the case. We are inventive, we have great management capacity abroad (and sometimes at home), the British working man is second to none, we are one of the freest societies in the world, especially with regard to the rights of the individual and our potential is very great. What we nonetheless fail to do is realise the potential.

The subject of this book is union power, but union power is not something to be considered in isolation: it has to be related to our industrial and productive performance and that is worse than the performance of our major western industrial competitors—the USA, Japan, West Germany and France. Most assessments of this difference in performance suggest a variety of reasons: that while Britain suffers from all the weaknesses referred to above, the West Germans, on the other hand, have a more sensible union structure; or the Americans are production-profit oriented. These particular arguments are important. Yet what is usually ignored or quickly passed over is the fact that Britain's main industrial rivals, despite their better *productive* performance, have to face at least as many social and political problems as we do in Britain. The recession is worldwide; the rest of Europe does not have Britain's North Sea oil; political discontent with the imbalances of existing systems is as much apparent among the youth of West Germany or the USA as in Britain; interest groups in France are as tenacious of their interests as are any in Britain. So what makes the difference?

Is it, as Nicholas Scott and Tom Jackson both imply, that we have opted perhaps at some unconscious national level for the easier life? Or is it that despite our many national virtues we are also possessed of some special defect peculiar to ourselves? Is the poor level of Britain's industrial performance today really because we industrialised first and must now face the penalties for winning the initial race? Or, as John Gorst argues, is it because we did not have the 'advantage' of defeat at the end of the Second World War with the subsequent opportunity to refurbish our industrial structure? When British unions attempt to use their influence to persuade governments to act according to their interests, are they behaving undemocratically or in markedly different fashion from unions elsewhere and is it wrong, as some on the political right would suggest, to use industrial action to further political aims?

Something like 90 per cent of strikes in Britain are unofficial and this fact, it is often argued, plays a far larger part in holding back production than strikes as such, for Britain is by no means at the top of the strike league among the industrialised nations. Why this indiscipline—if it is indiscipline? The return of union power to the shop-floor has been a major aspect of industrial development during the 1970s. The British are quick enough to lecture the outside world upon the benefits of democracy, yet when the workforce—not necessarily the unions—in fact becomes more democratic in its behaviour (rather than simply accepting the *diktat* of a powerful union boss from on high) we immediately talk of subversive elements or left wing shop stewards who are more interested in politics than the welfare of the workers they represent, forgetting when we make such judgements that politics is supposedly about our welfare anyway.

Many commentators of both left and right suggest that the law is not the way to reform the unions, yet from Barbara Castle's abortive attempt to introduce reforms with her 'In Place of Strife' through to Mr Prior's Bill of 1979, both political parties have been busy with the law as though despite their own expressed reservations laws nonetheless will cure or modernise union behaviour. They will not. As Lord Carr says, there has to be dialogue between government and unions—a fact which the sheer weight of the unions ought to make apparent—yet many members of the Tory Party appear to believe (even if it is not true) that such dialogue is not necessary. In Britain the unions simply cannot and should not be ignored.

Industrialists repeatedly refer to the restrictive practices of the unions which lead to overmanning and they are quite right. But again, to quote Lord Carr, what of the restrictive practices of management leading to overmanning at levels other than the shop floor? And more generally what of restrictive practices in such professions as the law? The unions are too easily made scapegoats for attitudes which prevail across the entire working life of the nation. One problem is the lack of esteem for industry. Does this attitude result solely from the nineteenth-century concern to educate an élite whose primary duty was to be 'service' to the nation, whether running the empire overseas or the government at home? Or is there some other cause?

Management, as politicians and industrialists point out, should manage. Why in so many areas of British industry has it apparently failed to do so? It is all very well to blame the unions for undisciplined behaviour, but how much is this precisely because over a lengthy period of time management has abnegated a substantial and crucial part of its role: the actual control of the conduct of its workforce. Indeed, on its own admission, management has often left a good deal of that task to the unions and now it is reaping the harvest of such neglect.

Tories and management complain that the unions are involved in politics. They protest at this state of affairs either with simulated amazement, as though such conduct is somehow undemocratic, or suggest that the unions took a wrong turn at some point in their history. Such an attitude is nonsense. In the first place, in a democracy such as ours everybody should be involved in politics all the time, and in other contexts Tory politicians are quick enough to talk of political apathy.

In the second place, unions *especially* are concerned with politics. That is why they came into being in the first place and as trade unionists point out, the second clause in any union membership normally concerns *bettering conditions* and this covers a wide spectrum of activity, political and social as well as conditions of work. Britain is a representative democracy which is politically designed to respond to pressure groups. The TUC is one of these pressure groups, as is the CBI. Many Tories imply and some say explicitly that it is an unfortunate aspect of British politics that

220

such close links exist between organised labour and the Labour Party. Those who take such a line should reflect more upon the sources of political funds for the Tory Party.

Many Tories and industrialists lay the blame for the growth of union power—in the sense of indiscipline and the inability of the union hierarchies to control their members—upon poor management and weak rather than strong union leadership at the top. They hanker after the days, now past, when a strong union leader made a deal on behalf of his union members with an equally strong management and subsequently ensured that everyone fell into line.

Disraeli gave the Tories the concept of 'one nation', a concept sadly absent at the present time. Within the scope of that idea it is possible to contain an alliance between trade unions and management, trade unions and the Tory Party, each striving to create more wealth to be shared by all: a united approach to national problems. Yet Tories seem especially shy of this idea today: in the years since 1945, although there have been periods of good Tory-union relations—most notably when Sir Walter Monckton was Minister of Labour—the party has otherwise done little to woo the unions to Tory principles, despite claiming that millions of trade unionists vote Tory. There has been Tory trade union tokenism, which has consisted year after year of one or two rather pathetic right wing union stalwarts being dutifully trotted out at the annual party conference where they give a rousing speech about the independent nature of the working man. They receive an especially rousing cheer which is always reserved for those whose aspirations the party is not about to meet, and then the conference returns to more weighty matters.

The Tory Party, which so often claims to be a national party, has in fact shown a singular inability in recent years to understand the aspirations of a large part of the population who, although they are trade unionists, are neither necessarily left wing or even supporters of the Labour Party.

The Tory MP John Stokes says the unions do not really understand capitalism and are not behind it. This could explain the failure of the Tory Party and the unions as well as management and the unions to come together in the way they do—or are reputed to do—in West Germany and the USA, to discuss the size of the national 'cake' and how it is to be divided. Trade unionists are likely to reply to Mr Stokes that they understand capitalism ony too well, which is why they behave in the way they do.

Political parties, among other things, are in the business of de-

221

livering the 'goods' for their supporters and, as Bob Hughes points out, there are members of the Labour Party who have a sneaking admiration for the way the Tories 'reward their friends'. Politicians like to present themselves as dealing with the national interest; in fact for most of the time they are advancing or retarding particular sectional interests and when a party too obviously lets down its key supporters it runs into electoral trouble, as did Labour with the trade unions in 1979.

The fortunes of the Labour Party and organised labour are in-extricably bound up with each other. Of equal importance is the fact that the trade union movement often has greater ability to help Labour achieve political power than to deliver better wages to its members. Objectively, over a long period of time, the role of the unions has been to defend wages and maintain a *status quo* rather than increase the real power and share of the national 'cake' that belongs to the workforce which the unions represent. As a result of their long history and their battles to ensure that wages did not drop (let alone increase), the unions have become essen-tially defensive in character. This, possibly more than anything else, explains why when they do suddenly find themselves in posi-tions of preponderant strength, as for example the NGA in Fleet Street today, unions go for everything they can get, imbued with the philosophy, however ultimately destructive, that 'it is my turn now'.

It is easy to argue in the abstract that a country should opt for either a planned or a free market economy, but solutions are rarely that simple. It is part of the British political genius—and its failing —to blur edges and not go for logical solutions in the way we like to imagine the French do (currently they have five-year plans for their economy which is in a good deal better shape than Britain's). The nearest we have come to a planned approach that also fits the mixed economy was the social contract of the years 1976–9. That contract failed. This is hardly surprising, since it too rapidly de-veloped into a one-side bargain under which the unions had to curb wages in a retracting economy while government aspects of the contract were not met. A social contract operated under an expanding economy could offer genuine 'social wage' improve-ments in return for trade union restraints in wage demands, and so prevent unbridled claims which depend solely upon the strength of a particular union. At the present time, however, though this approach offers future possibilities it is not the answer to British industrial problems.

Labour Party members and trade unionists may support the concept of a social contract, yet they also make another fundamental point: that confrontation is part of our national structure. As Eric Heffer says: 'We do live in a class society.' And as William Speirs of the STUC argues: 'There cannot be harmony between capital and labour.'

There is another vital question to be asked: does the trade union movement collectively or individually believe in the socialism that its rhetoric suggests? The insistence upon the maintenance of differentials is hardly a socialist principle, yet this is the cornerstone of much union activity. The determination of the strongest unions to use their powers to gain the maximum 'money on the table' may be entirely justified in relation to the interests of the members such unions represent, but it is also to play the capitalist market game of 'the most to the strongest'. It is not socialism. A good deal of dishonesty on this subject exists in trade union circles. Many trade unionists, when challenged about the non-socialist aspects of such behaviour, defend the use of trade union strength in the market in pursuit of the narrow interests of the group with the claim that as long as they are a part of a capitalist economy they are justified in using capitalist techniques. Such an answer evades the issue: when are they going to begin to match their rhetoric and actually behave like socialists? Were the miners to go on strike, for example, not so as to put up their own pay, but in order to secure equal pay with themselves for municipal road sweepers, it would then be possible for the first time to say that socialist principles of solidarity were being applied so as to bring the whole working movement a step closer to socialism. This suggestion will certainly be dismissed as utopian rubbish. Yet its converse exists in Britain today. Individual unions work the capitalist system in a capitalist way to obtain as much for their members as possible. It is precisely because they have been doing this that Mrs Thatcher's Government feels justified in pursuing its monetarist capitalist policies. As Tom Jackson claims, such policies are the obverse of the free collective bargaining that the union movement insists upon. This situation raises another question of whether the broad mass of the organised trade union movement wishes to be socialist at all. On present evidence the answer to that is a resounding no.

Businessmen would like the unions to be enterprise oriented: if they will accept the profit motive and join with management in devising ways to increase wealth for the benefit of everyone, then

223

in return capital would expect tough bargaining for rising wages. This capitalist picture of the two sides of industry working together to increase productivity and wealth is far from contemporary realities.

Some trade unionists see themselves taking part in such a scenario, but many more approach their relationship with capital in a quite different spirit. With the growth of the multinational corporation, for example, they see the decision making process getting further away from British boardrooms anyway, so they believe the chances of greater union or worker participation in board room decisions is receding rather than coming closer, while the management whose decisions ultimately affect their lives is becoming even more faceless than is often the case in the popular imagination at the present time.

A marked feature of trade unions attested to from all sides is their ability to stop things rather than readiness to initiate new developments. This negative aspect of the movement is almost certain to become increasingly dominant during the 1980s should the period continue to be one of recession. In such circumstances the size of the 'cake' for distribution will not grow, unemployment will increase and the new technoogy is likely to threaten many of the jobs that do exist; each of these factors inducing the unions to become more restrictive and negative in their attitudes. Should the unions find their numbers dropping at the same time, then the chances of union reform during the decade will recede still further.

Such developments during the 1980s will make it an uneasy decade for the union movement. If, in addition, the Labour Party remains in opposition as a result of its own internal divisions, then the movement may find itself still further weakened after ten or so years under governments unsympathetic to its cause. It is therefore possible that, contrary to the popular impression of the seventies, the massive and seemingly monolithic structure of the trade union movement will be transformed during the eighties into something weaker and more diffuse with individual unions much more concerned to obtain the best deals possible for their members than to use what strength they possess as part of a wider movement aiming to change the basis of society.

The moderate vision of trade unionists such as Weighell and Jackson, which sees a trade union movement dealing with the government on behalf of all its twelve million members in order to prevent the 'dog eat dog' approach of the strongest going for the most, may become increasingly utopian. There is no indication at present that the stronger unions will surrender any of their bargaining advantages in order to make the movement as a whole more effective.

As David Buckle says, there is no half way house between the capitalist approach and complete state ownership and worker control. If his assessment is correct, the outlook is gloomy: further divisive and damaging political confrontation about how the economy is to be run.

On the capital side of industry—management and the CBI—views are equally entrenched. The CBI is obsessed with the fact that bargaining power is weighted in favour of labour. This point is made repeatedly, yet is it true? As various trade unionists and Labour MPs point out, the share of wealth going to those represented by the labour movement has not greatly altered in fifty years, so how is greater union strength actually being used? Union power has certainly not altered the balance of wealth controlled by the two sides. It is true that labour can be and often is very disruptive—more than in the past—yet often this is a sign of weakness rather than strength. The Day of Action was the despairing activity of a movement that could not get its voice heard by more legitimate means. The 'winter of discontent', despite its ugliness, arose because considerable segments of our society at the bottom of the economic heap had been ignored for too long. They may then have behaved 'irresponsibly', but *what* had society ever done to persuade them to behave responsibly? The thirteen-week steel strike did not prevent mammoth redundancies. It is important to understand that the power to disrupt is not necessarily the power to alter, and this is often the case in the trade union movement at the present time.

Perhaps the greatest area of difficulty lies with attitudes rather than bad management, union restrictive practices or even government interference. There are endless examples of attitudes which inhibit worker-management co-operation. There are the obvious ones of education, public school and non-public school, *them* and *us*. There are far more subtle attitudes, so that sometimes it seems impossible to break through the barriers with which people surround themselves and sometimes people behave as though the one thing they do not want is actually to remove the barriers which exist. Two companies quoted in this book, United Biscuits, which is unionised, and Marks and Spencer which is not, have reputations for very good worker-management relations and lack of industrial strife. When I mentioned this fact to someone on the middle left of British politics, his reaction was a reflex class qualification: 'Well of course they are paternalist,' the single word 'paternalist' being sufficient in his eyes to dismiss their record without further examination. Such attitudes go deep.

There is the question of identification: do workers identify with their company first or their union? The trade union is a safeguard organisation designed to look after workers' interests and protect them against exploitation, and in this respect the unions have a vital role to play. But the union ought not (except for its full time officials) to be the first claim upon a workers' loyalty. In fact it often is, and there are two sorts of reason to explain this phenomenon. The first is negative and often stretches back many years: companies had, even if this is no longer the case, such bad reputations for the way they treated their workforces that these understandably turned first to their unions. Some of these attitudes which place union loyalty before the company, date back to a bleak past whatever changes have since occurred. They constitute an indictment of both the capitalist system in the past and of individual managements and companies. The second reason, arising out of the first, may be explained by the fact that only a proportion of modern managements even today have really worked at the task of securing the first loyalty of their workforce to the company —IBM (UK) may claim to be one such company. The extent to which workers do put their unions before their companies is an indictment of management; in many situations it appears more or less axiomatic that the workforce will regard the union as more deserving of its loyalty than the company.

Another attitude now appears to be deeply ingrained. It was demonstrated by Grenville Hawley, the national automotive officer of the TGWU (see above p. 181) when he accused BL management in November 1980 of storing up a great deal of trouble and bitterness by forcing workers to take a single figure increase for the third successive year. He said: 'In the interest of preserving jobs and keeping a viable BL we have had to take another totally unacceptable offer, but it cannot go on like this year after year.' The logic of Mr Hawley's statement is that had the men rejected the offer and gone on strike then the company would have ceased to be viable and jobs would have been lost. Yet despite his own logic, he argues that in future the men clearly must have larger settlements whether or not such logic still applies. This approach developed during the relative boom times when management constantly gave way—some would argue weakly—to union demands and final offers turned out not to be anything of the sort. If Sir Michael Edwardes is right in his economics and the company cannot afford more, a point Mr Hawley concedes in the first part of his statement, then the second part must be seen as irresponsible since he says in future they will demand more than the company can afford to pay. This attitude is all too prevalent at the present time: a company is seen as the means whereby workers' standards of living are kept abreast of inflation or equivalent to what those in other companies receive elsewhere in the economy whether or not the company itself is a viable proposition.

Politicians and management are ready enough to suggest that trade unions should act responsibly, what this usually means, in fact, is that they should not behave in a manner that adversely affects the interests of the company or of the economy as interpreted by the politicians then in power. But as Pat Lowry points out, it is not the business of trade unions to be 'responsible': it is their business to bargain on behalf of their members and like any other barganing group they go for the best possible terms they can secure. Primarily the unions are concerned to better the conditions of their members, some are a good deal more successful at doing this than others. It is part of their tradition that unions want to make society into a more equitable and socialist one. On present performance, however, while a great deal of rhetoric is spent upon the subject of socialism, the most practical union attention goes to improving or maintaining the position of their members within a mixed, though capitalist oriented, state.

Furthermore, a fair proportion of the unions and their leadership are uninterested in changing society: they are interested in bettering their own positions within the society in which they live. This, perhaps, is the most important facet of the trade union movement that the Tory Party appears to have lost sight of in recent years: the fact that the aspirations of many working men make them natural Tories rather than aspiring socialists.

It is a carefully cultivated myth of the political right that an unfortunate historical accident produced the union-Labour Party links which now exist. The implication behind this line is that industrial relations generally would be easier, the restrictive attitudes of a Labour oriented TUC would disappear and the country would overcome many of its industrial problems if that particular relationship were to disappear. This argument is dishonest: not so much in itself as in what it leaves out, that business is equally tied to the Tory Party even if the structural aspects of the links are far less formal. Nothing could make this more apparent than the unease in business circles when Sir Terence Becket gave his famous 'bare knuckle fight' speech at the CBI conference of November 1980. It is one thing to maintain the fiction that business is independent of the Tory Party or vice versa, but for a major business figure who is also the executive head of the CBI actually to behave as though the fiction were fact, was something quite different.

Britain's two major political parties are equally partisan in terms of their separate approaches to industry; as a result, half industry—the organised union movement—supports one political party and the other half of industry supports the other political party to which it looks for the furtherance of its capitalist aims. As Sir Charles Forte told the *Sunday Times** in reaction to the Sir Terence row: 'The CBI ought to support Margaret Thatcher's government in every way possible ' On the contrary: the CBI ought to be prepared to lobby any government and support or oppose the policies of any government depending upon how that government and its policies affect British industry. If this argument were applied to both the TUC and the CBI all the time without the reservations which each organization feels about putting too much pressure upon its 'own' government, British industry today might be considerably stronger and healthier.

Keith Wickenden, however, whose company did resign from the CBI, said something rather different: 'It's nice for the CBI leaders like Sir Terence to be in and out of Downing Street, but I'm opposed to industrialists getting directly to grips with government. It encourages the TUC to go for like treatment.' Would Mr Wickenden be happy, one wonders, for industrialists to have access to government if this did not encourage the TUC?

The chief merit of Mrs Thatcher's approach to the problems of the economy has been to concentrate the minds of everybody else upon alternatives. The Labour Party, the trade unions, most others who do not normally support the Tory Party, as well as considerable numbers of her own party do not believe that the tough line her government has pursued, generally described as monetarism, is in fact going to solve Britain's deep industrial malaise. The monetarist approach is a doctrinaire one and its critics tend to say it will not work for that reason. Implicit in such a criticism is the argument that no doctrinaire solution will solve the problem. Britain is a mixed economy; therefore solutions need

* *Sunday Times*, 16 November 1980. Article 'More Firms Threaten to Quit CBI', by Robert Eglin and Peter Stothard.

also to be mixed so as to achieve a consensus. In fact critics of the one doctrine normally advance equally doctrinaire alternatives.

In his Granada lecture, Tony Benn suggested that under Macmillan Britain reached the high watermark of consensus politics. Perhaps we did, but only in a negative sense. The one positive aspect of consensus politics from Attlee to Heath was the maintenance of full employment: that disappeared in the 1970s. The other aspect of consensus was rather different: acceptance of the fact that there would be 'left' and then 'right' policies depending upon which party was in power and that a proportion of the measures enacted by the one party would be accepted by their opponents when they in turn came into power and vice versa. That acceptance of part of the other side's programme is what has produced our mixed economy. There was no consensus about leaving industry alone or adopting a bi-partisan economic policy. The result has been thirty years of swings between more or less intervention, nationalisation, greater free enterprise and so on. In the end the only consensus left about the economy has been that each party on coming to office would try something new, as they did often more than once, during their term of government. It is not possible to argue that there has ever been a consensus approach to the economy: there has not

During November 1980 the *Sunday Times* ran a major series of articles about the economy, the first entitled 'Why Germany Beats Britain' by Harold Lever and George Edwards. There was plenty of excellent analysis. Then came the solutions: a much greater proportion of the national product to be reinvested; the banking system to be prepared (like that of Germany) to provide far more in loans on better terms to industry than it does at present. Few would argue with their plea for a greater amount of investment and many would support their argument that the banks should lend more to industry on easier terms. What the authors do not tell us is why this has not been happening for years. As L. J. Tolley of Renold claims (see above, page 155) there has never been any lack of finance in Britain. The money is here, but those who have the money too often do not wish to invest in industry. So the argument has to be taken back another stage.

It would be foolish to suggest that British industrialists do not want their businesses to compete successfully with the Japanese, Germans and Americans. They do. Therefore, if the investment has not been ploughed back into industry, there have to be other causes for such apparent short-sightedness. Two main reasons have been advanced. The first, that investment or re-investment in British industry is inhibited by union attitudes. They are said to be negative, defensive and restrictive because their primary concern is to prevent redundancies and defend jobs they see as threatened by the new technology that results from investment. There is much truth in this argument, and here part of the difficulty lies in union attitudes. Many trade unionists are prepared to argue that the movement needs to be reformed, yet trade union leaders will not initiate reforms themselves.

It is easy to argue for union reform, but how can a movement which officially represents twelve million people (nearly a quarter of the total population) with its enormous range of variations, interests and attitudes actually reform itself? Which big union is going to give the lead and surrender some of its power to a TUC that is to be given 'teeth'? And which unions will agree to merge themselves in others so there may be a move towards industrial unions? And how, in conditions of a contracting economy, are trade unionists to be persuaded to welcome massive new investments which almost certainly mean the introduction of technologies that will put large numbers of their membership on the dole queues? Looked at in such terms, it appears unlikely that the 1980s will witness major reforms carried out by the unions from within their own ranks. The alternative would be reforms forced upon them from outside. The unions have made very plain to their own political party, Labour, that they will not permit it to reform them and since that is the case they will certainly not submit to any basic reforms imposed upon them by the Tories.

Union reluctance to reform could be reinforced by the most important union development of the 1970s: the weakening of the central organisations of the great unions by the growth of shop-floor power. Many industrialists bemoan the days when agreements between management and a strong union were reached and the union subsequently made sure its members put these into practice. Those days are unlikely to return. Education and a greater sense of personal rights mean that more and more individuals and groups on the shop-floor are uninterested in being told by union bosses from outside what they should or should not do. The tough management style of a man like Sir Michael Edwardes may restore a semblance of that older approach as perhaps did the intervention of Terence Duffy, the President of the AUEW, in November 1980 which probably averted another strike by BL workers. Whether there will be a wider return to this way of doing things is open to doubt, principally because once people realise they have power they get the taste for using it. The men on the shop-floors have experienced that during the 1970s; they are unlikely to want to take a step back from a new and more involved role in the decision making processes which affect their lives. As Bob Ramsey of Ford argued in a paper he wrote in 1980*: 'The real problem is that the preponderance of power in the hands of employees is fragmented power. . . . Increasingly, they know they have the sectional power—and they use it.' At least some managements are coming to terms with the prospect that more and more of their bargaining in future will have to be with tough shop-floor groups rather than powerful central organisations.

The second reason advanced for the poor investment record in industry is the stop-go policies of successive governments. Frequent changes of policy between Tory and Labour have discouraged industrialists from long-term investments since they expect yet further changes to occur as soon as there is another change of government.

There are other reasons. Empire is undoubtedly one of these: the habit of overseas investment has been reinforced by the fact that investment possibilities are uncertain at home. Thus the British have been especially tempted to put money into profitable overseas markets with high returns, such as South Africa, rather than into home industries. British overseas investment has been far greater than, say, that of West Germany. The lifting of exchange controls by Sir Geoffrey Howe in 1979, forty years after their imposition, has made such investment outflows still more attractive.

The partisan nature of our approach to the economy crops up in almost every discussion. At the end of 1980 a government blueprint was being drawn up to overhaul the country's obsolete apprentice system—not before time. The TUC indicated support; the CBI was described as wary since industry would have to bear most of the cost. The result: yet another apparent divide between capital and labour.

In an H. G. Wells Memorial Lecture which he gave in November 1980, Peter Shore coined the apt phrase 'The Stalemate State' whose major ingredients, he argued, were capital, labour and government. Mr Shore's analysis of developments led him to conclude: 'This impasse between capital and labour, presided over by a weak state, is the reality of so-called "corporatism" in Britain.

* 'Industrial Relations and the Balance of Power', 25 April 1980.

231

This is our own sterile version of the "historic compromise" between capital and labour.' The analysis is excellent. Then, however, Peter Shore dismisses the Thatcher monetarist approach and in its place advances a series of policies which have all been tried before: lower interest rates; a reflation of the economy; devaluation; import control and in this connexion North Sea oil is to be used as the bargaining weapon with our EEC partners whose exports to us are presumably to be curbed—they will accept such curbs because they need our oil. And so Peter Shore offers a third —socialist way—of co-operation between government and the unions in the form of another social contract. This will allow collective bargaining but within agreed parameters—perhaps half an incomes policy.

The problem is a recurring one. The Tory Government of Mrs Thatcher set about applying what may be termed 'hard' Tory measures in 1979. Labour and the unions were horrified. Their response was to advance arguments for further doses of socialism. Thus the political polarisation increases. In the meantime, industry will continue to be buffetted first one way and then another.

If the Tories are right to offer the country the choice of a free economy as opposed to a planned economy—and there is much to be said for such logic—then Labour will be as justified in arguing for a totally planned economy. Either approach could solve the basic industrial problem. The difficulty Britain faces is, simply, that neither party will be allowed to remain in office long enough to put one or other of these solutions fully into practice. Not only are we a mixed economy but we are also a mixed democracy, in the sense that there is no clear political majority for either solution and little indication that such a majority will emerge in the foreseeable future.

The British penchant for muddling through is as much a part of our political approach as of anything else. Electoral swings are less in terms of an ideological decision—'Let us go for the planned economy solution' or 'Let us go for the free enterprise solution' than they are a matter of saying 'Let us try the other lot and see if for a few years they can do better than this government which we are now going to kick out'. There is a fundamental dispute between the two approaches; what there is not, however, is any fundamental determination of a majority of the British people to opt for one or other solution. This middle-of-the-road British approach to politics—the refusal to make an ultimate commitment to a logical and sustained economic policy (and much else besides) —possibly lies at the heart of the present malaise.

Tom Jackson said, correctly and with more honesty than many trade unionists, that the monetarist policies of the Thatcher Government are the obverse of unfettered free collective bargaining by trade unions and the one deserves the other. The British have had a habit of a particular kind of freedom for a very long time: the freedom for everyone to go along his own selected path, and this applies at least as much within the ranks of the trade union movement as it does within the ranks of the Tory Party. One result is curious. It is that even the most politically left wing trade unionists, who will argue fiercely for collective action by the movement, will also defend the freedom of unions to pursue their own interests. Such trade unionists do not at heart appear to believe in sinking the search for differentials in pursuit of a common socialist goal.

The same is true, if in different fashion, on the political right. Freedom is fine as long as its effects do not really hurt those who advocate such freedom. For a generation following the devaluation of the pound after the war by Sir Stafford Cripps, businessmen have bemoaned a weak international pound—a strong one would be a symbol of British greatness. When at last the North Sea oil bonanza gives Britain a strong pound, everyone complains about its effects upon exports. And Mr Nott, Secretary of Trade in Mrs Thatcher's Government, which arguably is the most freedom oriented since the war, nonetheless joins with his European colleagues to put pressure upon the Japanese to curtail their free penetration of the ailing and incompetent British car market.

John Biffen, a high Tory, poses a crucial question about the middle ground. Recognising the partisan nature of British politics and its effect upon industry, he asks whether a settled acceptance of a social market economy is possible: that is, whether each side will make concessions. The Tories, he says, would have to concede the social services and a substantial degree of government economic management; Labour would have to concede private ownership so that political control did not come from equity ownership. The chances of such two-way acceptance are fairly remote, not only because of the adversary nature of British industry and the adversary nature of our *them* and *us* culture, but still more because of the adversary nature of British politics, cultivated over generations within the parameters of our much vaunted two-party system. The result is a lack of impartiality. Very nearly everybody in British public life is committed to one or other side in the argument: to Labour, to the Tories, to the TUC, to the CBI, and hardly ever in this context to the best means of creating more wealth.

A broad consensus does exist as to the causes of the country's low performance when measured against the performance of her principal rivals. These causes fall under the following headings: that Britain was first to industrialise and is now the first to feel the effects of a 'run-down' or old age; that the unions are too weak rather than too strong and so are unable to control their rank and file; that the movement is basically reactive, negative and defensive; that there is a dangerous lack of investment in industry; and that management has often been weak and, for example, has abnegated its managerial responsibilities in good times by too readily conceding union demands, resulting in a belief on the part of the workforce that it can always win a wage demand if it presses hard enough. Further, that management has often relied upon the trade union movement to do its job for it by, for example, controlling the workforce when this is management's task.

There is the cultural divide, the *them* and *us* society whose ill effects have been attested to from both sides of industry. There is the complaint of government interference: or rather, less a complaint at interference since both sides of industry are happy if the interference suits them, than at the constant changes of ideology behind the interferences so that there is no continuous policy. There is the confrontation mentality, partly derived from the *them* and *us* divide but also arising out of the long-standing expectation that industrial affairs must be conducted on lines of confrontation anyway. And, finally, there is the soft option approach: why should we spend all our lives creating wealth and competing with the Japanese and Germans—there are other more interesting and rewarding things to do.

These, with numerous variations, are advanced as the main reasons for the British industrial-low-production malaise.

What are the solutions? Union reform is one. It is certainly possible, but to be effective it should come from within the movement and for that to happen four preconditions are essential. The first, a stronger union leadership than exists at present especially in the key unions with real power. The second, a growth economy that would remove at least some of the fears of unemployment, which at present ensure that the unions remain reactive and restrictive. One difficulty is that the second condition in part depends upon the first, so that it is necessary to break out of a circular restraint.

A new investment strategy is another solution; again the arguments will be circular. If union restrictive practices were less—which might happen in an expanding economic situation where fear of unemployment has been removed—then the incentive to invest would become greater. This will not happen under present circumstances. Even so, investment could still be greatly increased were government to adopt policies which forced reinvestment: in the public sector, for example, by devoting North Sea oil profits to it; in the private sector by legislation requiring a proportion of all profit automatically to be reinvested in the industry. Neither option will be adopted by a Tory Government.

The third precondition is a return to strong management. Weak management has been a major factor in the present decline; or, to put the matter in a different light: the primary responsibility for the state of British industry rests and must always rest with management—not the unions, and not the government. Sir Michael Edwardes has demonstrated what strong management can get away with in a notoriously difficult industry. More efficient and determined management is certainly possible.

The fourth precondition is the need for educational reform in the widest sense: not only is our system too much geared towards the humanities while industry is too little esteemed, but, as Sir Peter Parker points out, in other countries such as West Germany or the USA everybody can afford to *trust* his children to the state system. Arguments about the public schools tend to be sterile. Of course they are élitist, and their result is to encourage the *them* and *us* attitudes which are so damaging to our society, despite everything that may be adduced in their favour in terms of the quality of the academic education they offer. The problem of the public schools could be solved by so raising the standards of the education now available to the 95 per cent of the population which does not go to public schools, that only a fool would spend thousands of pounds buying what was equally available free.

Difficult as any of the above reforms may be to effect, they pale into insignificance beside the question of political partisanship. Britain is a mixed economy but less from choice than by accident. Because of the two-party system neither side in the capital and labour ideological argument has been in power long enough to ensure that its system takes over. The result has been a series of see-saws between two versions of how to manage the economy:

what has been left in the middle constitutes our mixed economy. This economy, however, is now so mixed that it could not easily be unscrambled even if that were desirable. Nonetheless it could be unscrambled, though the process would be a traumatic one for the nation. Equally, the establishment of full state control could be pursued, and the process of establishing that in full could also be traumatic.

What, then, are the options? They appear to be four in number. First, a move back to the right. Second, a move to the left. In either case this would mean the uncharacteristic adoption by Britain of a logical political decision and progression that would be revolutionary in its implications and probably in its results, given the kind of society we are now. So far, the logic of the two-party system has been to produce a mixed mess, since neither party has ever been in power long enough to ensure the full-blooded adoption of its own doctrinaire answer to the way the economy should be run.

The swing to the right under the government of Mrs Thatcher certainly represents the nearest approach to such a solution since the Attlee Government of 1945. Many doubt that the policies dubbed monetarist will work, and the doubters include a significant section of the Tory Party. Moreover, even Mrs Thatcher has not dared to talk of a wholesale unscrambling of the public sector, though that may come. Should her government be tempted to embark upon such a course later in the 1980s, this would be to invite a head-on and almost certainly catastrophically damaging collision with the unions. Nonetheless, a return to fullblooded free enterprise is one option. There is no indication that a majority of the British people want to follow such a course.

The logical alternative to such a course is full-blooded socialism. The greatest likelihood for socialism appears to depend upon whether or not Tony Benn ultimately gets control of the Labour Party. He and those who think like him in the Labour Party are its doctrinaire equivalents to Mrs Thatcher and Sir Keith Joseph. Some unions would go a considerable way along a path of greater nationalisation, yet the irony is that the most powerful unions— those most in sympathy with a policy of increased nationalisation —are also the ones most likely to insist upon their continuing right to indulge in free collective bargaining, which is the antithesis of genuine socialism anyway. There is no indication that a majority of the British people want to follow this course either.

The third, most damaging, possibility which also seems the most likely, is a continuation of the see-saw swings of the last thirty years. If the Thatcher approach breaks down and Labour returns to power in the mid-eighties, it will no doubt adopt a further round of middle-of-the-road Labour policies. The country will be back once again on its familiar see-saw with little or nothing resolved.

The only other possibility lies in seeking a consensus on the economy, which has never so far been attempted. Essentially this would require agreement between four elements: the two main parties; the trade unions represented by the TUC; and capital and management represented by the CBI. Much is said about tripartism, and bodies such as the NEDC do their best to bridge the gaps between capital and labour. But the possibilities for genuine tripartism to work—that is, government of whichever party, management and labour getting together to work for greater national productivity—only appear realistic if the two parties are willing to take the management of the economy out of the political arena.

Were the two political parties to agree to a moratorium upon the application of their economic remedies over twenty years, then within that framework it might be possible for unions and management or capital and labour, to work out new ways of co-operation: the primary consideration must be partnership and not confrontation. Any such approach requires acceptance by each political party of a substantial part of the other's case. This seems highly unlikely at the present time, though it is far from impossible.

The British have never particularly favoured logical solutions to problems, yet a very powerful case indeed can be advanced for depoliticising the approach to the economy. This, in turn, would require certain agreed policies, as mentioned in the preconditions outlined above: fundamental improvements in education; the use of North Sea oil revenues for re-investment in industry; adequate finance for the public sector; allowing industries now in private hands to remain there and to provide reasonable profits for their shareholders. In theory, a great deal of middle ground acceptable to both parties exists. Although the middle ground has been arrived at almost accidentally and represents what has been left behind after each change of government and swing in the alternative direction, nonetheless it is there.

Is there, however, any chance that such a consensus approach will be adopted as an alternative to increasingly bitter partisan political fighting which could result from a steadily declining British economy less and less able to fulfill the nation's aspirations?

237

The efforts of the Liberal Party to represent a middle ground over thirty years have failed conspicuously. Moreover, the above suggestions will be treated as anathema by the hard core of both Tory and Labour supporters. As Harold Macmillan said (see above p. 203) 'Both sides now seem to want confrontation.' If too many people believe that support of doctrine is more important than solving the problem, then there is no hope for this approach. Yet there are possibilities, and the greatest hope may come through the trade unions, for though they argue socialism they insist upon free collective bargaining and in this split personality of the union movement may be found the means to break the deadlock between the political extremes of the two parties. Capital or management would also have to make a major contribution to any consensus solution. Management wants restrictions removed without any parallel willingness to guarantee jobs. An essential aspect of any consensus policy must be to remove the basic union fear of redundancy, in so far as this is possible. Some companies make it a basic aspect of their policy to guarantee the jobs of their workforce as much as they conceivably can, and all companies should adopt similar policies. Another essential aspect of any consensus policy would be the surrender to it by every party of a proportion of what they now regard as their fundamental political or economic right or doctrine.

Almost everybody in Britain is firmly *parti pris*, and it is exceptionally difficult to find men or women of calibre and stature in public affairs who are not in fact committed to one or other side or group—to Labour, to the unions, to capital or to the Tories. Against such a background, what is a realistic appraisal of the possibilities during the 1980s? The decade is likely to be one of continuing recession, mounting unemployment in its turn exacerbated by the application of the new technology, with the unions increasingly on the defensive. Such developments are most likely to induce greater political polarisation, with each of the two major parties arguing fiercely that their approach is the only way to solve the nation's economic problems. If this turns out to be the case, our condition is likely to deteriorate. The prospects for the triumph of any one of the three positive possibilities—a full-blooded left wing solution, a full-blooded right wing solution or a real consensus solution—seem about equally unlikely. This leaves us with the fourth and least palatable non-solution: that, accepting the periodic political swings, Britain will simply continue to muddle downwards.

List of Abbreviations

ACAS	Advisory, Conciliation & Arbitration Service
AEU	Amalgamated Engineering Union
APEX	Association of Professional, Executive, Clerical & Computer Staff
ASLEF	Associated Society of Locomotive Engineers and Firemen
ASTMS	Association of Scientific, Technical & Managerial Staffs
ASRS	Amalgamated Society of Railway Servants (NUR)
AUEW	Amalgamated Union of Engineering Workers
BALPA	British Airline Pilots' Association
BIM	British Institute of Management
BL	British Leyland
BLMC	British Leyland Motor Corporation
CBI	Confederation of British Industry
CPSA	Civil & Public Servants' Association
DATA	Draughtsmen's and Allied Technicians' Association
ETU	Electrical Trades' Union
GMWU	General & Municipal Workers' Union
GNP	Gross National Product
IMF	International Monetary Fund
MLR	Minimum Lending Rate
NALGO	National & Local Government Officers' Association
NEDCO	National Economic Development Council
NEDO	National Economic Development Office
NGA	National Graphical Association

NUM	National Union of Mineworkers
NUPE	National Union of Public Employees
NUR	National Union of Railwaymen
OECD	Organisation of Economic Co-operation & Development
PSI	Policy Studies Institute
SOGAT	Society of Graphical & Allied Trades
STUC	Scottish Trades Union Congress
TASS	Technical, Administrative and Supervisory Section (of AUEW)
TGWU	Transport & General Workers' Union
TSSA	Transport Salaried Staffs Association
TUC	Trades Union Congress
UAW (US)	United Automobile Workers
UCATT	Union of Construction, Allied Trades and Technicians
UCW	Union of Communications Workers
UPW	Union of Postal Workers
USDAW	Union of Shop, Distributive & Allied Workers